# LEARNING

# BASIC

## FOR THE PERSONAL COMPUTER

**by DAVID A. LIEN**

International Standard Book Number: 0-932760-13-9

Library of Congress Catalog Card Number: 82-73471

10 9 8 7 6 5 4 3

*Printed in the United States of America*

# A Personal Note From The Author

*Learning IBM BASIC* incorporates the best of my earlier writings on the BASIC language plus much more, customized for use in the classroom with the IBM Personal Computer. It is written for the average person who has no experience with a Computer. The style is light and non-threatening since we have no insecurities to pass along. Learning should be fun, not intimidating...

*And why shouldn't learning be fun...?*

Sit back, relax, read slowly as though savoring a good novel, and above all, let your imagination wander. I'll supply all the routine facts and techniques we need. The real enjoyment begins when *your* imagination starts the creative juices flowing and the Computer becomes a tool in *your* hands. *You* become the master -- not the other way around. At that time it will evolve from just a pretty box of parts into an extension of your own personality!

Enjoy your new Personal Computer!

Dr. David A. Lien
San Diego -- 1984

# Acknowledgements

The following played key roles in the creation of this book:

**Technical Director:** Dave Waterman
**Project Coordinator:** Inez Goldberg
**Technical Researchers:**
Mike Hunter
Maria Melendrez
Morgan Davis
Mark Schaffroth
Peter Krause
Bill Smith
**Editorial Director:** Gary Williams
**Production Coordinator:** Janice Scanlan
**Production Assistant:** Suzanne Hartwell
**Cartoons:** Bob Stevens

# Introduction

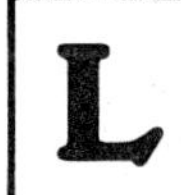

**earning IBM BASIC** is divided into 5 sections. Section A, the tutorial section, is divided into 9 parts:

**Part 1 -- Getting Started**
Teaches how to set the realtime clock and calendar, format disks, use the editor, and understand the different ways to use the keyboard.

**Part 2 -- Speak to Me, Oh Great Computer**
Teaches beginning BASIC. Covers math operators, using the Computer as a calculator and SAVEing and LOADing files with disk. It also teaches looping, formatting with TAB, INTeger functions and random numbers.

**Part 3 -- Strings**
Begins intermediate BASIC with a comprehensive look at Strings.

**Part 4 -- Variable Precision and Math**
Teaches the use of SiNGle and DouBLe precision numbers, trigonometric and defined functions.

**Part 5 -- Display Formatting**
Teaches the use of LOCATE, the power of INKEY$, INPUT$, and PRINT USING, and coloring in text mode.

**Part 6 -- Arrays**
Teaches how to create and use single and multi-DIMension arrays and SEARCH/SORT techniques.

**Part 7 -- Sound**
Teaches how to use IBM's sound feature.

**Part 8 -- Miscellaneous**
Teaches advanced features of BASIC such as PEEK and POKE, logical operators, and methods for saving, merging and chaining programs.

**Part 9 -- Program Control**
Teaches flowcharting and debugging techniques.

Sections B through E provide Answers to Exercises found in the Chapters, Ready-to-RUN User Programs, Appendices with helpful charts and lists, and a comprehensive Index.

# Table Of Contents

# SECTION A

# IBM BASIC TUTORIAL

# PART 1
# GETTING STARTED

Coming Attractions
IBM
IBM

# The Big Picture

**Learning IBM BASIC** teaches Elementary and Intermediate BASIC, up to but not including Random and Sequential File handling.

It is written specifically for a 64K 2 disk system, however nearly all of the exercises work on smaller machines, including a 16K non-disk machine. Some readers have only 1 disk drive, but that will cause no insurmountable problems. Those few programs that won't work on smaller machines are flagged so we won't waste time and become frustrated.

Since we write in specifics, not generalities, we have to make some assumptions. It is assumed you have the IBM monochrome Personal Computer Display so 80-column width is available. This further assumes you have the IBM monochrome display printer adapter installed in one of the expansion slots inside the "box".

If you have the Color Graphics Monitor Adapter, a regular TV set or video monitor can be used.

The use of HiRes Color Graphics, Game control adapter (joysticks), light pen, and asynchronous communications is covered in Vol. 3, a peripherals book. This volume in the IBM Learning Series will be available from CompuSoft in the near future.

If you are learning on a non-disk system, skip immediately to Appendix A for special instructions and meet the rest of us at Chapter 2 in a few minutes.

Everyone else move straight ahead to Chapter 1.

# Doesn't Everyone Have Disk?

You are fortunate to have a disk system. So you had to sell the second car -- this is the only way to fly! Having a disk system will be of some help in learning Elementary and Intermediate BASIC, but it's sort of like flying a Boeing 747 before mastering a Cessna 150.

Our non-disk readers must wrestle with slow and marginally reliable cassette tapes to store their programs and data. With a highly reliable disk system you may never experience the agony (and ecstasy?) of making a cassette system work. Count your blessings!

You will achieve an excellent mastery of Elementary and Intermediate BASIC in these 50+ bite-sized Chapters. The *advanced* features of Disk BASIC, (mainly File Handling), are covered in a 2nd volume entitled, *Learning IBM Disk BASIC*, which picks up where this one ends.

## A Real Turn On

Place the SYSTEM diskette (or a *copy* of it) with its label up, in drive A (the left drive), and close the door. Turn the Computer ON with the power switch located on the right side of the main box. The Computer will give itself a perfunctory check up, the disk drive(s) will whir and groan, and after BEEP-ing, the screen will ask us for the date:

```
Current date is Tue  1-01-1980
Enter new date:
```

DISK DRIVE!

Type in today's date using this format:

```
9-28-90        or        9/28/90
```

then press the [↵] key. The [↵] key is the one located directly above the key that says [PrtSc] on the right side of the keyboard.

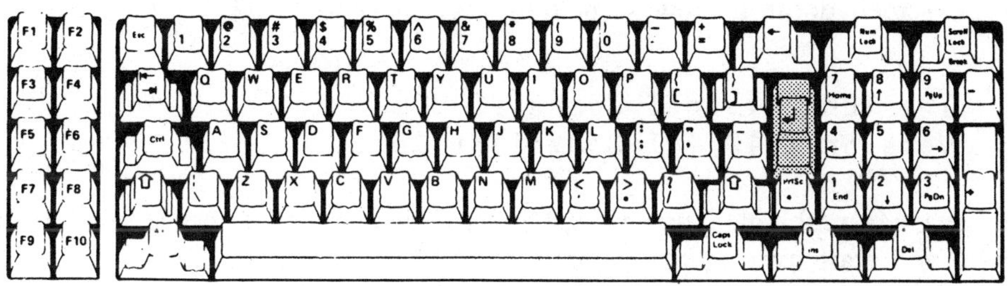


Then the screen may say:

```
Current time is  0:01:30.00
```

The "current time" is how long the Computer has been ON since it beeped, or since the time was set. The IBM Computer keeps track of time in to the 24 hour system, so 2:15 in the afternoon is written as:

```
14:15:00.00
```

accurate to 1/100 of a second. That's pretty accurate!

My wristwatch says 1:26 in the afternoon, so I'll type:

`13:26` and press [↵].

You type in your own time. The colon (:) which separates the hour and minute is found on the same key as the semicolon (;) and, as on an ordinary typewriter keyboard, requires that we press a [SHIFT] key (⇧ up-arrow on the keyboard) to type it.

The time the Computer remembers is no more accurate than the time we enter, but *hour* and *minute* are usually accurate enough for government work. The date and time are stored in memory for future reference, but have little value in our early study of BASIC.

Now that we've done it and know how to do it, we can tell this little secret: It's not mandatory to enter either the date or time. To bypass them, just respond to both opportunities by pressing [←┘].

If the screen doesn't show something like this:

```
The IBM Personal Computer DOS
Version 1.10 (C) Copyright IBM
```

we've got a problem. Turn off the big red switch, let it rest at least 15 seconds, and start over at the beginning of this Chapter.

Assuming all is well, the bottom Line will say:

```
A>_
```

"A>—" tells us that we are at the SYSTEM or COMMAND level of computer control. Drive A is "logged on" and ready for action. From this SYSTEM or DOS level we can do all sorts of things, but our mission in this book is **Learning IBM BASIC**. The *other* things we can do from SYSTEM level is left to other books.

---

The computer doesn't care if we use lower case or capital letters. Since computers traditionally use UPPER case, we will use UPPER case only throughout this book. To LOCK into the upper case mode, press the key marked [Caps Lock]. Each time it's pressed, the keyboard "toggles" between UPPER CASE ONLY and upper/lower case. In [Caps Lock] we need not use the ⇧ keys for capital letters -- only for characters *above* the numbers and other special keys.

---

## What's On The Disk?

Just for fun, look at the list of programs that came on the SYSTEM diskette in Drive A. This activity is called a "pulling a DIRectory". Type:

`DIR` and press [←┘]

A listing of about 2 dozen file names whiz by on the screen. Few are of interest to us in this book, but look for BASIC and BASICA. They can teach the Computer how to speak BASIC, and are what this book is all about.

Find the [Ctrl] and [Num Lock] keys. Type DIR again and while the listing is scrolling by, press both keys at the same time. This freezes the display so we can study it. To restart the listing, hit almost any key. Type:

```
DIR     [←]
```

again, freezing the display near its beginning, and look for a program named:

```
DISKCOPY
```

## Backup

Our first task is to make a complete *backup* (safety copy) of the original SYSTEM diskette. We'll use that *backup* copy as our *working master* and store the *original* away for safe keeping. This precaution may save a long drive down to the computer store to exchange a damaged diskette. As the owner, you are allowed to make as many copies of the SYSTEM diskette as needed for your personal use, subject to any provisions stated in the factory notice.

Check to be sure the SYSTEM diskette is protected by a write tab (or no notch), then insert it in drive A. Insert a *blank* and unprotected diskette in drive B.

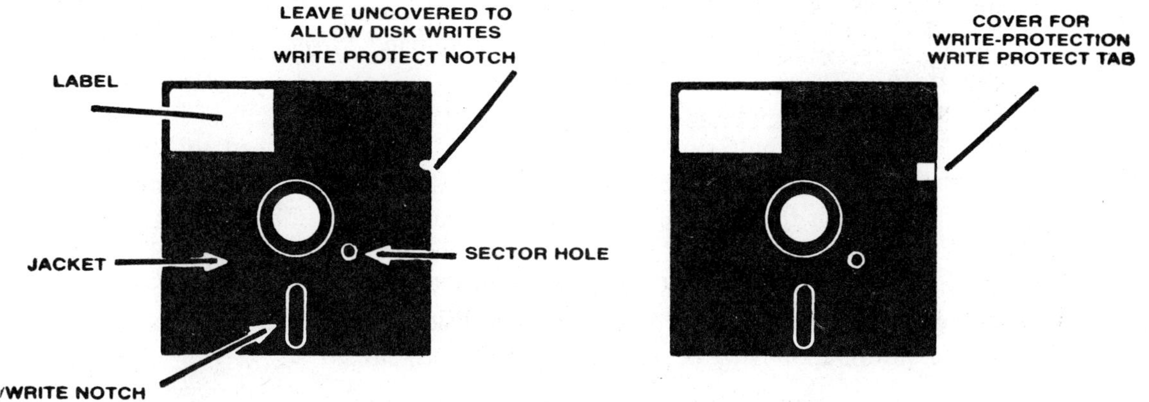

Before we BACKUP a diskette, it should be erased with a "bulk eraser" of the type commonly used to clean cassette tapes. That process ensures that any information previously saved is removed, and it thoroughly "agitates" the iron oxide particles making sure they are awake. The result is a better quality "recording". If you don't have a bulk eraser, buy one as soon as possible.

Type:

```
DISKCOPY A: B:
```

Single drive users simply type `DISKCOPY` .

When the DISKCOPY program is complete, it will say so.

## Backup Complete

The diskette created by DISKCOPY is identical to the *original*. Hide the original away in a safe location and place the new *working master* in drive A.

## Format

We will need a number of diskettes to store our programs and assignments. However, if we try to save a program on a blank diskette, the Computer won't know how to make it stick. The FORMAT program writes special magnetic race tracks on diskettes so they can remember.

We started this session by placing a copy of the Disk Operating System (DOS) diskette in drive A. Diskettes used in other drives need to contain a small amount of DOS information. The FORMAT command "writes" that information on them.

A big advantage of multi-drive systems is that there is no need to reserve large amounts of valuable diskette space for SYSTEM or DOS information on diskettes other than the working master. That leaves room for more program and data storage. Even a single drive system doesn't need all the SYSTEM information on every diskette. From now on, we will call a diskette containing the entire Disk Operating System a SYSTEM diskette. One that contains only Formatted information will be called a DATA diskette.

To FORMAT the DATA diskette, type:

```
FORMAT        [↵]
```

The FORMAT program is loaded into the Computer and it tells us to:

```
Insert new diskette for drive A:
and strike any key when ready
```

Remove the SYSTEM disk from drive A and insert a blank. Since we have to "write" on the blank, be sure there is *not* a write protect tab on it, then press any key.

The screen responds with:

```
Formatting...
```

Note the red light on drive A. Listen to the disk drive noises as they give a good hint of what's going on mechanically. Each of the clicks indicates recording of a magnetic stripe called a "track".

When the screen says:

```
Formatting...Format complete

160256 bytes total disk space
160256 bytes available on disk

Format another (Y/N)?
```

type N and replace the DATA diskette with the SYSTEM diskette.

---

Your system may show different numbers, depending on the type of disk drive.

---

## Getting Down to BASICs

The SYSTEM disk contains programs named BASIC and BASICA, either of which will teach the Computer to speak BASIC. To pour these instructions inside the Computer's head, type:

```
A:BASICA
```

Which means "load in the program named BASICA from the diskette found in drive A".

The Computer responds with:

```
The IBM Personal Computer Basic
Version A1.10 Copyright IBM Corp
33402 Bytes free
OK
-
```

If your machine has more or less than 64K bytes of memory, the "free bytes" number will be more or less than 33402.

---

Why did we choose BASICA (Advanced BASIC) instead of BASIC (Regular BASIC)? We chose Advanced, because even though it occupies a little more memory space, it is the "top of the line" BASIC furnished with the machine. Let's go for it!

---

## Why Disk BASIC?

So-called "DISK BASIC" has all the regular IBM "ROM BASIC" features plus a few special ones of concern with the use of diskettes. In this book we will be concerned only with SAVE, LOAD, CHAIN and MERGE and will learn to use them in due course.

Just because we have a disk system doesn't mean we have to start right off using Disk BASIC. If at this point you would really rather learn the straight old BASIC like our non-disk readers, turn the system OFF (per the directions below) then back ON with disk drives empty. Cassette or ROM BASIC will automatically appear. This option isn't really recommended if you have a disk system.

## Turning The Disk System Off

**Always** remove the diskette(s) before turning the system OFF. Punishment for failure to do so may be a "zapped" disk, one with some of its information accidentally erased or scrambled. Move now to Chapter 2 and join our non-disk friends who came from their own separate briefing.

### Learned In Chapter 1

| Commands | Miscellaneous |
| --- | --- |
| DIR | Turning the Computer ON and OFF |
| FORMAT | Setting the DATE |
| | Entering BASIC |

# Chapter 2

# Computer Etiquette

From the moment we turn it on, our IBM Personal Computer follows a well-defined set of rules for coping with us, the "master". This makes it an exceptionally easy computer to use. To a large extent, all we have to do is say the right thing (via the keyboard) at the right time. Of course, there are lots of "right things" to say; putting them together for a purpose is called *programming*.

In this Chapter we'll start a conversation with our Computer and teach it some simple social graces. At the same time, you'll learn the fundamentals of computer etiquette. You'll even write your first computer program!

## Getting "READY"

If you turned the Computer OFF, turn it back ON as described in Chapter 1. After entering the date and time, type:

```
BASICA        [↵]
```

to enter BASIC.

When:

```
Ok

_
```

appears, we're set to "go" again. The blinking dash is called the *cursor*. The

Computer is saying:

*"I'm ready -- it's your turn!"*

To make sure we start off with a clean slate -- erasing all traces of prior programs or tests -- type NEW and press [↵]. The Computer responds by erasing the screen and printing:

```
OK

_
```

Type in FRE(Ø) and [↵]. This is a very simple test to see that the Computer "powered up" properly. The display should read:

```
NEW

PRINT FRE(Ø)

 334Ø2

OK

_
```

---

If the number is not 334Ø2 (or whatever is reasonable for your system), turn the Computer OFF. Wait for about 10 seconds and turn it ON again. Repeat the test and verify that the number is in the ball park. If not, it's off to the repair center.

---

## What Is a Computer Program?

A program is a sequence of instructions the Computer stores until we command it to follow (or "execute") them. Most programs for the IBM are written in a language called BASIC, and its very name tells how easy it is to learn!

Let's write a simple one-Line program to let the Computer meet us.

GO AHEAD, POKE AWAY - I WON'T BYTE!

Don't bother to use the shift key -- letters are always *capital* unless we "toggle" the [Caps Lock] key.

Type the following Line, *exactly* as shown:

```
10 PRINT "YOU ARE A COMPUTER PROGRAMMER."
```

Do *not* hit the [←┘] key yet!

If you made a typing error, don't worry. Just use the backspace key ←. Each time you press this key, the rightmost character will be erased. If the error was at the beginning of the Line, erase way back to that point then retype the rest of the Line. (If you hold the backspace key down longer than a second it will erase many letters very quickly.)

Study *very carefully* what you typed:

1. Is everything after the word PRINT enclosed in quotation marks?

2. Are there any extra quotation marks?

If everything's okay, press [←┘]. The flashing _ cursor will move to the left edge, telling us "I got the message".

## If It's Too Late

If you found an error after pressing [←┘], the backspace key cannot correct it. best way to fix it is by retyping the *entire* Line, correctly. When the [←┘] key is pressed, this new Line will replace the old one since they both share the same starting number (in this case, 10). In several Chapters we'll learn how to "EDIT" out errors instead of retyping entire Lines.

## "Allow Me To Introduce You"

Let's tell the Computer to execute or RUN our program. The BASIC command for this is simple: RUN. So type:

```
RUN
```

and press [←┘]

If we made no mistakes, the bottom Line will read:

```
YOU ARE A COMPUTER PROGRAMMER.
```

If it doesn't work, try typing RUN again. If RUN still doesn't produce the greeting, there's something wrong in your program. Type NEW [↵] to clear it out, then type it in and RUN again.

If it did work -- let out a yell!

*"I are now a REAL computer programmer!"*

This is very important, because you have tasted success with computer programming, and it may be the last you are heard from in some time.

## In Summary

Note that the word PRINT is not displayed, nor are the Line number nor the quotation marks. They are part of the BASIC Language program's *instructions* and we didn't intend for them to be printed. Everything inside the quote marks is printed, including blank spaces and the period.

Type the word RUN again and hit [↵].

Type RUN [↵] to your heart's content, watching the magic machine do as it's told. When you feel you've got the hang of all this, get up and stretch, walk around the room, look out the window -- the whole act. You'll soon be absorbed in programming and won't have time for such things.

Whether typing in a program, or giving direct commands like RUN, we have to hit [↵] to tell the Computer to look at what we typed, then act accordingly.

### Learned in Chapter 2

| Commands | Statements | Miscellaneous |
|---|---|---|
| NEW | PRINT | |
| RUN | [↵] | _ cursor |
| | | ◀ backspace key |
| | | " " quotation marks |

*Commands* (like RUN) are executed as soon as we type them and press [↵] .

*Statements* (like PRINT) are executed only after we type the RUN [↵] command.

**Special message for people who can't resist the urge to play around with the Computer and skip around in this book.** (There always are a few!)

It is possible to "lose control" of the Computer so it won't give a READY message. To regain control, just press [Break]. If that doesn't work, push the RESET button. If that doesn't work, turn the Computer OFF for 10 seconds, then turn it back ON again.

---

Be sure to remove all diskettes before turning the Computer OFF!

---

# Chapter 3

# Expanded Program

**W**e now have a program in the Computer. It's only a one-Liner, so let's expand it by adding a second Line. In BASIC, every Line in the program *must* be numbered, and the instructions are executed in order from the lowest Line number to the highest. Type:

```
20 PRINT "YOU HAVE A COMMAND, MASTER?"
```

Check it carefully -- especially the quote marks, then:

```
RUN
```

---

Have you noticed that we use Ø for the number zero so we can distinguish between the letter O and number Ø? The Video Display does it this way -- and it's standard throughout Computerdom.

---

If all was correct, the screen will read:

```
YOU ARE A COMPUTER PROGRAMMER.
YOU HAVE A COMMAND, MASTER?
OK
_
```

If it ran Ok, answer the question by typing:

```
YES
```

Oh -- sorry about that! It “bombed”, didn’t it? The screen says:

```
Syntax error
```

We deliberately “set you up” to demonstrate the Computer’s *error* trouble-shooter. The Computer is smart enough to know when *we’ve* made a mistake in telling it what to do, and it PRINTs a clue as to the nature of the error.

“Syntax” is an obscure word that refers to the pattern of words in a language. *Error* means we have made one. The Computer is expecting a new program Line or a BASIC command. The word “YES” is neither. A bit later we’ll learn how to make the Computer accept a “YES” or “NO” and respond accordingly.

There are many possible errors we can make, and in good time we will learn to understand the built in “ERROR CODES”.

---

A complete listing of ERROR CODES is provided in Appendix E.

---

Meanwhile, there is one other important *error* situation which we must be able to recognize to pry ourselves out of accidental trouble. Let’s type a temporary Line 30 and deliberately make a spelling error:

```
30 PRIMT "TESTING."
```

and

```
RUN
```

OH, COME NOW. I HATE TO SEE A GROWN MAN CRY... SO YOU 'BOMBED' — LET'S GIVE IT ANOTHER SHOT!

Again we get an *error* message:

```
Syntax error in 30
```

but after Ok, we see:

```
30 PRIMT "TESTING"
```

the "bad" Line number.

This tells us that the error is in Line 30. Pressing the [↵] key a few times will move the cursor down giving us some breathing room. (Shhh! If you know what the flashing cursor under the Line number will let us do, don't say anything. We don't want to confuse anyone with too much too soon.)

To erase the bad Line, type:

```
30        [↵]
```

and it's gone.

## And The Program Grows

It is customary, traditional (and all that) to space the Lines in a program 10 numbers apart. Note that our two-Line program uses the numbers 10 and 20. The reason ... it's much easier to modify a program if we leave room to insert new Lines inbetween the old ones. There is no benefit to numbering the Lines more closely (like 1,2,3,4). *DON'T DO IT.*

RUN again and look at the Video Display. What if we'd rather not have the two Lines PRINTed so close together, but would like to have a space between them? Type in the new Line:

```
15 PRINT
```

Then:

```
RUN
```

It now reads

```
YOU ARE A COMPUTER PROGRAMMER.


YOU HAVE A COMMAND, MASTER?
```

---

Note: To make this book easier to read, we are using more space between all our program Lines than you actually see on the screen.

---

Looks neater, doesn't it? But what about Line 15? It says PRINT. PRINT what? Well -- PRINT *nothing*. That's what followed PRINT, and that's just what it PRINTed. But in the process of PRINTing nothing it automatically inserted a space between the PRINTing ordered in Lines 10 and 20. (Hmmm...so *that's* how we space between lines.)

---

*Didn't that room between Lines 10 and 20 come in handy?*

---

Another important program statement is REM, which stands for REMark. It is often convenient to insert REMarks into a program.

Why? So you or someone else can refer to them later, to help remember complicated programming details, or even what the program's for and how to use it. It's like having a scratch-pad or notebook built into the program. When we tell the Computer to execute the program by typing RUN [↵], it skips right over any numbered Line which begins with a REM. *A REM statement has no effect whatsoever on the program.* Insert the following:

```
5 REM *THIS IS MY FIRST COMPUTER PROGRAM* [↵]
```

---

You might be wondering why the asterisks(*) in Line number 5? The answer is ... they're just for decoration. Let's give this operation some class! Remember, *anything* on a line that follows REM is ignored by the Computer.

---

Then:

RUN 

The "video printout" reads just like the last one, totally unaffected by the presence of Line 5. Did it work that way for you?

Well, this programming business is getting complicated and I've already forgotten what is in our "big" program. How can we get a LISTing of what our program now contains? Easy. A new BASIC command. Type:

```
LIST
```

The screen reads:

```
5 REM *THIS IS MY FIRST COMPUTER PROGRAM*
10 PRINT "YOU ARE A COMPUTER PROGRAMMER."
15 PRINT
20 PRINT "YOU HAVE A COMMAND MASTER?"
```

## Where Is The END Of The Program?

The end of a program is, quite naturally, the last statement we want the Computer to execute. Many computers require placing an END statement at this point so the Computer will know when to stop. But with our IBM, an END statement is optional. Remember though, if you want to RUN BASIC programs on fussier computers, they will probably need END statements.

> When we get into more complex programs, we'll use END statements to *force* execution to END at specified points.

Let's take a closer look at END. By the rules governing its use, most dialects of BASIC which require END insist that it be the last statement in a program, telling the computer "That's all, folks". By tradition, it is given the number 99, or 999, or 9999 (or larger), depending on the largest number the specific computer will accept. Our IBM accepts Line numbers up to 65529.

Let's add an END statement:

Type:

```
99 END
```

Then:

```
RUN
```

The sample RUN should read:

```
YOU ARE A COMPUTER PROGRAMMER.

YOU HAVE A COMMAND, MASTER?
```

**Question:** "Why didn't the word END PRINT?" **Answer:** Because nothing is PRINTed unless it is the "object" of a PRINT statement. So, how could we make the Computer PRINT THE END at the end of the program execution? Think for a minute before reading on, and typing the next Line.

```
98 PRINT "THE END"
```

...and RUN.

> This assumes that Line 98 is the last PRINT statement in the program. We now have an END statement (Line 99) and a PRINT "THE END" statement (Line 98). 98 says it; 99 does it.

## Erasing Without Replacing

Just for fun, let's move the END statement from Line 99 to the largest usable Line number our IBM will accept, 65529. It requires two separate steps.

First, we erase Line 99. Note that we're not just making a change or correcting an error in Line 99 -- we want to completely eliminate it from the program. Easier done than said.

Type:

```
99
```

The Line is erased. How can we be sure? Think about this now. Got it? Sure

-- "pull" a LISTing of the entire program by typing:

```
LIST      [⏎]
```

The screen should show the program with Lines 5, 1Ø, 15, 2Ø, and 98. 99 should be gone. Any entire Line can be erased the same way.

The second step is just as easy. Type:

```
65529 END      [⏎]
```

...and the new Line is entered. Pull a LISTing of the program to see if it was. Was it? Now RUN the program to see if moving the END statement changed anything. Did it? It shouldn't have.

## Other Uses For END

Move END from number 65529 to Line number 17, LIST then RUN.

What happened? It ENDed the RUN after PRINTing Line 1Ø and a space. RUN it several times.

Now move END to Line 13, LIST and RUN. Then to Line 8, LIST and RUN.

Do you see the effect END has, depending where it is placed (even temporarily) in a program? Feel like you are really gaining control over the machine? You ain't seen nothin' yet!

### Learned In Chapter 3

| Commands | Statements | Miscellaneous |
|---|---|---|
| LIST | PRINT (Space) | Error Messages |
| | REM | Line Numbering |
| | END | |

# Chapter 4

# Using The EDITor

n extraordinarily valuable capability of our BASIC is a feature called the EDITor. Its purpose is as simple as its name. It lets us "EDIT", or make changes in a program.

The IBM EDITor gives us the best of 2 worlds. We get the ease of use of a "Line editor" plus the power of a "screen editor". Since our EDITor edits letters and numbers in only one Line at a time we have nearly the power of a word processor on that one Line. It is so easy to use but so powerful you'll never again want to use a computer without one.

Clear out the current program by typing NEW [↵]. Then type in this Line (errors and all):

```
10 PRINT "THIS HEAR ARE SHORE A FLOXY CONFUSER."
```

...and RUN.

NOTE: From now on, we will not specify [↵], except in special circumstances. We all know that a RUN or LIST requires an ENTER to make it work.

The program should RUN just fine, and if that's the way we usually talk we probably don't see the need for EDITing out some errors. If, on the other hand, we wish to change the sentence to something like:

```
THIS IS SURE A FOXY COMPUTER.
```

NOW THAT YOU'VE LEARNED TO SPEL- WHAT SAY WE TAKE UP EDITing?

then we need to do some EDITing in Line 10.

In the earlier Chapters we would solve the problem by just retyping the entire Line, hoping we didn't make more mistakes than we eliminated. This particular example has so much to change it might be just as easy to retype it, but our purpose here is to "exercise" the EDITor, so type:

```
EDIT 10        [←]        (don't omit the space before the 10!)
```

and see what happens.

Hokay...we get:

```
10 PRINT "THIS HEAR ARE SHORE A FLOXY CONFUSER."
```

The flashing cursor under the 1 is a good (but not perfect) sign the Computer is in the EDITor mode.

To get out of the EDITor we can simply hit [←], like we did several Chapters ago when we blundered into it by mistake.

But being in EDITor isn't like being in BASIC. We only use [←] when we are DONE EDITing and want to RETURN to BASIC. The EDITor is *not* part of BASIC. It's a special feature we call up from BASIC using the word EDIT. Don't hit [←] until the EDITing is finished.

Since we want Line 10 to read THIS IS SURE A FOXY COMPUTER, let's first get rid of the words HEAR ARE. Tap (or hold down) the right arrow ➧ (number 6 on the keypad) and watch the cursor move. When it is under the H in HEAR, stop.

```
10 PRINT "THIS HEAR ARE SHORE A FLOXY CONFUSER."
```

Press the key that says [Del] (the "." on the keypad) 9 times. It will Delete the H and 8 characters to its right. Line 10 now reads:

```
10 PRINT "THIS SHORE A FLOXY CONFUSER."
```

If a number of 6's appear on the screen instead of characters being Deleted, press the [Num Lock] key once. It "toggles" the keypad between the Numbers on it and the arrows which control the cursor, similar to the way in which the [Caps Lock] handles upper and lower case letters. Retype Line 10 to get rid of the unwanted 6's.

We now have to insert the word IS between THIS and SHORE. Position the blinking underline cursor below the S and Press [Ins] (0 on the keypad). Notice that the cursor is now a big block instead of an underline. This means the EDITor is in Insert mode. Type the letters:

```
IS
```

and press the space bar once. The screen now reads:

```
10 PRINT "THIS IS SHORE A FLOXY CONFUSER."
```

We inserted the IS and a space following it, but must now LEAVE the Insert mode. We can always completely bail out of the EDITor at any time by hitting [↵], but since we have a lot more work to do on this Line, press the right arrow to move the cursor under the H in SHORE. Hitting any of the EDITor arrow keys bails us out of Insert, as does hitting the INS key again. It too acts as a "toggle".

Now Delete the H and type the letter U. By typing U we *changed* the O to a U. *Changing* a letter or number is done simply by such "overstriking". It now reads:

```
10 PRINT "THIS IS SURE A FLOXY CONFUSER."
```

If it seems we're going slowly, you're right! The EDITor is so important but so simple we may as well learn to use it right the first time. You know the old story, "there's never time to do it right the first time, but always time to do it over."

Hit the right arrow 6 times to put the cursor under the L in FLOXY.

```
10 PRINT "THIS IS SURE A FLOXY CONFUSER."
```

Think for a moment. How can we change FLOXY to FOXY?

The easiest way is to just press:

[Del] to Delete the L.

Next, move the cursor under the N.

```
10 PRINT "THIS IS SURE A FOXY CONFUSER."
```

Only one final change is needed, changing CONFUSER to COMPUTER. Should we go into the word CONFUSER and Delete the N and F and Insert M and P, or would it be easier to just Change those letters instead?

What about the S? Think it thru.

Of course! It usually takes fewer keystrokes to Change than to Delete then Insert, so we always change or overstrike when possible. Move the cursor under the N and type MPUT.

Whew! Finally done. But wait -- we're still in the EDITor. Press [↵], see the cursor drop down, and know that we're back in BASIC. RUN to be sure all is well.

It is *very important* to hit [↵] when done EDITing a Line. This tells the Computer:

*"Ok, I'm done EDITing this Line. Lock the changed Line into memory as the NEW program Line"*.

A *very* common mistake is to EDIT a Line, then instead of hitting [↵] use the down arrow (2 on the keypad) to go down to EDIT another Line. If we do that the Computer has no way of remembering the changes we made on the first Line. We *must* hit [↵] to save the changes!

Despite our taking each editing task one step at a time, it is possible to make all these EDITing changes in only one pass through the Line. The purpose of an editor is *to save time*.

Since you're now the "ace of the base" when it comes to flying this EDITor, let's type:

```
NEW
```

and type in old Line 10 again, then EDIT it in one pass.

```
10 PRINT "THIS HEAR ARE SHORE A FLOXY CONFUSER."
```

If we blow it, start all over by retyping Line 10.

Pretty slick, huh? With some practice it will take you less than 10 seconds. From here on, we should always use the EDITor for changes, especially in long Lines. Compare the time it would take to change only one letter or number in a very long and complex Line by retyping it, with the speed of doing it with the EDITor.

Several other keys can help us in EDIT. Type:

```
LIST
```

and tap the [↵] key until Line 10 is at the top of the screen.

The cursor is now at the bottom of the screen. But suppose we want to EDIT Line 10. Instead of typing EDIT 10 we can just hit the [Home] key (7 on the keypad). This immediately moves the cursor to the top left hand corner of the screen, or sends it HOME. We can now EDIT Line 10. Try it.

If we use the [Ctrl] key with either the right or left arrows, it will jump to the *beginning* of each word in that direction. Try it. (The [Ctrl] key doesn't work with the up or down arrows.)

The [End] key (1 on the keypad) moves the cursor to the End of the current Line, and [Ctrl] [End] *erases* to the End of the Line. Position the cursor in the middle of the Line and try it.

Very often we want to clear the screen because it can get very confusing while we're EDITing. Hitting [Ctrl] [Home] moves the cursor up to the top left *and* clears the entire screen. It doesn't erase the program, just the screen. Try it.

**EXERCISE 4-1:** Type NEW [↵], then use the EDITor to change:

```
10 PAINT "WE CAN TAKE CREDIT FOR CONSUMER PROGRESS."
```

to:

```
10 PRINT "WE CAN EDIT COMPUTER PROGRAMS."
```

Try working this one out on your own. The answers to later Exercises will be provided in Section B, along with further comments.

## The Editor -- Second Semester

We could probably live happily ever after thinking we are in fat city with what we've learned, but the EDITor has a number of other powerful features. One which will certainly arise is typified by the following Lines. Erase the memory with NEW and type:

```
10 PRIMT "THAT ISN'T HOW TO SPELL PRINT!"
```

...and RUN.

```
Syntax error in 10
Ok
10 PRIMT "THAT ISN'T HOW TO SPELL PRINT!"
```

means there is a syntax error in Line 10. The Computer is telling us:

*What? -- I don't understand what you are saying,*

and, *automatically* puts us in the EDITor mode at the Line which contains the error. This always happens when there is a syntax error. (More on Syntax and other errors in later Chapters.) Proceed normally to change the "M" to an "N" and type:

[⏎] to return to BASIC.

There is a third and often convenient way to enter the EDIT mode. It is particularly valuable when experimenting ... switching back and forth between BASIC and EDIT to test programming changes.

For example, we just EDITed Line 10. To enter EDIT 10 again, simply type:

```
EDIT .
```

(note the space and the period)

Try it.

EDIT followed by a period is just an abbreviation for EDIT followed by the Line number of the Line LAST EDITed. It's great for short memories. Obviously, if we didn't recently EDIT a Line, this feature has no meaning.

## Learned In Chapter 4

| Commands | Miscellaneous |
| --- | --- |
| EDIT | Editing Features |
| EDIT . | |

## Chapter 5

# Automatic Line Numbering And Renum

### They Laughed When I Sat Down At The Computer To Play

Clean out the old program by typing:

```
NEW       [↵].
```

As the artist approaches a blank canvas with only a gleam in his eye, so we approach our empty Computer and type:

```
AUTO       [↵]
```

It responds with:

```
10 _
```

We are in the AUTOmatic Line Numbering Mode. Type:

```
PRINT "WHAT IS GOING ON HERE?"       [↵]
```

and

```
20 _
```

pops up on the screen.

Type:

```
PRINT "THIS IS RIDICULOUS."        [↵]
```

and

```
30 _
```

appears.

Well, it's obvious at this point that we're being fed new Line numbers as fast as we can use them. Hit the [↵] key a few more times and watch them jump up.

Okay -- how do we get OUT of AUTO? Hit: [Ctrl] [Break] or [Ctrl C]

Type LIST and see that only those Line numbers we actually used (10 and 20) contain anything.

Type NEW, then:

```
AUTO 1000
```

and

[↵] a few times. Line spacing "defaults" to 10. Hit [Ctrl] [Break], then:

```
AUTO 1000,200
```

Hit the [↵] key a half dozen times or so and the pattern becomes immediately clear. The "1000" established the *beginning* Line number, and the "200" determined the spacing between Lines.

[Break] out of AUTO and start again with:

```
AUTO 3000,1
```

and a few [↵] s. Very handy for very big programs requiring lots of Line Numbers.

[Break] again, and:

```
AUTO 17,4
```

plus a few [↵] s and [Break].

You get the idea. It is even possible to use AUTO as a statement inside a program, though I can't think of any reasonable excuse for putting it there. Can you?

Unless we specify otherwise, AUTO will always begin numbering with Line 10 and always space the Lines 10 numbers apart.

One important caution. Whenever we get fooling with something that's automatic, a degree of personal control is lost. Enter this quickie, using AUTO and the Line Numbers shown:

```
10 PRINT"NOW WHAT ARE WE UP TO?"
20 PRINT"BEATS ME!"
40 REM
80 REM
99 END
```

Then type:

```
AUTO
```

...oh, oh! What does the

`10*` mean?

W-H-A-T I-S G-O-I-N-G O-N H-E-R-E?
BEATS ME!

The asterisk means there is **already** a Line Number 10, and if we hit [Enter] without typing anything, the cursor will advance to Line 20 without altering the existing Line 10.

The AUTO command is not just for the lazy. It can be a real time saver (and save mental energy as well). For the touch typist who doesn't have to look at the screen when typing fast, it's a real delight.

Insert Line 60 by typing

```
60 REM
```

then type

```
AUTO .        (put a space between AUTO and the period)
```

AUTO . starts automatic Line numbering with the *highest* or *last* Line number entered in the program.

[Break] out of it.

## RENUMbering

In addition to the AUTOmatic Line Numbering feature, we can also RENUMber program Lines by simply typing:

```
RENUM      [Enter]
```

our entire program is RENUMbered by tens, starting with Line 10. Try it, then LIST to see the result.

To RENUMber by fives, try:

```
RENUM ,,5
```

Try it, and LIST.

If we need to RENUMber only part of a program, use:

```
RENUM 5000,25
```

This command will RENUMber from Line 25 to the end of the old program, starting with a new Line 5000. The RENUMbering will be by tens. Line 25 needn't actually be in the program. If it isn't, renumbering will start with the next highest existing Line Number. Try it and LIST.

RENUM also changes all of the GOSUBs and GOTOs (yet to be studied) along with the new Line numbers.

For computer types who thrive on cryptics, the entire RENUM syntax is:

```
RENUM newLine,startLine,increment
```

## Learned In Chapter 5

| Commands | Miscellaneous |
|---|---|
| AUTO | Automatic Line Numbering |
| AUTO . | |
| RENUM | |

# Chapter 6

# The Keyboard

## Special Function Keys

On the far left side of the keyboard are 10 keys labeled F1 - F10. These are "Special Function" Keys, sometimes called "Soft Keys", and each can call up an entire command or series of commands with just a touch of the key. The function of each is displayed at the bottom of the screen. Look at them.

So far, the only two that look familiar are LIST and RUN, but we will discover the uses for the rest of the keys as needed.

Let's give it a whirl. Type in the following NEW program:

```
10 PRINT "I WONDER WHAT THESE KEYS ARE FOR?"
20 PRINT "MAYBE THEY'RE GOOD FOR SOMETHING."
```

Now hit the key labeled [F1].

```
LIST _
```

appears on the screen. Since we want to LIST the entire program, just hit [←].

Voila. We see the program on the screen.

Now hit [F2].

NO! NO! THAT'S NOT A "SOFT" KEY- YOU'VE GOT GUM ON YOUR FINGER!

What happened? Why didn't we have to hit [←┘] ? Look carefully at the bottom of the screen next to the word RUN. See the left arrow? This means that the key [F2] types RUN on the screen *plus* an [←┘]. Keys [F5], [F7], and [F8] also have arrows after them. More on them in due course.

## The Whole Enchilada

Hit [F9] then [F1]. The screen will display:

```
KEY LIST
```

Hit [←┘]. The instructions associated with each key are PRINTed out in complete detail. Notice that [F10] says `SCREEN 0,0,0`. However, on the bottom right hand side of the screen it says only:

```
0 SCREEN
```

Each KEY is allowed to have 15 characters associated with it, but there is only room on the screen to display the first 6.

The "Soft Keys" are here to aide the computer programmer (that's us) in writing and executing programs. If we want to assign *our* own set of characters to the Keys, the Computer is perfectly willing. That's why the keys are called "SOFT". Unlike the rest of the keys, they can be easily reprogrammed to do special things.

Suppose for example, we want Key 6 to say MY CLEVER IBM!. All we have to do is type:

```
KEY 6, "MY CLEVER IBM!"
```

Do it. Look at bottom of the screen after the number 6.

Type KEY LIST again (or [F9] [F1]) and hit [←┘]. This time Key 6 displays MY CLEVER IBM!

To prove that this really works, type:

```
30 PRINT "[F6]"
```

[F6] means "Press key F6". Don't type in F6! *Do* include the quotes.

and RUN. ( [F2] does RUN [↵], remember?)

## Alternate Keys

In addition to the special function Keys, almost every letter key has a BASIC keyword associated with it. A keyword is a BASIC *command, function* or *statement*. We will make the distinctions in future Chapters.

For example, in the last Chapter we learned about AUTOmatic Line Numbering. Now we'll see an easier way to do it. Type NEW.

Now hold down the [Alt] key and hit the letter A. AUTO magically appears on the screen. Hit [↵] a few times to convince yourself that we're really in AUTO Line numbering mode, then [Break] out of it.

The chart below shows the [Alt] keywords corresponding to the letter keys A-Z.

```
A - AUTO            B - SAVE            C - COLOR
D - DELETE          E - ELSE            F - FOR
G - GOTO            H - HEX$            I - INPUT
J - (not used)      K - KEY             L - LOCATE
M - MOTOR           N - NEXT            O - OPEN
P - PRINT           Q - (not used)      R - RUN
S - SCREEN          T - THEN            U - USING
V - VAL             W - WIDTH           X - XOR
```

Y and Z are also not used. If you can't type well but can remember the keywords, the Alternate keys are great time savers.

The [Ctrl] key on the left side of the keyboard is used for very special purposes. It allows us to do some interesting things. For example, hold down the [Ctrl] key and hit the letter G. This is called [Ctrl G] (pronounced Control Gee). The speaker speaks!

Now try [Ctrl M]. The cursor moves down one Line each time. The same thing happens with [Ctrl J].

Now try [Ctrl I]. The cursor moves over 8 spaces at a time. And [Ctrl H] moves the cursor back one space. For the finale, hit [Ctrl L], and the screen is cleared. The program, however, is unchanged.

Take a quick look back at Appendix B, the so-called ASCII chart. We will study this Chart intensively in later Chapters.

Notice the relationship between codes 7-13 and the actions we just performed. [Ctrl G] made a beep and code 7 is a beep. G is the seventh letter of the alphabet. And H is the eighth letter, [Ctrl H] performed a backspace, and Appendix B says code 8 is a backspace. Stay tuned for more information.

There are several more important keys we'll just mention briefly. On the right side is a key that says [Num Lock]. Hit [Num Lock] and we can have all the keys needed for a calculator on the numeric keypad, complete with a + and −. Hit [Num Lock] again and we're toggled back to the EDITor arrows.

The [Esc] stands for Escape key. It is used to erase everything on the Line con-
taining the cursor. Set the cursor on a Line then hit [Esc]. It disappears from the screen only. The program is not affected.

There are a couple more keys that we'll not need in this book. They are [Pg Up] and [Pg Dn] which stand for Page Up and Page Down and are used primarily with word processor and electronic spreadsheet programs.

## Learned In Chapter 6

### Miscellaneous

Special Function keys
Alternate keys
[Ctrl]
[Esc]
[Num Lock]

# PART 2

# SPEAK TO ME, OH GREAT COMPUTER

# Chapter 7

# Math Operators

## But Can It Do Math?

Yes, it can. Basic arithmetic is a snap for the IBM. So are highly complex math calculations -- when we write special programs to perform them -- and we will.

The BASIC Computer language uses the 4 fundamental arithmetic operations, plus 4 more complex ones which are just modifications of the others:

1. ADDITION, using the symbol +

2. SUBTRACTION, using the symbol − *(See -- nothing to this. Just like grade school. I wonder whatever happened to old Miss... Well, ahem -- anyway)*

3. MULTIPLICATION, using the special symbol * *(Oh drat, I knew this was too easy to be true!)*

4. DIVISION, using the symbol / *(Well, at least it's simpler than the ÷ symbol)*

and

5. EXPONENTIATION, using ^ (unveiled in the next chapter)

6. NEGATION, (meaning "multiply times minus one") using the − symbol

OH, COME NOW-YOU CAN LEARN THAT * MEANS "TIMES" and / MEANS DIVISION. SAY TO YOURSELF I WILL.

7. MODulo. Of interest primarily to pure math-computer types. (We'll discuss it in Chapter 30)

8. INTEGER DIVISION, using the backslash \. (Taught in Chapter 18)

Of course, we also need that old favorite, the equals sign (=). But wait! The BASIC language is very particular about how we use this sign! Math expressions (like 1 + 2 * 5) can only go on the *right-hand* side of the equals sign; the left-hand side is reserved for the *result* of the math equation. We say 4 = 2 + 2. (This may seem a little strange, but it's really quite simple, as we'll discover in the next few pages.)

We *cannot* use an "X" for multiplication. Unfortunately, a long time ago a mathematician decided to use "X", which is a letter, to mean multiply. We use letters for other things, so it's much less confusing to use a "*". Confusion is one thing a computer can't tolerate. To computers, "*" is the *only* symbol which means multiply. After using it a while, you too, may feel we should do away with X as a multiplication symbol.

Putting all this together in a program is not difficult, so let's do it. First, we have to erase the "resident program" from the Computer's memory.

---

"Resident program" is computer talk for "what's already in there".

---

Type the command:

```
NEW       [↵]
```

Then type:

```
LIST      [↵]
```

to check that it's really gone. The Computer will respond with a simple:

```
OK
```

## Putting The Beast To Work

We'll now use the Computer for some very simple problem solving. That means using equations. (Oh -- panic). But then, an equation is just a little statement that says "what's on one side of an equals sign amounts to the same as what's on the other side." That can't get too bad.

We'll use that old standby equation,

"*Distance* traveled equals *Rate* of travel times *Time* spent traveling."

If it's been a few years, you might want to sit on the end of a log and contemplate that for awhile.

To shorten the equation, let's choose letters (called variables) to stand for the 3 quantities. Then we can rewrite the equation as a BASIC statement acceptable to the Computer. Type in:

```
40  D = R * T        [ENTER]
```

Remember, you have to use a * to specify multiplication.

What's that 40 doing in our equation? That's the program Line Number. Remember, every step in a program has to have one. We chose 40, but another number would have done just as well.

The extra spaces in the Line are there just to make the equation easier for us to read; BASIC ignores them. Later, when writing very long programs, you may want to eliminate extra Line spaces because they take up memory space. For learning, they are helpful, so leave them in.

Here's what Line 40 means to the Computer: "Take the values of R and T, multiply them together, and assign the resulting value to the variable D. So until further notice, D is equal to the result of R times T.

We *could not* reverse the equation and write: R*T=D. It has no meaning to the Computer. Remember, the left-hand side of the equation is reserved for the Line Number and the value we are *looking for*. The right-hand side is the place to put the values we *know*.

Any of the 26 letters from A through Z can be used to identify the values we know, as well as those we want to figure out. Whenever possible, it's a good idea to choose letters that are abbreviations of the things they stand for -- like the D, R, and T for the Distance, Rate, Time equation.

To complicate this very simple example, there's an optional way of writing the equation, using the BASIC statement LET:

```
40  LET D = R * T
```

This use of LET reminds us that making D equal R times T was *our* choice, rather than an eternal truth like 2 = 1 + 1. Some computers are fussy, and always require the use of LET with programmed equations. Our IBM says, "Whatever you want".

Okay -- let's complete the program.

Assume:

> Distance (in miles) = Rate (in miles per hour) multiplied by Time (in hours). How far is it from San Diego to London if a jet plane traveling at an average speed of 500 miles per hour makes the trip in 12 hours?

(Yes, I know you can do that one in your head but that's not the point!)

Use AUTO, and type in the following:

```
10 REM  * DISTANCE, RATE, TIME PROBLEM * [↵]
20 R = 500   [↵]
30 T = 12   [↵]
40 D = R * T   [↵]
```

LIST and check the program carefully, then:

```
RUN    [ENTER]
```

Hum de dum...ho-hum...(this sure is a slow computer).

```
Ok
_
```

All it says is Ok. **The Computer Doesn't Work!**

Yes it does. *It worked just fine.* The Computer multiplied 500 times 12 just like we told it, and came up with the answer of 6000 miles. But *we* forgot to tell it to give *us* the answer. Sorry about that.

**EXERCISE 7-1:** Can you finish this program without help? It only takes one more Line. Give it a good try before reading on for the answer. That way, the answer will mean more to you. (Hint: We've already used PRINT to PRINT messages in quotes. What would happen if we said `50 PRINT "D"`? ... No, we want the *value* of D, not "D" itself. Hmmmm, what happens when we get rid of the quotes?)

---

**Don't Read Beyond This Point Until You've Worked On The Above Exercise!**

Look in Section B of this Manual for an answer for this 1st Exercise. Also some notes and ideas.

Well, the answer 6000 is correct, but its "presentation" is no more inspiring than the readout on a hand calculator. This inevitably leads us back to where we first started this foray into the unknown -- the PRINT statement.

---

Did you find out the hard way that a space must be placed between the PRINT and the variable D? It *can't* be eliminated.

---

Note that we said `50 PRINT D`. There were no quotes around the letter D like we had used before. The reason is simple but fairly profound. If we want the Computer to PRINT *the exact words* we specify, we enclose them in quotes. If we want it to PRINT the *value* of a variable, in this case D, we leave the quotes off. That simple message is worth serious thought before continuing on.

Did you think seriously about it? Then on we go!

Now suppose we want to include both the *value* of something *and* some exact words on the same Line. Pay attention, as you will be doing more and more program designing yourself, and PRINT statements give beginners more trouble than any other single part of computer programming. Type in the following:

```
50 PRINT "THE DISTANCE (IN MILES) IS",D    [ENTER]
```

Then:

```
RUN    [ENTER]
```

(REMEMBER: Typing in a statement with a Line Number that already exists erases the original Line completely -- and that's what we want to do here. Could we have used the EDITor instead of retyping? Yes.)

The Display says:

```
THE DISTANCE (IN MILES) IS   6000
```

How about that! The message enclosed in quotes is PRINTed exactly as we specified, and the letter gave us the value of D. The comma told the Computer that we wanted it to PRINT two separate items on the *same* Line. We can PRINT up to **6** items on the same Line, simply by inserting commas between them.

With this in mind, see if you can change Line 50 so the Computer finishes the program with the following message:

```
THE DISTANCE IS              6000           MILES.
```

**Answer:** Break up the message words into two parts, and put the number variable in between them on the same PRINT Line. (Use the EDITor).

```
50 PRINT "THE DISTANCE IS",D,"MILES."
```

Why is there all that extra space on both sides of the 6000 in the PRINTout? The reason is that the Computer divides up the screen width into 5 zones of 14 characters each, plus a 6th zone which can hold 10 characters. That adds up to 80 columns. When a PRINT statement contains two or more items separated by commas, the Computer automatically PRINTs them in adjacent PRINT zones. *Automatic zoning* is a very convenient method of outputting TABular information, and we'll explore the subject in detail later on.

It's possible to eliminate the extra spaces in the display. EDIT the last version of Line 50, substituting semi-colons (;) for the 2 commas.

(Careful -- don't replace the period with a semi-colon.)

RUN 

Perfection, at last:

```
THE DISTANCE IS 6000 MILES.
```

Look carefully at the new Line 50. There is no blank space between the S in IS, the D, and the M in MILES. But in the display printout, there *is* a space between IS and 6000, and another space between 6000 and MILES. Why?

**Reason:** When a *number* is PRINTed, (the *value* of D), leading and trailing blank spaces are automatically inserted. As we do more programming, this feature will become very important.

*WHEW!*

Well, we have already covered more than enough Commands, Statements and Math Operators to solve a myriad of problems.

*Math Operators?* -- they're the = + - * ^ / and \ symbols we mentioned earlier.

Now let's spend some time actually writing programs to solve problems. There is no better way to learn than by doing, and *everything* covered so far is fundamental to our success in later Chapters. Don't jump over these exercises! They will plunge you right into the thick of programming, where you belong. Sample answers are in Section B, along with further comments.

**EXERCISE 7-2:** Write a program which will find the TIME required to travel by jet plane from London to San Diego, if the distance is 6000 miles and the plane travels at 500 MPH.

______________________________________________

______________________________________________

______________________________________________

______________________________________________

**EXERCISE 7-3:** If the circumference of a circle is found by multiplying its diameter times $\pi$ (3.14) write a program which will find the circumference of a circle with a diameter of 35 feet.

______________________________________________

______________________________________________

______________________________________________

______________________________________________

**EXERCISE 7-4:** If the area of a circle is found by multiplying $\pi$ times the square of its radius, write a program to find the area of a circle with a radius of 5 inches.

______________________________________________

______________________________________________

______________________________________________

______________________________________________

**EXERCISE 7-5:** Your checkbook balance was $225. You've written three checks (for $17, $35 and $225) and made two deposits ($40 and $200). Write a program to adjust your old balance based on checks written and deposits made, and PRINT out your new balance.

## Learned In Chapter 7

| Statements | Math Operators | Miscellaneous |
|---|---|---|
| LET (Optional) | = | , |
| | + | ; |
| | − | Variable Names |
| | * | |
| | / | |
| | \ | |
| | ^ | |

Remember, we can use any of the 26 letters as variables, not just D, R, and T (they were just convenient for our problem).

# Chapter 8

# Scientific Notation

## Are There More Stars Or Grains Of Sand?

In this mathematical world we are blessed with very large and very small numbers. Millions of these and billionths of those. To cope with all this, our Computer uses "exponential notation", or "standard scientific notation" when the number sizes start to get out of hand. The number 5 million (5,000,000), for example, can be written "5E+06" (E for Exponential). This means, "the number 5 followed by six zeros."

Technically, $5*10^6$, which is 5 times ten to the sixth power: 5*10*10*10*10*10*10

If an answer comes out "5E-06", that means we must shift the decimal point, which is after the 5, six places to the *left*, inserting zeros as necessary. Technically, it means 5 X $10(^{-6})$ or 5 millionths, (.000,005).

In our BASIC, that's 5/10/10/10/10/10/10

This is really pretty simple once you get the hang of it, and makes it very easy to keep track of the decimal point. Since the Computer *insists* on using it with very large and very small numbers, we can just as well get used to it right now.

Type NEW, then type and RUN the following:

```
10 PRINT 5*10^7
```
(The caret ^ is located above the 6 key)

NO MORE NAGGING!
IT'S ↵ AFTER
EACH LINE OR
COMMAND – TA DA

The answer is:

```
5E+07
```

Type NEW before solving the following exercises:

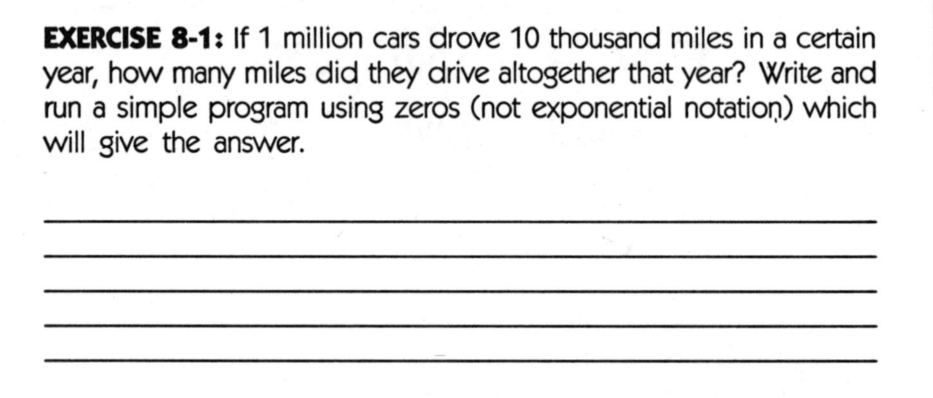

**EXERCISE 8-1:** If 1 million cars drove 10 thousand miles in a certain year, how many miles did they drive altogether that year? Write and run a simple program using zeros (not exponential notation) which will give the answer.

---

Didn't forget the [↵] did you? Up till now we've been reminding you to [↵] after each Line or command -- but from now on, we'll assume you've got that little routine down pat.

---

Before going on, LIST the program. Look at Line 20. What's that exclamation point doing at the end of the Line? It turns out that the Computer automatically converts all whole numbers over 32767 into *single precision variables*. The exclamation point is a *Type Declaration Character* that means *single precision*. Don't worry about it! We'll explain it in Part 4.

## Learned In Chapter 8

### Miscellaneous

E - notation

---

(E stands for "exponent" and in our case it refers to the exponent of 10, i.e. the number of zeros to the right or left of the main number.)

---

# Chapter 9

# Using ( ) And The Order Of Operations

arentheses play an important role in computer programming, just as in ordinary math. They are used here in the same general way, but there are important exceptions.

1. In BASIC, parentheses can enclose operations to be performed. Those operations which are within parentheses are performed before those *not* in parentheses.

2. Operations buried deepest within parentheses (that is, parentheses inside parentheses) are performed first.

---

To be sure equations are calculated correctly, use ( ) around the operations which must be performed first.

---

3. When there is a "tie" as to which operation the Computer should perform *after* it has solved all problems enclosed in parentheses, it works its way along the program Line from *left to right* performing the *multiplication* and *division.* It then starts at the left again and performs the *addition* and *subtraction.*

Recall the old memory aid, "My Dear Aunt Sally"? In math we do Multiplication and Division first (from left to right), then come back for Addition and Subtraction (left to right). IBM BASIC follows the same sequence.

INT, RND and ABS functions are performed before multiplication and division. (We haven't used them yet, but just to be completely accurate...)

4. An operation written as (X)(Y) will *not* tell the Computer to multiply. X * Y is the only scheme recognized for multiplication.

EXAMPLE: To convert temperature expressed in degrees Fahrenheit to Celsius (Centigrade), the following relationship is used:

The Fahrenheit temperature equals 32 degrees plus nine-fifths of the Celsius temperature. Or, maybe you're more used to the simple formula:

$$F = \frac{9}{5} * C + 32$$

Assume we have a Celsius temperature of 25. Type in this NEW program and RUN it:

```
10 REM * CELSIUS TO FAHRENHEIT CONVERSION *
20 C = 25
30 F = (9/5)*C + 32
40 PRINT C;"DEGREES (C) =";F;"DEGREES (F)."
```

SAMPLE RUN:

```
25 DEGREES (C) = 77 DEGREES (F).
```

Remember what the semi-colons are for?

MY DEAR AUNT SALLY- I DIDN'T KNOW YOU WERE PART OF THIS!
THIS IS MY S-L-O-W NEPHEW!

Notice first that Line 40 consists of a PRINT statement followed by 4 separate expressions -- 2 variables and 2 groups of words in quotes called "literals" or "strings". Notice also that everything within the quotes (including spaces) is PRINTed.

Next, note how the parentheses are placed in Line 30. With the 9/5 securely inside, we can multiply its quotient times C, then add 32.

Now, remove the parentheses in Line 30 and RUN again. The answer comes out the same. Why?

1. On the first pass, the Computer started by solving all problems within parentheses, in this case just one (9/5). It came up with (but did not PRINT) 1.8. It then multiplied the 1.8 times the value of C and added 32.

2. On our next try, without the parentheses, the Computer simply moved from left to right performing first the division problem (9 divided by 5), then the multiplication problem (1.8 times C), then the addition problem (adding 32). The parentheses really made no difference in this example.

Next, change the +32 to 32+ and move it to the front of the equation in Line 30 to read:

```
30 F = 32 + (9/5)*C
```

RUN it again, without parentheses.

Did it make a difference in the answer? Why not?

**Answer:** Execution proceeds from left to right, multiplication and division first, then returns and performs addition and subtraction. This is why the 32 was *not* added to the 9 before being divided by 5. **Very Important!** If they had been added, we would, of course, have gotten the wrong answer.

**EXERCISE 9-1:** Write and RUN a program which converts 65 degrees Fahrenheit to Celsius. The rule tells us that "Celsius temperature is equal to five-ninths times what's left after 32 is subtracted from the Fahrenheit temperature."

$$30\ C = (F - 32) * \frac{5}{9}$$

**EXERCISE 9-2:** Remove the first set of parentheses in the Ex. 9-1 answer and RUN again.

**EXERCISE 9-3:** Replace the first set of parentheses in program Line 30 and remove the second pair of parentheses, then RUN. Note how the answer comes out -- correctly!

**EXERCISE 9-4:** Insert parentheses in the following equation to make it correct. Write a program and check it out on the IBM.

30 - 9 - 8 - 7 - 6 = 28

## Learned In Chapter 9

### Miscellaneous

( )
Order of Operations

Chapter 10

# Relational Operators

**I**f you liked the preceding Chapters, **then** you're going to love the rest of this book!

...because we're really just getting into the good stuff like IF-THEN and GOTO statements that let the Computer make decisions and take, um, er, executive action. But first, a few more operators.

**Relational Operators** allow the Computer to compare one value with another. There are only 3:

1. Equals, using the symbol =

2. Is greater than, using the symbol >

3. Is less than, using the symbol <

Combining these 3, we come up with 3 more operators:

4. Is not equal to, using the symbol <>

5. Is less than or equal to, using the symbol <=

6. Is greater than or equal to, using the symbol >=

Example: A<B means A is less than B. To help distinguish between < and >, just remember that the *smaller* (pointed) part of the < symbol points to the *smaller* of the two quantities being compared.

By adding these 6 *relational* operators to the *math* operators we already know, plus new *statements* called IF-THEN & GOTO, we create a powerful system of comparing and calculating that becomes the central core of everything that follows.

The IF-THEN statement, combined with the 6 relational operators above, gives us the *action* part of a system of logic. Enter and RUN this NEW program:

```
10 A = 5
20 IF A = 5 THEN 50
30 PRINT "A DOES NOT EQUAL 5."
40 END
50 PRINT "A EQUALS 5."
```

The screen displays:

```
A EQUALS 5.
```

This program is an example of using an IF-THEN statement with only the most fundamental relational operator, the equals sign.

## The Autopsy

Let's examine the program Line by Line.

Line 10 establishes the fact that A has a value of 5.

Line 20 is an IF-THEN statement which directs the Computer to GOTO Line 50 *if the value of A is exactly* 5, skipping over whatever might be inbetween Lines 20 and 50. Since A *does* equal 5, the Computer jumps to Line 50 and does as it says, PRINTing `A EQUALS 5`. Lines 30 and 40 were not used at all.

Now, change Line 10 to read:

```
10 A = 6
```

...and RUN.

The screen says:

```
A DOES NOT EQUAL 5.
```

Taking it a Line at a time:

Line 10 establishes the value of A to be 6.

Line 20 tests the value of A. If A equals 5, THEN the Computer is directed to GOTO Line 50. But "the test fails", that is, A does *not* equal 5, so the Computer proceeds as usual to the next Line, Line 30.

Line 30 directs the Computer to PRINT the fact that A DOES NOT EQUAL 5. It does not tell us what the *value* of A is, only that it does *not* equal 5. The Computer proceeds to the next Line.

Line 40 ENDs the program's execution. Without this statement separating Lines 30 and 50, the Computer would charge right on to

Line 50 and PRINT its contents, which obviously are in conflict with the contents of Line 30.

## IF-THEN Vs GOTO

IF-THEN is what is known as a *conditional* branching statement. The program will "branch" to another part of the program *on the condition that* it passes the IF-THEN test. If it fails the test, program execution simply passes to the next Line.

GOTO is an *unconditional* branching statement. If we were to replace Line 40 with:

```
40 GOTO 99
```

SORT OF LIKE A FAMILY TREE!
GOTO
IF-THEN

and add Line 99:

```
99 END
```

...whenever the Computer hit Line 40 it would *unconditionally* follow orders and GOTO 99, ENDing the RUN. Change Line 40 as discussed above and RUN.

Did the program work Ok as changed? Did you try it with several values of A? Be sure you do! We will find many uses for the GOTO statement in the future.

## Optional THEN With GOTO

When the IF-THEN statement is used with a GOTO statement, either THEN or GOTO or both can be used. This can be useful in long program lines. For example, either of these Lines will work in place of Line 20 in our program:

```
20 IF A = 5 THEN GOTO 50
```

or

```
20 IF A = 5 GOTO 50
```

**EXERCISE 10-1:** Change the value of A in Line 10 back to 5 then rewrite the resident program using a "does-not-equal" sign in Line 20 instead of the equals sign. Change other Lines as necessary, so the same results are achieved with your program as with the one in the example.

________________________________________

________________________________________

________________________________________

________________________________________

________________________________________

**EXERCISE 10-2:** Change Line 10 to give A the value of 6. Leave the other four Lines from Exercise 10-1 as shown. Add more program Lines as necessary so the program will tell us whether A is larger or smaller than 5 and RUN.

**EXERCISE 10-3:** Change the value of A in Line 10 at least three more times, RUNning after each change to ensure that your new program works correctly.

No sample answers are given since you are choosing your own values of A. It will be obvious whether or not you are getting the right answer.

## Learned In Chapter 10

| Statements | Relational Operators | Miscellaneous |
| --- | --- | --- |
| IF-THEN | = | Conditional branching |
| GOTO | > | Unconditional branching |
| | < | |
| | <> | |
| | <= | |
| | >= | |

# Chapter 11

# It Also Talks And Listens

By now you have probably become tired of having to retype Line 10 each time you wish to change the value of A. The INPUT statement is a simple, fast and more convenient way to accomplish the same thing. It's a biggie, so don't miss any points.

Enter this NEW program:

```
10 PRINT "THE VALUE I WISH TO GIVE A IS"
20 INPUT A
30 PRINT "A =";A
```

...and RUN

The Computer will print:

```
THE VALUE I WISH TO GIVE A IS
? _
```

See the question mark on the screen? It means, "It's your turn -- and I'm waiting..."

Type in a number, press [↵] and see what happens. The program responds exactly the same way as when we changed values within a program Line. RUN several more times to get the feel of the INPUT statement.

Pretty powerful, isn't it?

Let's add a touch of class to the INPUT process by changing Line 10 as follows:

```
10 PRINT "THE VALUE I WISH TO GIVE A IS";
```

Look at that Line very carefully. Do you see how it differs from the earlier Line 10? It is different -- a *semi-colon* was added at the end.

---

Did you use the EDITor to add the semi-colon? Search for [↵].

---

Think back a bit. We used semi-colons before in PRINT statements, but only in the *middle,* to hook several together to PRINT them on the same Line. In this case, we put a semi-colon at the *end,* so the *question mark* from the Line 10 will PRINT on the *same* display Line rather than on a second line. After changing Line 10 as above, RUN. It should read:

```
THE VALUE I WISH TO GIVE A IS?
```

We cannot use a semi-colon indiscriminately at the end of a PRINT statement. It is only meant to hook two Lines together, *both* of which will PRINT something. The INPUT Line PRINTs a question mark. We will later connect two long Lines starting with PRINT by a "trailing semicolon" so as to PRINT everything on the same Line.

The IBM BASIC *interpreter* speaks "The King's BASIC" as well as a variety of dialects. The first of the many "short-cuts" we will learn combines PRINT and INPUT into one statement.

---

INTERPRETER -- is the program we loaded in from disk which allows us to "rap" with the Computer in the English language. The program is called BASIC, which stands for Beginners All-purpose Symbolic Instruction Code.

---

Sometimes the word "dialect" is used when talking about the different variations of a computer language. Just as with dialects in "human" languages, there are differences in the way different computers use BASIC words. That's why I wrote *The BASIC Handbook, Encyclopedia of the BASIC Language* available at better Computer and Bookstores everywhere in English, and translated into French, German, Swedish, Norwegian, Dutch, Italian, Spanish and Hebrew.

Change Line 10 to read:

```
10 INPUT "TYPE IN A VALUE FOR A";A
```

delete Line 20 by typing:

```
20        [↵]
```

...and RUN.

The results come out exactly the same, don't they? Here is what we did:

1. Changed PRINT to INPUT
2. Placed both statements on the same Line
3. Eliminated an unnecessary Line

In the long programs which we will be writing, running and converting, this shortcut will be valuable.

## Endless Love

Up to now, all our programs have been strictly one-shot affairs. You type RUN, the Computer executes the program, PRINTs the results (if any) and comes back with an `Ok`. To repeat the program, we have to type RUN again. Can you think of another way to make the Computer execute a program two or more times?

No -- don't enlarge the program by repeating its Lines over and over again -- that's not very creative!

BY GEORGE! I THINK I'VE GOT IT !!
LISSEN, I'LL KEEP ASK-IN' FOR MORE UNTIL YOU HIT CTRL and SCROLL LOCK

We'll answer that question by upgrading our Celsius-to-Fahrenheit conversion program (Chapter 9). If you think GOTO is a powerful statement in everyday life, wait 'til you see what it does for a computer program!

Type NEW and the following:

```
10 REM * IMPROVED (C) TO (F) CONV. PROGRAM *
20 INPUT "WHAT IS THE TEMP IN DEGREES (C)";C
30 F = (9/5)*C + 32
40 PRINT C;"DEGREES (C) =";F;"DEGREES (F)."
50 GOTO 20
```

...and RUN.

Hit [Ctrl] [Scr Lock] to exit the program loop.

The Computer will keep asking for more until we get tired, or the power goes off (or some other event beyond its control). This is the kind of thing a computer is best at -- doing the same thing over and over. Modify some of the other programs to make them self-repeating. They're often much more useful this way.

These have been 5 long and "meaty" lessons, so go back and review them all, repeating those assignments where you feel weak. We are moving out into progressively deeper water, and complete mastery of these *fundamentals* is your only life preserver.

## Learned In Chapter 11

| **Statements** | **Miscellaneous** |
|---|---|
| INPUT and<br>INPUT with built-in PRINT | ; Trailing semi-colon |

# Chapter 12

# Calculator Or Immediate Mode

## Two Easy Features

Before continuing exploration of the nooks and crannies of the Computer acting as a *computer*, we should be aware that it also works well as a *calculator*. If we *omit* the Line number before certain statements and commands, the Computer will execute them, and display the answer on the screen. What's more, it will work as a calculator even when another computer program is loaded, *without disturbing that program*. All we need, to be in the calculator mode, is the cursor _.

EXAMPLE: How much is 3 times 4? Type in:

```
PRINT 3 * 4        [←]
```

...the answer comes back:

```
12
```

EXAMPLE: How much is 345 divided by 123?

Type:

```
PRINT 345/123        [←]
```

...the answer is:

```
2.804878
```

Spend a few minutes making up routine arithmetic problems of your own and use the calculator mode to solve them. Any arithmetic expression which can be used in a program can also be evaluated in the calculator mode. This includes parentheses and chain calculations like A*B*C.

Try the following:

```
PRINT (2/3)*(3/2)
```

The answer is:

```
1
```

## Calculator Mode For Troubleshooting

Suppose a program isn't giving the answers we expect. How can we troubleshoot it? One way is to ask the Computer to tell us what it knows about the variables used in the resident program.

EXAMPLE: If our program uses the variable X, we can ask the Computer to:

```
PRINT X
```

The Computer will PRINT the present value of X.

---

Keep this handy tip in mind as you get into more complex programs.

---

Another thought: *Something* is stored in every memory cell (even if *you* have not put anything there). Enter this instruction in the calculator mode:

```
PRINT A,B,C,D,E,F,G,H,I,J,K,L,M,N,O,P,Q,R,S,T,
U,V,W,X,Y,Z
```

The answers depend on the values last given those variables -- even from

Y'KNOW, ALL THIS IS UNNECESSARY FOR TROUBLE SHOOTING!

much earlier programs. If we turn the Computer off, then on again, all variables will be reset to Ø. Typing RUN also "initializes" all variables to Ø.

We will get all zeros if the machine was turned OFF since the last RUN.

## The FRE(Ø) Command

Since programs do occupy space in the Computer's memory, and program size is limited to how much memory is installed, it may be important to know how much memory is left. That's what the FRE(Ø) Command is for.

In a "16K" computer there are about 16,000 different memory locations available to store and process programs. "16K" is just a shortcut phrase for the exact amount of memory, which is 16384. With "64K" of memory, the number is 65536.

This book is for the computer operator and programmer, so we are studiously avoiding computer electronics theory -- when possible.

The Computer uses some of the memory for program control. To see the actual amount of memory available for our use, type:

```
NEW            [↵]

PRINT FRE(Ø)        [↵]
```

...and the answer is:

```
33402
```

With no program loaded, it means there are 33402 memory locations available for use. The difference in memory space between 33402 and 65536 is used by the BASICA language interpreter and overall management and "monitoring" of what the Computer is doing.

Type in this simple program:

```
10 A = 25
```

then measure the memory remaining by typing:

```
PRINT FRE(Ø)        [←┘]
```

Ø is a "dummy" value used with FRE. Any number or letter can be used.

...the answer is:

```
33391
```

The program we entered took 33402 - 33391 = 11 bytes of space. Here is how we account for it:

1. Each Line number and the space following it (regardless of how small or large that Line number is) occupies 4 memory cells. The "carriage return" at the end of the Line takes 1 more byte, even though it does not PRINT on the screen. Thus, memory "overhead" for each Line, short or long is 5 bytes.

2. Each letter, number and space takes 1 byte. In the above program 5 bytes for overhead + 6 bytes for the characters = 11 bytes.

Now, type RUN, then check the memory again with PRINT FRE(Ø). It changed to 33383, 8 more bytes! When RUN, a simple variable like the A takes up 4 bytes and the numerical value takes another 4, totaling 8.

BYTE -- is the basic unit of storage for the IBM and most other microcomputers. In the IBM it is a string of eight **bi**nary digi**ts** (bits). Thus a byte = 8 bits.

We will be studying memory requirements in more detail later.

Obviously, the short learning programs we have written so far are not taking up much memory space. This changes quickly, however, as we move to more sophisticated programming. Make a habit of typing `PRINT FRE(Ø)` when completing a program to develop a sense of its size and memory requirements.

## Learned In Chapter 12

**Functions**

FRE(∅)

**Miscellaneous**

Calculator Mode
Memory
Byte

# Chapter 13

# Saving and Loading Using Disk

big advantage of having disk drives is that programs can be SAVEd on or LOADed from disk very quickly and reliably.

On a one-drive system, programs are automatically SAVEd on the diskette in drive A, unless it has a write-protect tab on it. In multi-drive systems, we have to specify use of any other drive. In our case, that's always Drive B:.

Remember: Diskettes must be "formatted" before they can be used. The master disk in drive A is, of course, already formatted. See Chapter 1 for use of the FORMAT command.

Type in this short BASIC program:

```
10 REM * DISK BASIC PROGRAM *
20 PRINT "HELLO THERE, DISK USER!"
99 END
```

then, with our blank formatted diskette in Drive B:

```
SAVE "PROGRAM1"
```

WELL, OUR SAVINGS PROGRAM DOES NOT INCLUDE DISKS!
TELLER

Oh-oh! The screen says:

```
Disk Write Protected
```

The program didn't SAVE on diskette B because Drive A is the "default" drive. It couldn't SAVE on Drive A because we deliberately (and permanently) have that diskette write protected. Now what do we do?

Using this special SAVE command, SAVE the program to Drive B.

```
SAVE "B:PROGRAM1"
```

Aha. It worked. By incorporating the Drive designation, B: into the SAVE command, we overrode the default drive designation and SAVEd the day. Remember this little lesson well. It will be useful again.

How do we know it worked? Easy. Type:

```
FILES "B:*.*"
```

and see the name:

```
PROGRAM1.BAS
```

listed. But where did the .BAS come from? The Computer automatically adds .BAS to any program saved from the BASIC interpreter. We don't have to use it when either SAVEing or LOADing a program to or from disk. When the disk has many programs on it, it's nice to be able to look at a FILES listing and know which are written in BASIC.

The *.* are 2 "wild cards". It essentially says, "ALL programs of whatever name *before* the period, and ALL programs of whatever name *after* the period." We will study some other wild cards later in the book.

With the program SAVEd and the FILES checked, let's see if we can LOAD the program back from disk into memory. Type NEW to remove it from memory first, then LIST to be sure it's gone, then:

```
LOAD "B:PROGRAM1"
```

and the Computer says Ok. Type LIST to see if it's back in memory. How about that?

Just for fun, let's see what's on Drive A. Type:

```
FILES
```

and there they are. Do you rememb
Using DIRectory. From BASIC we
hard. Most are the subject of a wh

Well, having learned our lesson by a
gram, let's go back to DOS and rede
make life a little easier. Type:

```
SYSTEM
```

and

```
B:
```

and the deed is done. Now let's go b... with:

```
BASICA
```

What's this? It doesn't recognize the BASIC command? The shoe is now on the other foot. With B as the default, if we want something to happen that involves Drive A, we have to specify it. So:

```
A:BASICA
```

and we're back home in BASIC again.

As a final test, let's load in our PROGRAM1 again, but without using any drive designators:

```
LOAD "PROGRAM1"
```

and

```
LIST
```

How sweet it is!

With B as the default drive, we can easily SAVE and use FILES to check what's on the diskette that's getting all the use.

## Learned in Chapter 13

**Commands**

SAVE
LOAD
FILES

**Miscellaneous**

"pulling a DIRectory"
from BASIC
Wild Cards
Forced Drive Designation

## Chapter 14

# FOR-NEXT Looping

A major difference between a Computer and a calculator is the Computer's ability to do the same thing over and over an outrageous number of times! This single capability (plus, a larger display) more than any other feature distinguishes between the two.

The FOR-NEXT loop is of such overwhelming importance in putting our Computer to work that few of the programming areas we explore from here on will exclude it. Its simplicity and variations are the heart of its effectiveness; and its power is truly staggering.

Type NEW and then the following program:

```
20 PRINT "HELP! MY COMPUTER IS BERSERK!"
40 GOTO 20
```

...and RUN.

The Computer is PRINTing:

```
HELP! MY COMPUTER IS BERSERK!
```

and will do so indefinitely, until we tell it to STOP. When you have seen enough, hit [Ctrl] [Break]. This "breaks" the program RUN.

## Endless Loop

We created what is called an "endless loop". Remember our earlier programs which kept coming back for more INPUT? They were in a very similar "loop".

Line 40 is an unconditional GOTO statement which causes the Computer to cycle back and forth ("loop") between Lines 20 and 40 forever, if not halted. This idea has great potential if we can harness it.

Modify the program to read:

```
10 FOR N = 1 TO 5
20 PRINT "HELP! MY COMPUTER IS BERSERK!"
40 NEXT N
60 PRINT "NO --- IT'S UNDER CONTROL."
```

...and RUN it.

The Line:

```
HELP! MY COMPUTER IS BERSERK!
```

was PRINTed 5 times, then:

```
NO --- IT'S UNDER CONTROL.
```

The FOR-NEXT loop created in Lines 10 and 40 caused the Computer to cycle through Lines 10, 20, and 40 exactly 5 times, then continue through the rest of the program. Each time the Computer hit Line 40 it saw "NEXT N". The word NEXT caused the value of N to increase (or STEP) by exactly 1. The Computer "conditionally" went back to the `FOR N =` statement that *began* the loop.

Execution of the NEXT statement is "conditional" on N being less than or equal to 5, because Line 10 says FOR N = 1 TO 5. After the 5th pass through the loop, the built-in test fails, the loop is broken and program execution moves on. The FOR-NEXT statement harnessed the endless loop!

## The Step Function

There are times when it is desirable to increment the FOR-NEXT loop by some value other than 1. The STEP function allows it. Change Line 10 to read:

```
10 FOR N = 1 TO 5 STEP 2
```

...and RUN.

Line 20 was PRINTed only 3 times (when N=1, N=3, and N=5). On the first pass through the program, when NEXT N was hit, it was incremented (or STEPped) by the value of 2, instead of the default value of 1. On the second pass through the loop, N equaled 3. On the third pass N equaled 5.

FOR-NEXT loops can be STEPped by any decimal number, even negative numbers. Why we would want to STEP with negative numbers might seem vague at this time, but that too will be understood with time. Meanwhile, change the following Line:

```
10 FOR N = 5 TO 1 STEP -1
```

...and RUN.

Five passes through the loop stepping *down* from 5 to 1 is exactly the same as stepping *up* from 1 to 5. Line 20 was still PRINTed 5 times. Change the STEP from -1 to -2.5 and RUN again.

Amazing! It PRINTed exactly twice. Smart Computer. Change the STEP back to -1.

---

You *are* using the EDITor aren't you?

---

## Modifying The FOR-NEXT Loop

Suppose we want to PRINT both Lines 20 and 60 five times, alternating between them. How will you change the program to accomplish it? Go ahead and make the change.

HINT: If you can't figure it out, try moving the NEXT N Line to another position.

Right -- we moved Line 40 to Line 70 and the screen reads:

```
HELP! MY COMPUTER IS BERSERK!
NO --- IT'S UNDER CONTROL.
HELP! MY COMPUTER IS BERSERK!
NO --- IT'S UNDER CONTROL.
```

... etc., 3 more times.

How would you modify the program so Line 20 is PRINTed 5 times, then Line 60 is PRINTed 3 times? Make the changes and RUN.

The new program might read:

```
10 FOR N = 1 TO 5
20  PRINT "HELP! MY COMPUTER IS BERSERK!"
40 NEXT N
50 FOR M = 1 TO 3
60  PRINT "NO --- IT'S UNDER CONTROL."
70 NEXT M
```

We now have a program with *two* controlled loops, sometimes called *DO-loops*. The first do-loop *DOes* something 5 times; the second one *DOes* something 3 times. We used the letter N for the first loop and M for the second, but any letters can be used. In fact, since the two loops are totally separate we could have used the letter N for both of them -- not an uncommon practice in large programs where many of the letters are needed as variables.

HELP! MY COMPUTER'S
GONE BERSERK!
HELP! MY COMPUTER'S
GONE BERSERK!
HELP! MY COMPUTER'S
GONE BERSERK!
HELP! MY COMPUTER'S
GONE BERSERK!
HELP! MY COMPUTER'S
GONE BERSERK!
MY
BERSERK!
MY OMPUTER'S
BERSERK!

RUN the program. Be sure you understand the fundamental principles and the variations. Then SAVE on disk as "DOLoop".

## Incremental Looping

There is nothing magic about the FOR-NEXT loop, in fact, you may have already thought of another (longer) way to accomplish the same thing by using features we learned earlier. Stop now, and see if you can figure out a way to construct a workable do-loop substituting something else in place of the FOR-NEXT statement.

---

**Answer:**

```
10 N = 1
20 PRINT "HELP! MY COMPUTER IS BERSERK!"
30 N = N + 1
40 IF N < 6 THEN 20
60 PRINT "NO --- IT'S UNDER CONTROL."
```

Line 10 *initializes* the value of N, giving it an *initial* or beginning value of 1. Without initializing, N could have been any number from a previous program or program Line. Note that typing RUN automatically resets all variables back to 0 before the program executes.

> *Initialize:* initially, or at the beginning, establishes the value of a variable.

Line 30 *increments* it by 1, making N one more than whatever it was before. Line 40 uses one relational operator, <, to check that the new value of N is within the bounds we have established. If not, the test fails and the program continues.

> *Increments:* STEPs (increases or decreases) values by specific amounts: by 1's, 3's, 5's, or whatever.

Note that in this system of *incrementing* and testing we do not send the program back to Line 10 as was the case with FOR-NEXT. What would happen if we did?

**Answer:** We would keep re-initializing the value of N to equal 1, and would again form an endless loop.

The opposite of *incrementing* is *decrementing*. Change the program so Line 30 reads:

```
30 N = N - 1
```

To *decrement* is to make smaller.

... then make other changes as needed to make the program work.

The changed Lines read:

```
10 N = 6
30 N = N - 1
40 IF N>1 THEN 20
```

## Putting FOR-NEXT To Work

It isn't very exciting just seeing or doing the same thing over and over. The FOR-NEXT loop has to have a more noble purpose. It has many, and we will be learning new ones for a long time.

Suppose we want to PRINT out a chart showing how the time it takes to fly from London to San Diego varies with the speed at which we fly. (Remember, the formula is D = R*T). Let's PRINT out the flight time required for each speed between 100 mph and 1500 mph, in increments of 100 mph. The program might look like this:

```
10 REM * TIME VS RATE FLIGHT CHART *
20 CLS
30 D = 6000
40 PRINT "      LONDON TO SAN DIEGO"
50 PRINT "   DISTANCE =";D;"(MILES)"
```

```
60 PRINT "RATE (MPH)","TIME (HOURS)"
70 PRINT
80 FOR R=100 TO 1500 STEP 100
90    T = D/R
100   PRINT R,T
110 NEXT R
```

Type in the program and RUN.

---

How about that...? Try doing that one on the old slide rule or hand calculator!

---

It is really solving the D = R*T problem 15 times in a row, for different values, and PRINTing out the result. The screen should look like this:

```
        LONDON TO SAN DIEGO
      DISTANCE = 6000 (MILES)
RATE (MPH)      TIME (HOURS)


 100             60
 200             30
 300             20
 400             15
 500             12
 600             10
 700             8.571428
 800             7.5
 900             6.666667
 1000            6
 1100            5.454546
 1200            5
```

```
1300          4.615385
1400          4.285714
1500          4
```

## Analyzing The Program

Look through the program and observe these many features before we do some exercises to change it:

1. The REM statement identifies the program for future use.

2. Line 20 uses the CLS (CLear Screen) statement to erase the screen so we have a nice place to write. It allows us to write in a *top-down* manner. (RUN the program again leaving out this Line to contrast *top-down* with *scroll* mode, then, put it back in.) CLS is a very unfussy statement which you will want to use often just to make your PRINTouts neat and impressive.

3. Line 30 *initializes* the value of D. D will remain at its initialized value.

4. Lines 40 through 70 PRINT the chart heading.

5. Line 60 uses *automatic zone spacing* to place those column headings (the comma).

---

*Remember zone spacing?* The comma (,) in a PRINT statement automatically starts the PRINTing in the next 14-space PRINT zone.

---

6. Line 80 established the FOR-NEXT loop complete with a STEP. It says, initialize the rate (R) at 100 mph, and make passes through the "do-loop" with values of R incremented by values of 100 mph until a final value of 1500 mph is reached. Line 110 is the other half of the loop.

7. Line 90 contains the actual formula which calculates the answer.

8. Line 100 PRINTs the two values. They are positioned under their headings by automatic zone spacing (the commas).

9. Lines 90 and 100 are indented from the rest of the program text. This is a simple programming technique high-lights the do-loop, and makes reading and troubleshooting easier. *Try to adopt good programming practices like this* as you do the exercises. Indenting does take up a little memory space, and on long programs is sometimes omitted.

Take a deep breath and go back over any points you might have missed in this lesson. SAVE the program onto Disk as "LONDON1" because we will use it in the next Chapter, continuing our study of FOR-NEXT loops.

## Learned In Chapter 14

| Statements | Miscellaneous |
|---|---|
| FOR-NEXT | Increment |
| CLS | Decrement |
| STEP | Initialize |
| | "Top down" Display |
| | "Scroll" Display |
| | "Do-Loop" |

# Chapter 15

# Son Of FOR-NEXT

his is heady stuff. If you turned the Computer off between Chapters, LOAD in the LONDON1 program which we SAVEd in the last Chapter.

Modify the program so the rate and time are calculated and PRINTed for every 25 mph increment instead of the 100 mph increment presently in the program.

...and RUN.

---

**Answer:** `80 FOR R = 100 TO 1500 STEP 25`

## Trouble In The Old Corral

What a revolting development! The PRINTout goes so fast we can't read it, and by the time it stops, the top part is cut off. *Aught'a known you can't trust these computers!*

## Solutions For Sale

Several solutions are available:

1. Pressing the [Ctrl] and the [Num Lock] keys *at the same time* will halt program execution or a LISTing. Pressing almost any other key will start it again. RUN the program several times, and practice stopping and starting using this method.

There's another solution we must try. While the program is RUNning, -- press [Ctrl] [Break] for an execution BREAK. While [Ctrl] [Num Lock] can be thought of as just pressing in the clutch, a BREAK is more like turning off the engine.

To restart execution after a BREAK, either type RUN to start all over again from the beginning, or type CONT to CONTinue execution from the "break-point". CONTinue does *not* reset all variables back to zero, which can be an important consideration. [F5] does the same as CONT [↵].

2. If we want a classy display we can build a "pause" *into the program*. The screen will fill, pause a moment, then automatically continue if we don't interrupt execution.

## The Timing Loop

It takes time to do everything. Even this foxy box takes time to do its thing, though we may be awed by its speed.

We are going to write and experiment with a timing program using Lines 1-9 without erasing the one already resident. The new one must END without plowing ahead ito the "LONDON1" program, thus, Line 9. Type:

```
4 PRINT "DON'T GO AWAY"
5 FOR X = 1 TO 8000
6 NEXT X
7 PRINT "TIMER PROGRAM ENDED."
9 END
```

...and RUN.

Remember back when we learned *not* to do this (number Lines in tight sequence)? Well ... if we *hadn't* followed that rule with our "LONDON1" program, we wouldn't have this nice space to demonstrate the point.

How long did it take? Well, it did take time, didn't it? About 10 seconds? The IBM Personal Computer can execute approximately 800 FOR-NEXT loops per second. That means, by specifying the number of loops, we can build in as long a time-delay as we wish.

Change the program to create a 30-second delay. Time it against your watch or clock to see how accurate it is.

SHHHH
DON'T DISTURB
'IM! HE'S IN
THE MIDDLE
OF A LOOP!

**Answer:** `5 FOR X = 1 TO 24000`

**EXERCISE 15-1:** Using the space in Lines 1 through 8, design a program which:

1) Asks us how many seconds delay we wish, allows us to enter a number, then executes the delay and reports back at the end that the delay is over, and how many seconds it took. A sample answer is in Section B.

______________________________

______________________________

______________________________

## How To Handle Long Program LISTings

We now have **two** programs in the Computer. Let's pull a LIST to look at them. My, my -- they almost fill the screen. Wonder what would we do if the programs were a few Lines longer so they couldn't both fit on the screen at the same time?

Rather than wring our hands about the problem, let's add some dummy Lines and learn how. Add:

---

Remember how to use AUTO?

---

```
1000 REM
2000 REM
3000 REM
4000 REM
5000 REM
6000 REM
7000 REM
8000 REM
```

```
9000 REM

10000 REM
```

and LIST. Sure enough, the first Lines of the first program are chopped off.

## For Every Problem, A Solution

Try each of the following variations of the LIST command, and study the screen very carefully as each version does its thing:

LIST 50 (Lists only Line 50)

LIST -50 (Lists all Lines up through 50)

LIST 50- (Lists all Lines from 50 to end)

LIST 30-70 (Lists all Lines from 30 thru 70)

LIST 15-85 (Note that these numbers are not even in the program)

LIST . (Lists 80, the last Line number printed)

LIST .- (Lists the current or last Line number to end)

How's that for something to write home about?

**Question:** How would you look at the resident program only up through Line 9?

---

**Answer:** Type LIST -9 (Talk about a give-away!)

## Is There No End To This Magic?

To RUN the first program resident in the Computer -- we just type RUN. To RUN the second one we have a foxy variation of RUN called:

```
RUN ###
```

The ###'s represent the number of the Line we want the RUN to start with.

...and as you might suspect, it is similar to LIST ###. To RUN the program starting with Line 1Ø, type:

```
RUN 1Ø
```

...and that's just what happens.

---

Don't forget the space between RUN and 1Ø. The IBM is fussy about some of these things. Note that we can't use key [F2] since it always starts RUNs with the first program Line.

---

Will wonders never cease? If there are 20 or 30 programs in the Computer at the same time, we can RUN just the one we want, provided we know its starting Line number. What's more, we can start any program in the middle (or elsewhere) for purposes of troubleshooting -- something we will do as our programs get longer and more complicated.

## Meanwhile, Back At The Ranch

We got into this whole messy business trying to find a way to slow down our RUN on the flight times from London to San Diego. In the process we found out a lot more about the Computer and learned to build a timer loop. Now let's see if we can build a pause right into the Distance program. First, erase the test program by typing:

```
DELETE 1-9          [←┘]
```

and

```
DELETE 1ØØØ-1ØØØØ          [←┘]
```

---

Don't forget the space after DELETE.

---

Now:

```
LIST
```

Wow! How's that for power? It DELETEd those Lines, without having to type each individual Line Number.

## Wrong Way Computer

One way to STOP the fast parade of information is to put in a STOP. Type in:

```
85 IF R = 500 THEN STOP
```

...and RUN.

We know R is going to increment from 100 to 1500. 500 is about a third of the way to the end. See how the chart PRINTed out to 475 mph, then hit the STOP as 500 came racing down to Line 85? The screen displays the first third of the chart and:

```
Break in 85
```

This means the program is STOPped, or broken in Line 85. To restart the program merely type:

```
CONT        [←]
```
(or press [F5])

...and it automatically picks up where it left off and PRINTs the rest of the chart, or executes until it hits another STOP. Where would you place the next STOP?

Yep.

```
87 IF R = 1000 THEN STOP
```

...and RUN.

## At Last

The ultimate plan is to build timers into the program so as not to completely STOP execution, but merely delay it for study.

For the first timer, add:

```
83 IF R<> 500 THEN 90
```

```
84  FOR X = 1 TO 4000
85  NEXT X
```

...and RUN.

*Hey! It really works!* As long as R does *not* equal 500 the program skips over the delay loop in Lines 84 and 85. When R *does* equal 500, the test "falls through" and Lines 84 and 85 "play catch" 4000 times, delaying the program's execution for about 5 seconds.

You have learned enough to design the 2nd delay at Line 1000 by yourself. Have fun.

## Time For A Cool One

It's been a long and tortuous route with numerous scenic side trips, but we finally made it. You picked up so many smarts in these 2 lessons on FOR-NEXT, that it's your turn to put them to work.

**EXERCISE 15-2:** Modify the resident program so that in this heading, (MPH) appears *below* RATE, and (HOURS) appears *below* TIME. This one should be a breeze.

**EXERCISE 15-3:** Design, write and RUN a program which will calculate and PRINT income at yearly, monthly, weekly and daily rates, based on a 40-hour week, a 1/12th-year month, and a 52-week year. Do this for yearly incomes between $5,000 and $25,000 in $1,000 increments. Document your program with REM statements to explain the equations you create.

Some of the exercise programs are becoming too long to leave work space for your ideas. From now on, use a pad of paper for working up the answers.

**EXERCISE 15-4:** Here's an old chestnut that the Computer really eats up: Design, write and RUN a program which tells how many days we have to work, starting at a penny a day, so if our salary doubles each day we know which day we earn at least a million dollars. Include columns which show each day number, its daily rate, and the total income to-date. Make the program stop after PRINTing the first day our daily rate is a million dollars or more. (After that ... who cares?)

Answers to these exercises are found in Section B.

## The "Brute Force" Method

### (Subtitled: Get A Bigger Hammer)

Much to the consternation of some teachers, a great value of the Computer is its ability to do the tedious work involved in the "cut and try", "hunt and peck" or other less respectable methods of finding an answer (or attempting to prove the correctness of a theory, theorem or principle). This method involves trying many possible solutions to see if one fits, or to find the closest one, or establish a trend. Beyond that, it can be a powerful learning tool by providing reams of data in chart or graph form which would simply take too long to generate by hand. For example:

**EXERCISE 15-5:** You have a 1000 foot roll of fencing wire and want to make a *rectangular* pasture.

Using all of the wire, determine what length and width dimensions will allow you to enclose the maximum number of square feet? Use the brute force method; let the Computer try different values for L and W and PRINT out the Area fenced by each pair of L and W.

The formula for area is Area = Length times Width, or A=L*W.

**EXERCISE 15-6:** *Extra credit problem for "electronics types"*

As a further example (more complex and tends to prove the point better) try this final (optional) assignment. It involves a problem confronted by every electricity student who has studied SOURCES (batteries, generators) and LOADS (lights, resistors).

The *Maximum D.C. Power Transfer Theorem* states,

"Maximum DC power is delivered to an electrical load when the resistance of that load is equal in value to the internal resistance of the source."

And then the arguments begin...

> "Use a HIGH resistance load because it will drop more voltage and accept more power." ($P=V^2/R$)
>
> "No, use a LOW resistance load so it will draw more current and accept more power." ($P=I^2*R$)
>
> "Use a load value somewhere in between." ($P=I*V$)

Don't necessarily shy away from this problem if electricity doesn't happen to be your bag. Enough information is given to write the program. The principle, the optimizing of a value, is applicable to many fields of endeavor and is little short of profound.

With the values given in the schematic, design, write and RUN a program which will try out values of load resistance ranging from 1 to 20 ohms, in 1 ohm increments, and PRINT the answers to the following:

1. Value of Load Resistance (from 1 to 20 ohms)
2. Total circuit power (circuit current squared, times circuit resistance) $= I^2 * (10 + R)$
3. Power lost in source (circuit current squared, times source resistance) $= I^2 * 10$
4. Power delivered to load (circuit current squared, times load resistance) $= I^2 * R$

Note: Circuit current is found by dividing source voltage (120 volts) by total circuit resistance (load resistance + 10 ohms source resistance). Everything follows Ohms Law ($V=I*R$) and Watts Law ($P=I*V$)

GOOD LUCK! Don't look at the answer until you've got it whipped.

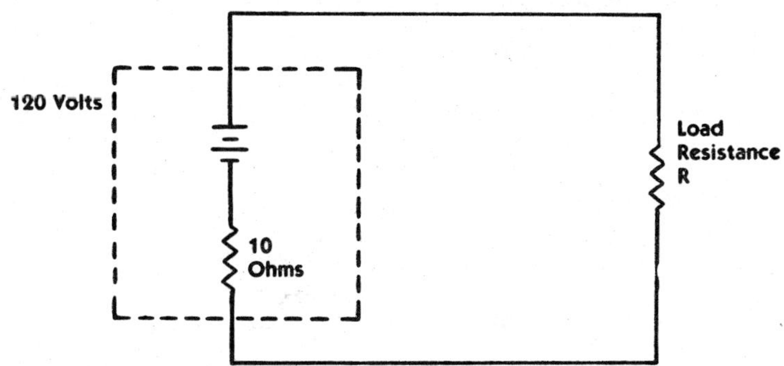


## Learned In Chapter 15

| Commands | Statements | Miscellaneous |
|---|---|---|
| LIST ### | STOP | Timer Loop |
| RUN ### | | "Brute Force" method |
| DELETE ### | | |
| CONT | | |

# Chapter 16

# Formatting With TAB

fter those last few Chapters it's time for an easy one.

We already know 3 ways to set up our output PRINT format.

We can:

1. Enclose what we want to say in quotes, inserting blank spaces as necessary.
2. Separate the objects of the PRINT statement with semi-colons so as to PRINT them tightly together on the same Line.
3. Separate the objects of the PRINT statement with commas to PRINT them on the same Line in the 6 different PRINT "zones".

A 4th way is by using the TAB function, which is similar to the TAB on a regular typewriter. TAB is especially useful when the output consists of columns of numbers with headings. Type in the following NEW program and RUN:

```
10 PRINT TAB(5);"THE";TAB(20);"TOTAL";
         TAB(35);"SPENT"
20 PRINT TAB(5);"BUDGET";TAB(20);"YEAR'S";
         TAB(35);"THIS"
30 PRINT TAB(5);"CATEGORY";TAB(20);"BUDGET";
         TAB(35);"MONTH"
```

Z
HEY! THE MAN JUST SAID TO TAKE IT EASY- LET'S NOT GO OVERBOARD!

The RUN should appear:

```
THE                 TOTAL              SPENT

BUDGET              YEAR'S             THIS

CATEGORY            BUDGET             MONTH
```

**EXERCISE 16-1:** EDIT the above program using the 3 ways we know (so far) to format PRINTing. Here is a start:

```
10.PRINT"THE                      TOTAL                 SPENT"

20.PRINT"BUDGET","YEAR'S","THIS"

30.PRINT TAB( );"CATEGORY";TAB( );

"BUDGET";TAB( );"MONTH"
```

Use ordinary spacing for the first Line of the heading, zone spacing for the second Line and TABbing for the third Line.

HINT: This isn't as easy as it looks, so it may require extensive editing. Since automatic zone formatting is not adjustable, the other formats will have to be keyed to it.

A semi-colon is traditionally used following TAB, as shown above. Most newer BASIC interpreters permit a blank, quote marks or even no symbol, instead.

```
10 PRINT TAB(10) "OOPS, NO SEMICOLON!"
```

RUNS just fine. **Leave out semi-colons at your own peril.**

The Computer will start PRINTing TAB(##) spaces to the right of the left margin. It is important to remember when using TABs that whenever numbers or numeric variables are PRINTed, the Computer inserts one additional space to the left of the number to allow for the – or + sign.

Type this NEW program:

```
10 A = 3
```

```
20 B = 5

30 C = A + B

40 PRINT TAB(10);"A";TAB(20);"B";TAB(30);"C"

50 PRINT TAB(10);A;TAB(20);B;TAB(30);C
```

...and RUN.

Appears:

```
A         B         C
 3         5         8
```

The numbers are indented one space beyond the TAB(##). Keep this in mind when lining up (or indenting) headings and answers.

Change Line 20 to read:

```
20 B = -5
```

...and RUN.

See why numbers indent one space?

Whole numbers are most commonly used as TAB values, but on those rare occasions when a fraction is used, the Computer rounds the fraction up to a whole number before TABbing.

All of the rules we have seen so far for TABbing apply whether the TAB value is an actual number or a numeric variable.

## The Long Lines Division

Have you ever wondered what would happen if we had to PRINT a great number of headings or answers on the same Line -- but didn't have enough room on the program Line to neatly hold all the TAB statements? You have? Really? You're in luck because it's easy. Type and RUN the following NEW program. It stretches the "leaving out of semi-colons" to the limits of prudence.

```
10 A = 0
20 B = 1
30 C = 2
40 D = 3
50 E = 4
60 F = 5
70 G = 6
80 H = 7
90 I = 8
100 PRINT "A"TAB(10)"B"TAB(20)"C"TAB(30);
110 PRINT "D"TAB(40)"E"TAB(50)"F";
120 PRINT TAB(60)"G"TAB(70)"H"TAB(80)"I"
130 PRINT A;TAB(10)B;TAB(20)C;TAB(30)D;
140 PRINT TAB(40)E;TAB(50)F;TAB(60)G;
150 PRINT TAB(70)H;TAB(80)I
```

The trailing semi-colons (;) in Lines 100, 110, 130 and 140 do the trick. They make the end of one PRINT Line continue right on to the next PRINT Line without activating a carriage return. The combination of TAB and trailing semi-colon allows us almost infinite flexibility in formatting the output.

But do you see 2 other unrelated problems in the display?

1. There is a space between the "label" Line and the "numbers" Line, but there is no PRINT statement which specified it. What happened?

When we specified `TAB(80)` we pushed the letter to be printed right up against the right hand side of the screen. After `"I"` was printed, the cursor "overflowed" onto the next Line, only to be hit by the normal end-of-Line Carriage Return and Line Feed which moved the cursor to the far left and down one line. The result is the same as if there were 2 Line Feeds, thus the blank row.

Change Line 120 to:

```
120 PRINT ... TAB(79)"I"
```

and RUN again. It proves the point.

2. The next problem is even worse. The number 8 is printed one Line too low, and indented one space. To print it on the same Line as the other numbers, change Line 150 to:

```
150 PRINT ... TAB(78)I
```

...and RUN.

These 2 extra lessons from the program are timely, and raise the flag of caution whenever the limits of either a screen or printer width are pushed. Plan ahead...

Finally, to see the program crash when one too many liberties are taken with semicolons, remove the only one in Line 150 and RUN.

That's enough fooling around with Mother Nature.

**EXERCISE 16-2:** Rework the answer to Exercise 15-3 to include the *hourly* rate of pay in the PRINTout. Use the TAB Function to have the chart display all 5 columns side by side.

**EXERCISE 16-3: (Optional)** Rework the special program 15-6 answer using the TAB Function so the PRINTout includes the internal resistance in a fifth column.

## Learned In Chapter 16

| Print Modifiers | Miscellaneous |
|---|---|
| TAB | Trailing semi-colon |

# Chapter 17

# Grandson Of FOR-NEXT

he FOR-NEXT loop didn't go away for long. It returns here more powerful than ever. Type this NEW program:

```
10 FOR A = 1 TO 3
20   PRINT "A LOOP"
30    FOR B = 1 TO 2
40     PRINT ,"B LOOP"
50    NEXT B
60 NEXT A
```

...and RUN.

---

For good program readability, add 2 blank spaces in Line 20 before PRINT; 3 in Line 30 before FOR; 4 in 40 before PRINT; and 3 in 50 before NEXT.

---

The result is:

```
A LOOP
               B LOOP
               B LOOP
```

```
A LOOP
                    B LOOP
                    B LOOP
A LOOP
                    B LOOP
                    B LOOP
```

This display vividly demonstrates operation of the nested FOR-NEXT loop. "Nesting" is used in the same sense that drinking glasses are "nested" when stored to save space. Certain types of portable chairs, empty cardboard boxes, etc. can be nested. They fit one inside the other for easy stacking.

Let's analyze the program a Line at a time:

> Line 10 establishes the first FOR-NEXT loop, called A, and directs that it be executed 3 times.
>
> Line 20 PRINTs `A LOOP` so we will know where it came from in the program. See how this program Line is indented to make it stand out as being nested in the "A loop"?
>
> Line 30 establishes the second loop, called B, and directs that it be executed twice. It is indented even more so we can instantly see that it is buried even deeper in the "A" loop.
>
> Line 40 PRINTs two items: "nothing" in the 1st PRINT zone, then the comma kicks us into the 2nd PRINT zone where `B LOOP` is PRINTed. Makes for a clear distinction on the screen between A loop and B loop, eh?
>
> Line 50 completes the "B" loop and returns control to Line 30 for as many executions of the "B" loop as Line 30 directs. (So far we have PRINTed one "A" and one "B".)
>
> Line 60 ends the first pass through the "A" loop and sends control back to Line 10, the beginning of the A loop. The A loop has to be executed 3 times before the program RUN is complete, PRINTing "A" 3 times and "B" six times (3 times 2).

Study the program and the explanation until you completely comprehend. It's simple but powerful magic.

Okay, to get a better "feel" for this nested loop (or loop within a loop) business, let's play with the program. Change Line 10 to read:

```
10 FOR A = 1 TO 5
```

...and RUN.

Right! A was PRINTed 5 times, meaning the "A" loop was executed 5 times, and B was PRINTed 10 times -- twice for each pass of the "A" loop. Now change Line 30 to read:

```
30 FOR B = 1 TO 4
```

...and RUN

Nothing to it! A was PRINTed 5 times and B PRINTed 20 times. Do you remember what to do if the A's and B's whiz by too fast? Press the [Ctrl] and [Num Lock] keys *at the same time* to temporarily freeze the display.

## How To Goof-Up Nested FOR-NEXT Loops

The most common error beginning programmers make with nested loops is improper nesting. Change these Lines:

```
50  NEXT A
60 NEXT B
```

...and RUN.

The Computer says:

```
NEXT without FOR in 60
```

Looking at the program we quickly see that the B loop is *not* nested within the A loop. The FOR part of the B loop is inside the A loop, but the NEXT part is outside it. That doesn't work! A later chapter deals with something

NOW HE'S
INTO NEST-
ED LOOPS

called "flow charting", a means of helping us plan programs to avoid this type of problem. Meanwhile we just have to be careful.

## Breaking Out Of Loops

Improper nesting is illegal, but breaking out of a loop when a desired condition has been met is OK. Add and change these Lines:

```
50   NEXT B
55  IF A = 2 GOTO 100
60 NEXT A
99 END
100 PRINT "A EQUALLED 2. RUN ENDED."
```

...and RUN.

As the screen shows, we "bailed out" of the A loop when A equaled 2 and hit the Test Line at 55. The END in Line 99 is just a precautionary block set up to STOP the Computer from executing into Line 100 unless specifically directed to go there. That would never happen in this simple program, but we will use *protective ENDs* from time to time to remind us that Lines which should be reached only by specific GOTO or IF-THEN statements must be protected against accidental "hits".

We'll be seeing a lot of the *nested* FOR-NEXT loop now that we know what it is and can put it to use.

**EXERCISE 17-1:** Re-enter the original program found at the beginning of this Chapter. It contains a B loop nested within the A loop. Make the necessary additions to this program so a new loop called "C" will be nested within the B loop, and will PRINT "C LOOP" 4 times for each pass of the B loop.

**EXERCISE 17-2:** Use the program which is the answer to Exercise 17-1. Make the necessary additions to this program so a new loop called "D" will be nested within the C loop, and will PRINT "D LOOP" 5 times for each pass of the C loop.

# WHILE - WEND

A more obscure variation on the FOR-NEXT idea is the WHILE-WEND statement. WHILE is the beginning statement in a series which is executed repeatedly until a certain WHILE condition becomes *false.*

The loop which begins with WHILE must be closed by a WEND. Type in this NEW program:

---

When writing programs, be sure to indent Lines to highlight nesting or program flow. It helps when reading them -- and is a great aid when debugging (troubleshooting) problems. End of message.

---

```
10 X = 1
20 WHILE X<>0
30    INPUT X
40    S = S + X
50 WEND
60 PRINT "SUM =";S
```

...and RUN.

INPUT several non-zero numbers, then INPUT a 0. As long as X does not = 0, WEND keeps returning execution to WHILE. When X is INPUT as 0, the WHILE statement in Line 20 interprets the 0 as its "bail-out" cue, and exits the loop via WEND. Line 60 PRINTs the sum of the numbers INPUT.

And with that, let's WEND our way towards the next Chapter.

## Learned In Chapter 17

| Statements | Miscellaneous |
|---|---|
| WHILE-WEND | Nested FOR-NEXT loops |
| | Protective END blocks |

# Chapter 18

# The INTeger Function

**I** **nteger?** "I can't even pronounce it, let alone understand it." Oh, come, come. Don't let old nightmares of being trapped in Algebra class stop you *now*. It's pronounced (IN-teh-jur) and simply means a *whole* number like -5, 0, or 3, etc. How difficult can that be? Come to think of it, some folks make a whole career of complicating simple ideas. We try to do just the opposite.

The INTeger function, INT(X), allows us to "round off" any number, large or small, positive or negative, into an INTeger, or *whole* number.

---

Careful -- we're not talking about ordinary rounding. Ordinary rounding gives us the *closest* whole number, whether it's larger or smaller than X. INT(X), on the other hand, gives us the ***largest** whole number which is **less than** or **equal to** X*. This is a very versatile form of rounding -- in fact, we can use it to produce the other "ordinary" kind of rounding.

---

Type NEW to clear out any old programs, then type:

```
10 X = 3.14159
20 Y = INT(X)
50 PRINT "Y =";Y
```

...and RUN.

The display reads:

```
Y =  3
```

Oh -- success is so sweet! It rounded 3.14159 off to the whole number 3. Change Line 10 to read:

```
10 X = -3.14159
```

...and RUN.

Good Grief! It rounded the answer *down* to read:

```
Y = -4
```

What kind of rounding is this? Easy. The INT function *always* rounds *down* to the next *lowest whole number*. Pretty hard to get that confused! It makes a positive number less positive, and makes a negative number more negative (same thing as less positive). At least it's consistent.

Taking it a Line at a time:

> Line 10 set the value of X (or any of our other alphabet-soup variables) equal to the value we specified, in this case $\pi$.
>
> Line 20 found the INTeger value of X and assigned it to a variable name. We chose Y.
>
> Line 50 PRINTed an identification label (Y =) followed by the value of Y.

## Not Content To Leave Well Enough Alone

We can do some foxy things by combining a FOR-NEXT loop with the INTeger function.

Change the program to read:

```
10 X = 3.14159
```

```
20 Y = INT(X)

30 Z = X - Y

40 PRINT "X =";X

50 PRINT "Y =";Y

60 PRINT "Z =";Z
```

Save this as "INTEGER1"...and RUN.

AHA! I don't know what we've discovered but it must be good for something. It reads:

```
X = 3.14159

Y = 3

Z = .1415899
```

We've split the value of X into its INTeger (whole number) value (called it Y), and its decimal part (called it Z).

Lines 40, 50, and 60 merely PRINTed the results.

## Hold The Phone

Oh - oh! Why doesn't Z equal the exact difference between X and Y? Where did that "899" in the decimal value come from? So what gives?

The slight difference has nothing to do with the INT function. You have discovered the Computer's limit of accuracy. Just like a calculator (or a person), a computer can never be perfectly accurate all the time. For short arithmetic expressions, the IBM is accurate to six digits. In longer, more complex expressions, such a minute error in the sixth digit can be magnified to where it becomes significant. All programmers have to cope with this kind of built-in error.

There *is* a way to control the accuracy of our results. It involves artificially rounding the fraction to the desired number of decimal places, and then forcing the Computer to PRINT out only those digits which are "properly rounded".

For example, suppose we need π accurate to only 3 decimal places. (Of course, we can specify it as 3.142, but that's not the point.) Type NEW, then enter and RUN the following program:

```
10 X = 3.14159
20 X =  X + .0005
30 X = INT(X * 1000)/1000
40 PRINT X
```

Adding .0005 in Line 20 gives our fraction a "push in the right direction". If this fraction has a digit greater than 4 in its 10-thousandths-place, then adding .0005 will effectively increase the thousandths-place digit by 1. Otherwise, the added .0005 will have no effect on the final result. This results in what's called "4/5 rounding".

Try using other values than π for X (just make sure X*1000 isn't too large for the INT function to handle).

It's easy to change the program to round accurately to a number of decimal places. For example, to round X off at the hundredths-place (2 digits to the right of the decimal point), change Lines 20 and 30 to read:

```
20 X = X + .005
30 X = INT(X * 100)/100
```

...and RUN, using several values for X.

---

This trick is very useful when PRINTing out dollars-and-cents. It prevents $39.995 type prices.

---

## HMMMM!!!

Do you suppose there is any way to separate each of the digits in 3.14159, or in any other number? Do you suppose we would have brought it up if there wasn't? After all (mumble, mumble).

It's really your turn to do some creative thinking, but we'll get it started and see if you can finish this idea. First, wipe out the resident program and reLOAD and RUN INTEGER1.

```
10 X = 3.14159
20 Y = INT(X)
30 Z = X - Y
40 PRINT "X =";X
50 PRINT "Y =";Y
60 PRINT "Z =";Z
```

It split X into an INTeger and fractional part.

Now, if we multiply Z by 10, then Z will become a whole number plus a decimal part: 1.4159. We can then take *its* INTeger value and strip off the decimal part, leaving the left hand digit standing alone. Let's label the Left-hand digit L and see what happens. Enter:

```
70 Z = Z * 10
80 L = INT(Z)
90 PRINT "L =";L
```

...and RUN.

Hmmm! It reads:

```
X = 3.14159
Y = 3
Z = .1415899
L = 1
```

We peeled off the leftmost digit in the decimal. Can you think of a way we might use a FOR-NEXT loop in order to strip off the rest?

---

Time Out For Creative Thinking!

---

 (...brief interlude of recorded music...) 

---

After all, these digits might not be just an accurate value of pi, but a coded message from a cereal box. If you don't have the decoder ring it's tough luck, Charlie -- unless you have a computer!

---

 (...More recorded music...) 

**Enough thinking there on company time!** Add these Lines:

```
75 FOR A = 1 TO 5
100 Z = Z - L
110 Z = Z * 10
120 NEXT A
```

SAVE as INTEGER2 and RUN.

VOILA! The "PRINTout" reads:

```
X = 3.14159
Y = 3
Z = .1415899
L = 1
L = 4
L = 1
L = 5
L = 8
```

# TIME OUT FOR CREATIVE THINKING

They are all there, but what's with the last value of L? L = 8? It's supposed to be 9!

Well, let's analyze the program first, then worry about that little detail.

Line 75 began a FOR-NEXT loop with 5 passes, one for each of the 5 digits right of the decimal.

Line 100 creates a new decimal value of Z by stripping off the INTeger part. (Plugging in the values, Z = 1.415899 − 1 = .415899)

Line 110 does the same as Line 70 did, multiplying the new decimal value times 10 so as to make the left-hand digit an INTeger and vulnerable to being snatched away by the INT function. (Z = .415899 * 10 = 4.15899)

Line 120 sends control back to Line 75 for another pass through the clipping program and the rest is history.

Now about that little detail ... the wrong value in the last digit. We already talked out the accuracy of the Computer. We can plow head-on into that problem. To understand it better, change Line 75 to read:

```
75 FOR A = 1 TO 10
```

...and RUN.

Where did all those extra numbers come from? (Beats me.) Again, the last digit or 2 at the end of a number is not to be trusted.

But there is a solution. Change Line 75 back as it was, then change Line 10 to read:

```
10 X = 3.1415900
```

...and RUN.

SAVE as INTEGER3.

Whew! Had us a little nervous there for awhile. By declaring that the accuracy of X to be a few decimal places greater than actually needed, digits we *do* need will be reliable. There are better ways to do this and we will learn to use them later.

Now "pull" a LIST of the program. Line 10 says:

```
10 X = 3.14159#
```

The # sign at the end is a "type Declaration" character. Since we typed in more than 6 digits, the Computer converted the number from "Single Precision" to "Double Precision". We'll talk *much* more about this concept in a later Chapter, but let's not be diverted from the main theme of *this* Chapter.

## Is This Too Hard To Follow?

No -- it isn't hard to follow, and we could go through and calculate every intermediate value just like I did before and it would be perfectly clear (to coin a phrase). Let's instead learn a way to let the Computer help us understand what it is doing.

We can insert temporary PRINT Lines anywhere in any program to follow every step in its execution. The Computer can actually overwhelm us with data. By carefully indicating exactly what we want to know, it will display the inner details of any process. Start by adding this Line:

```
72 PRINT "#72 Z =";Z
```

...and RUN.

The essentials of this "test" or "debugging" or "flag" Line are:

1. It PRINTs something.

2. The PRINT tells the *Line number*, for analysis and easy location for later erasure.

3. It tells the *name* of the variable we are watching at that point in the program.

4. It gives the *value* of that variable at *that point*.

This "flagging" is such a wonderful tool for troubleshooting stubborn programs that you will want to make a habit of never forgetting to use it when the going gets tough.

It can be very helpful when inserted in FOR-NEXT loops -- so:

```
77 PRINT "#77 A =";A
```

...and RUN.

Wow! The information comes thick and fast! It tells what is happening during each pass of the loop. Hard to keep track of so much, and we've barely begun. Is there some way to make it more readable?

Yes, there are lots of ways. Indenting is one simple way to separate the answers from the troubleshooting data. Change Lines 72 and 77 as follows:

```
72 PRINT ,"#72 Z =";Z
77 PRINT ,,"#77 A =";A
```

...and RUN.

Ahh. How sweet it is. That is so easy to read, let's monitor some more points in the program. Type in:

```
105 PRINT ,,,"#105 Z =";Z
115 PRINT ,,,,"#115 Z =";Z
```

SAVE as INTEGER 4

...and RUN.

Egad, Igor! We've created a monster!

Well, there it is. All the data we can handle (and then some). By using the [Ctrl] and [Num Lock] keys to temporarily halt execution, we can study the data at every step to understand how the program works (or doesn't). Do it. Understand this program and all its little lessons completely. When you are satisfied, go back and erase out the "flags".

## INTeger Division

And if that isn't quite enough to keep the mind reeling, there *is* another way to get the INTeger value of the result of an equation without using the INT function! It is called "INTeger division", and instead of using the normal slash /, we use a backslash \.

Type NEW. Then enter this example:

```
10 X = 23.987
20 Y = 2.567
30 PRINT "X/Y =";X/Y
40 PRINT "INT(X/Y) =";INT(X/Y)
50 PRINT "X\Y =";X\Y
```

...and RUN. It should produce:

```
X/Y = 9.34437
INT(X/Y) = 9
X\Y = 8
```

Eight? Is that right? Yep. INTeger division actually modifies the value of each variable in the equation *before the calculation is made*. In this case, both X and Y are rounded to the nearest whole numbers, 24 and 3, then division is performed producing the INTeger value of 8. Hmmm, did that sink in?

Take a breather. You have learned quite enough in this Chapter.

**EXERCISE 18-1:** Enter this straightforward NEW program for finding the area of a circle.

```
10 P = 3.14159
20 PRINT "RADIUS", "AREA"
30 PRINT
40 FOR R=1 TO 10
50  A = P * R * R
```

```
60  PRINT R,A

70 NEXT R
```

...and RUN.

Area equals $\pi$ times the radius squared (that is, the radius times itself).

Pretty routine stuff -- huh? Problem is, who needs all those little numbers to the far right of the decimal point. *Oh, you do?* Well, there's one in every crowd. The rest of us can do without them. Without giving any big hints, modify the resident program to suppress all the numbers to the right of the decimal point.

**EXERCISE 18-2:** Now, knowing just enough to be dangerous, and in need of a lot of humility, change Line 55 so that each value of *area* is rounded (down) to be accurate to one decimal place. For example:

```
RADIUS                    AREA
 1                          3.1
```

**EXERCISE 18-3:** Carrying the above Exercise one step further, modify the program Line 55 to round (down) the value of area to be accurate to 2 decimal places.

## Learned In Chapter 18

**Functions**

INT(X)
\

**Miscellaneous**

Flags
INTeger Division

# Chapter 19

# More Branching Statements

## It Went That-A-Way

Enter this NEW program:

```
10 INPUT "TYPE A NUMBER BETWEEN 1 AND 5";N
20 IF N = 1 GOTO 100
30 IF N = 2 GOTO 120
40 IF N = 3 GOTO 140
50 IF N = 4 GOTO 160
60 IF N = 5 GOTO 180
70 PRINT "THE NUMBER YOU TYPED WAS NOT"
80 PRINT "BETWEEN 1 AND 5 --- DUMMY!"
90 END
100 PRINT "N = 1"
110 END
120 PRINT "N = 2"
130 END
140 PRINT "N = 3"
150 END
```

```
160 PRINT "N = 4"

170 END

180 PRINT "N = 5"
```

SAVE as ONGOTO1 and RUN it a few times to feel comfortable and be sure it is "debugged". Be sure to try numbers outside the range of 1-5, including 0 and a negative number.

---

*Debugged* is an old Latin word which, freely translated, means "getting all the errors out of a Computer program."

---

This program works fine for examining the value of a variable, N, and sending the Computer off to a certain Line number to do what it says there. If there are lots of possible directions in which to branch, however, we will want to use a greatly improved test called ON-GOTO which cuts out lots of Lines of programming.

DELETE Lines 20, 30, 40, 50 and 60. Remember how? (DELETE 20-60).

Enter this new Line:

```
20 ON N GOTO 100,120,140,160,180
```

SAVE as ONGOTO2 and RUN a few times, as before.

Works the same, doesn't it?

Using the ON-GOTO statement is really pretty simple, though it looks hard. Line 20 says:

IF the "rounded" value of N is 1 THEN GOTO Line 100.

IF the "rounded" value of N is 2 THEN GOTO Line 120.

IF the "rounded" value of N is 3 THEN GOTO Line 140.

IF the "rounded" value of N is 4 THEN GOTO Line 160.

IF the "rounded" value of N is 5 THEN GOTO Line 180.

AW, LET'S NOT DRAG OUT THAT OL' CHESTNUT FOR "DE-BUGGING"!

IF the "rounded" value of N is not one of the numbers LISTed above, THEN move on to the next Line ... Line 7Ø.

The ON-GOTO statement has a built-in standard rounding system. If the number INPUT is less than halfway between 2 INTegers, rounding is downward to the *lower* INTeger. If it is halfway or larger, rounding is to the next *higher* INTeger.

RUN again and type in the following values of N to prove the point:

```
2.4

1.5

3.7

4.499

4.5

Ø.5
```

Get the picture?

## Variations On A Theme

Lots of tricks can be played to milk the most from ON-GOTO. For example, if we wanted to branch out to 15 different locations but didn't want to type that many different numbers on a single ON-GOTO Line, we could use several Lines, like this (don't bother to do it):

```
2Ø ON N GOTO 1ØØ,12Ø,14Ø,16Ø,18Ø

3Ø ON N-5 GOTO 2ØØ,22Ø,24Ø,26Ø,28Ø

4Ø ON N-1Ø GOTO 3ØØ,32Ø,34Ø,36Ø,38Ø
```

and, of course, fill in the proper responses at those Line numbers.

In Line 3Ø, it was necessary to subtract 5 from the number being INPUT as N, since each new ON-GOTO Line starts counting again from the number 1.

In Line 3Ø, since we had already provided for INPUTs between 1 and 10, we subtract 10 from N to cover the range from 11 through 15.

We could have used any letter after "ON", not just N. N can be the value of a letter variable, or a complete expression, either calculated in place, or calculated in a previous Line.

## Give Me A SGN(X)

Using ON-GOTO along with a new function called SGN (it's pronounced "sign") plus a modest amount of imagination produces a useful little routine. But first, let's learn about SGN.

The SGN function examines any number to see whether it is negative, zero, or positive. It tells us the number is negative by giving us a (−1). (In computer language, "it returns a −1"). If the number is zero it returns a (Ø). If positive, it returns a (+1). SGN is a very simple function.

In order to sneak easily into the next concept, we will simulate the built-in SGN function with a SUBROUTINE.

## So What Is A Subroutine?

Funny you should ask. A sub-routine is a short but very specialized program (or routine) which is built into a large program to meet a specialized need. The BASIC interpreter incorporates many of them which we never see.

As an example of how to create functions that are *not* included in our BASIC, we will use a 5-Line subroutine instead of the "SGN" function to accomplish the same thing. (Even though IBM BASIC has its own "SGN" function, you should complete this Chapter to be sure you learn about subroutines. We don't want to turn out dummies, you know.)

"Scratch" the program now in memory by typing NEW, then -- very carefully, type in this SGN subroutine:

```
30000 END
30010 REM SGN(X) INPUT X, OUTPUT T=-1,0, OR +1
30020 IF X < 0 THEN T = -1
30030 IF X = 0 THEN T = 0
30040 IF X > 0 THEN T = +1
30050 RETURN
```

## "CALLING" A Subroutine -- (Sort of like calling hogs.)

GOSUB directs the Computer to go to a Line number, execute what it says there and in the Lines following, and when done, RETURN back to the Line containing that GOSUB statement. We will use Line 20 here.

```
20 GOSUB 30020
```

RETURN is to GOSUB what NEXT is to FOR.

The RETURN statement is always at the end of a subroutine, and ours is at Line 30050. We have reserved Line number 30000 to hold a protective END block for all of our subroutines, so the Computer doesn't come crashing into them when it is done with the main program. (Try taking it out when we're done and see what happens.)

## Getting Down To Business

Okay, now let's combine GOSUB with the SGN subroutine to see what all this fuss is about. Add:

```
10 INPUT "TYPE ANY NUMBER";X
20 GOSUB 30020
30 ON T+2 GOTO 50,70,90
40 END
50 PRINT "THE NUMBER IS NEGATIVE."
60 END
70 PRINT "THE NUMBER IS ZERO."
80 END
90 PRINT "THE NUMBER IS POSITIVE."
```

...and RUN.

Try entering negative, zero and positive numbers to be sure it works. Most of the program workings are obvious, but here is an analysis:

Line 10 INPUTs any number.

Line 20 sends the Computer to Line 30020 by a GOSUB statement. This is different from an ordinary GOTO, since a GOSUB will return control to the originating Line like a boomerang when the Computer hits a RETURN. The call to GOSUB is not complete and will not move on to the next program Line until a RETURN is found.

Lines 30020 through 30040 contain this simple logic routine.

Line 30050 holds RETURN, which sends control back to Line 20, which silently acknowledges the return and allows execution to move to the next Line.

Line 30 is an ordinary ON-GOTO statement, but adds 2 to the value of its variable, in this case "T". Line 30 really says,

> "If T is -1 THEN GOTO Line 50. If it is zero THEN GOTO Line 70, and If it is +1 GOTO Line 90."

By adding 2 to each of the values from SGN we "matched" them up with the 1, 2, and 3 series which is built into the ON-GOTO statement.

Lines 40, 60, and 80 are routine protective END blocks.

---

By the way, many subroutines are not this simple -- as a matter of fact, they often contain very hairy mathematical derivations. We won't bother trying to explain any of them -- if you're heavily into Math, you go right ahead and play with the numbers.

---

## ON-GOSUB

ON-GOSUB is a variation on the ON-GOTO and GOSUB schemes. It allows branching to a variety of *subroutines* from a single GOSUB statement. If we had 3 subroutines and had to choose which one to use based on the value of X, here is how the program might be structured. (Don't bother to type it in).

```
10 INPUT X
20 ON X GOSUB 1000,2000,3000
30  REM - CALCULATIONS HERE
60  REM - PRINT RESULTS HERE
99 END
1000 REM - 1ST ROUTINE GOES HERE.
1099  RETURN
2000 REM - 2ND ROUTINE GOES HERE.
2099  RETURN
3000 REM - 3RD ROUTINE GOES HERE.
3099  RETURN
```

## Preview Of Coming Attractions?

Like so much of what we are learning, this is just the tip of the iceberg. The ON-GOTO and ON-GOSUB functions have many more clever applications, and they will evolve as we need them. As a hint for restless minds, note that the *value* of X (which we INPUT) was not used, but it didn't go away. All we did was find its SGN. Hmmm...

## Routines Vs Subroutines

In this Chapter we studied a special-purpose routine used as a SUBroutine. It was easy to understand. All routines, understandable or not, can be built directly into any program instead of being set aside and "called" as subroutines. The main value of subroutines is that they can be "called" repeatedly from different parts of a program, which is often desirable. Ordinary routines are usually only used once, so use of GOSUB and RETURN with them often doesn't make good programming sense.

One value of using routines as subroutines is that some are exceedingly complex to type without error, and if each is typed once and SAVEd on disk, it can be quickly and accurately LOADed back into the Computer as the first step in creating a new program, or added to an existing one.

---

We'll have more to say in a later Chapter. When you see just how powerful subroutines are, you'll feel like your IBM is even smarter than it thinks it is.

---

Now it's your turn.

**EXERCISE 19-1:** Remove all traces of the subroutine from the resident program. Use the SGN function to accomplish the same thing we have been doing with a subroutine. Hint: T = SGN(X)

## Learned In Chapter 19

| Functions | Statements | Miscellaneous |
|---|---|---|
| SGN(X) | ON-GOTO | Debugging |
| | GOSUB | Calling a subroutine |
| | ON-GOSUB | Routines |
| | RETURN | |

# Chapter 20

# Random Numbers

## At RANDOM

A *random* number is one with a value which is unpredictable. A "Random Number Generator" is a device which pulls *random numbers* "out of a hat". Our Computer has an RND generator, and it works this way:

```
N = RND(X)
```

Where N is the random *number*

RND is the symbol for *RaNDom* Function

X is a dummy value, either negative, zero, or positive, which can be either placed between the parentheses or brought in as a variable from elsewhere in the program.

Type this NEW program:

```
20 FOR N = 1 TO 10
30  PRINT RND(1)
40 NEXT N
```

...and RUN. Did you observe:

1. A different number appeared each time?

2. All numbers were between 0 and 1?
3. *Very* small numbers were expressed in Exponential notation.

RND behaves exactly the same as RND(X), when X is a positive number. Since this is almost always how it is used, we almost always omit (X). Put a semi-colon behind the PRINT statement and increase the FOR-NEXT loop to 100 passes to put more numbers on the screen at one time.

```
20 FOR N = 1 TO 100
30  PRINT RND;
40 NEXT N
```

...and RUN.

The Computer uses an internal "seed number" to produce a "random number" series. The seed for RND is always the same.

You get the idea.

Now type:

```
PRINT RND(0)        [ENTER]
```

and the *last* RaNDom number PRINTed is repeated. Hmmm...

## This Is Fairly Exciting!

*Well, maybe so, but you ain't seen nothin' yet!* Virtually all computer games are based on RND(X), and we'll soon play and design our own.

## RND With Racing Stripes

In most real-life cases we need a Random INTeger, not a Random Number between 0-1. To create numbers larger than 1, we have to resort to mathematical chicanery.

Change Line 30 to read:

```
30 PRINT INT(RND * 15 + 1);
```

...and RUN.

Wow! That's more like it -- real live random INTegers. They all have values between 1 and 15. Figured out the scheme? Pretty simple, isn't it?

This equation specifies the *range* of INTegers RND will output:

```
R = INT(RND * (B-A+1) + A)
```

Where R = The RaNDom number
B = the *largest* INTeger
A = the *smallest* INTeger

## Pseudo-Random

Random numbers are unpredictable; properly functioning computers are not. So how do we get truly random numbers from the Computer? We usually don't: we get *pseudo-random* numbers.

RUN the program several times and study the screen. The numbers from each RUN are the same as from the previous RUN! They may be random, but are certainly predictable!

Change Line 3Ø and RUN several times using negative seed numbers, like:

```
3Ø PRINT RND(-2Ø);
```

We get different sets of numbers -- but all with the same value. RUNning again, the numbers are unchanged. Using a different negative seed with RND produces the same result, but the value will change slightly.

When RUNning game programs using RND, it's a good idea to set the *seed* to an unpredictable value. To ensure that a different pseudo-random number sequence is used each time the Computer uses RND(X), we need to find a source of unpredictable numbers somewhere in the Computer.

[Ctrl] [Break] and type the following:

```
PRINT TIME$
```

Hmmm, that's interesting. If we could somehow separate the seconds from the rest of the time, we would have essentially unpredictable numbers between 0 and 59. That would give us 60 different seed numbers. Here's how to do it:

```
PRINT VAL(RIGHT$(TIME$,2))
```

The mechanics of that statement will be covered in detail in a later Chapter, but for those too curious to wait here is a short analysis: RIGHT$(TIME$,2) means "Peel off the 2 right-most characters from TIME$". VAL means "Make sure those 2 characters are numbers so we can use them in a numeric variable.

We now have the tools to write a subroutine for "randomizing" the INPUT to RND. Type the following:

```
10 GOSUB 10000          (to our own Randomizer)
20 FOR N = 1 TO 10
30  PRINT RND;
40 NEXT N
99 END
10000 S = VAL(RIGHT$(TIME$,2))
10010 FOR N = 1 TO S
10020  D = RND
10030 NEXT N
10040 RETURN
```

and here's how it works:

Line 10000 picks off a number between 0-59.

Lines 10010-10030 "burn off" the first "S" numbers in the RND series.

Line 10040 RETURNs execution to the main program where:

Line 30 continues RND, and PRINTs the next 10 numbers.

If you don't believe any of this, insert a temporary Line:

```
10005 S = 25
```

which sets the number of burn-offs to a specific value. Then RUN several times. The same 10 numbers appear each time, so it must be working.

Remove Line 10005 and RUN a few more times. Ahhh! Now we've got it. Instead of only one, we now have 60 versions. We have developed a viable RANDOMIZER routine.

## Randomizer

With a RANDOMIZE statement at the beginning of the program, the Computer will "shuffle" or "reseed" the series of random numbers. Type this NEW program:

```
10 RANDOMIZE
20 FOR N = 1 TO 10
30  PRINT RND;
40 NEXT N
```

...and RUN.

Oh, Oh! More decisions needed. RANDOMIZE allows the selection of 65536 different seed values. Even so, whoever picks the seed controls the numbers series.

## Variable Randomizer

To increase the possibility that a different seed number will be selected each time RANDOMIZE is encountered, we can let the Computer make that selection for us. The RANDOMIZE statement can be followed by a variable. A numeric value between −32767 and +32767 can be read into that variable. In the routine below, we set up a simple FOR-NEXT loop between those extremes and start it RUNning. When the [↵] key is pressed, execution breaks out of the loop and the value of R *at that time* is picked up by RANDOMIZE. Pretty clever, huh?

Since it takes over 5 minutes for the loop to execute from one extreme to the other, there's plenty of time for even the slowest player to press [↵].

```
10 GOSUB 20000
20000 FOR R = -32767 TO 32767
20010  R$ = INKEY$
20020   IF R$ = "" THEN 20040
20030  GOTO 20050
20040 NEXT R
20050 RANDOMIZE R
20060 RETURN
```

We will study INKEY$ in detail in a future Chapter, but for now just understand that if we press the [↵] key, execution will break out from Line 20020 to 20040. The value of R at breakout will seed RANDOMIZE, and upon RETURN to the main program, a string of random numbers from a variety of over 65,000 choices will be executed.

The "randomness" of this scheme is based on the unpredictability of the time from start of RUN to pressing of the [↵] key. Over 500 values of R whiz by each second. That's random enough to satisfy an eagle-eyed Las Vegas pit boss!

## The Old Coin Toss Gambit

We could toss a thousand heads in a row and the odds on the next toss are *exactly 50/50* that a head will come up next. The outcome of every toss is totally independent of what happened before. **It is too!**

In the *long run* however, the number of heads and tails should be exactly the same. (Casinos live off people who go broke waiting for their particular scheme to pay off ... "in the long run".) The Computer can provide an education in "odds" and various games of chance, and allow us to prove or disprove many ideas involving probability. This is known as computer "modeling" or "simulation."

Type in this coin toss simulation:

```
10 RANDOMIZE
```

```
20 INPUT "NUMBER OF COIN FLIPS";F
30 PRINT "STAND BY WHILE I'M FLIPPING"
40 FOR N=1 TO F
50  X = INT(RND * 2 + 1)
60  ON X GOTO 90,110
70  PRINT "WAS NEITHER A HEADS NOR TAILS."
80   END
90  H = H + 1
100  GOTO 120
110  T = T + 1
120 NEXT N
130 PRINT "HEADS","TAILS","TOTAL FLIPS"
140 PRINT H,T,F
150 PRINT 100*H/F;"%",100*T/F;"%"
```

...and RUN.

Seed the generator with the number 1 and "Flip the coin" 100 times. RUN a number of times, changing the seed. When it's time for lunch, try 25,000 flips or more.

Line 10 allows INPUT of a seed value.

Line 20 INPUTs the number of flips desired.

Line 30 Prints a "Standby" statement.

Line 40 begins a FOR-NEXT loop that RUNs "F" times.

Line 50 is the RND generator. We told it to generate INTegers between 1 and 2, and that restricts it to just the numbers 1 and 2. is "1" and Tails is "2".

Line 60 has an ON-GOTO test sending X=1 to Line 90 where the "Heads" are counted, and X=2 to Line 110 where the "Tails" are counted.

I GUESS I CAN'T COMPLAIN – I ASKED FOR RANDOM NUMBERS

Lines 70 is the default Line. If X = other than 1 or 2, the error message will be PRINTed and execution will END. It will never happen, but here is the proof.

Line 90 sets up H as a counter. Each time the ON-GOTO tests sends control to this Line because X=1, H is incremented by one and keeps count of the "Heads".

Line 100 sends control to Line 120 where only the first statement, NEXT N, is executed. When the N Loop has gone through all "F" number of passes, control drops to Line 130.

Until then, Line 50 generates another RaNDom number (1 or 2). If the next X = 2...

Line 60 sends control to Line 110.

Line 110 keeps track of the "Tails".

Line 130 PRINTs the Headings.

Line 140 PRINTs the values of H, T and F.

Line 150 calculates and PRINTs the percentage of heads, and percentage of tails.

Save this program as COINTOSS.

## More Than One Generator At A Time

It is possible to generate more than one random number in a program by using more than one generator. This has special value when the ranges of the generators are different, but is helpful even if their ranges are the same.

It could also be done with a single generator, but that wouldn't make the point.

To make the point, we will simulate the game of "Craps" -- where 2 dice are "rolled". Each "die" has six sides, and each side has 1,2,3,4,5 or 6 dots. When the 2 dice are rolled, the number of dots showing on their top sides are added. That sum is important to the game. Obviously, the lowest number that can be rolled is 2, and the highest number is 12. We will set up a separate Random Number Generator for each die, give each a range from 1 to 6, and call them die "A" and die "B".

Type NEW, then the following:

```
10 A = INT(RND*6+1)
20 B = INT(RND*6+1)
30 N = A + B
40 PRINT N,
50 GOTO 10
```

...RUN.

Each number PRINTed falls between 2 and 12. We only need to PRINT N since the dice are both thrown at the same time, and only the *sum* of the 2 is what counts.

Remember to press [Ctrl] [Break] to stop the Computer.

Why would the following by wrong? It creates numbers between 2 and 12.

```
10 PRINT INT(RND*11+2)
```

**Answer:** Adding random numbers created by two generators, each picking numbers between 1 and 6 will create many more sums which equal 3,4,5,6,7,8,9,10 and 11 than a single generator which picks an equal amount of numbers 0 through 10, to which we add 2, to make the range 2 through 12. To simulate 2 dies, the generator range must be 1-6, twice.

## Rules Of The Game

In its simplest form, the game goes like this:

1. The player rolls the two dice. If the sum is 2 (called "snake eyes"), a 3 ("cock-eyes"), or a 12 ("boxcars"), on the first roll, he loses and the game is over. That's "craps".

2. If the player rolls 7 or 11 on the first throw, (called "a natural"), he wins and the game is over.

3. If any other number is rolled, it becomes the player's "point". He must keep rolling until he either "makes his point" by getting the same number again to win, or rolls a 7, and loses.

**EXERCISE 20-1:** You already know far more than enough to complete this program. Do it. Put in all the tests, PRINT Lines, etc. to meet the rules of the game and tell the player what is going on. It will take you awhile to finish, but give it your best before we turn over to Section C (User's Programs) under CRAPS for a sample solution. Good luck!

**EXERCISE 20-2:** Add a RANDOMIZE subroutine to the CRAPS game. Test the game to be sure it's different each time it's RUN.

## Learned in Chapter 20

| Functions | Miscellaneous |
|---|---|
| RND(X) | Seed numbers |
| RANDOMIZE | Pseudo-random |

# Chapter 21

# READing Data

e have learned how to insert numeric values into programs by two different methods. The first is by building them into the program:

```
10 A = 5
```

The second is by using an INPUT statement to enter them through the keyboard:

```
10 INPUT A
```

The third principal method uses the DATA statement.

Type in this NEW program:

```
10 DATA 1,2,3,4,5
20 READ A,B,C,D,E
30 PRINT A;B;C;D;E
```

...and RUN.

The DATA statement is in some ways similar to the first method in that a Line holding the values is part of the program. It's different, however, since each DATA Line can contain many numbers, or pieces of data, each separated by a comma. Each piece of DATA must be read by a READ statement. Each

READ Line can hold a number of READ statements, each separated by a comma.

The display shows that all 5 pieces of DATA in Line 10, the values 1,2,3,4 and 5 were READ by Line 20, assigned to variables A through E, and PRINTed by Line 30.

---

Keep in mind these important distinctions: DATA Lines can be read *only* by READ statements. If more than one piece of DATA is placed on a DATA Line, they must be separated by commas. INPUT statements are used to enter data directly from the keyboard.

---

DATA Lines are always read from left to right by READ statements; the first DATA Line first (when there is more than one), and *it does not matter where they are in the program*. This may seem startling, but do the following and see:

1. Move the DATA Line from Line 10 to Line 25 and RUN. No change in the PRINTout, right?

2. Move the DATA Line from Line 25 to Line 10000. Same thing -- no change in the PRINTout.

*DATA Line(s) can be placed anywhere in the program.*

This fact leads different programmers to use different styles. Some place all DATA Lines at the beginning of a program so they can be read first in a LISTing and found quickly, to change the DATA.

Others place all DATA Lines at a program's end where they are out of the way and there are additional Line numbers available to add more DATA Lines as the need arises. Still others scatter the DATA Lines throughout the program, next to the READ Lines. The style you select is of little consequence -- *but consistency is comfortable.*

## The Plot Thickens

Since we now know all about FOR-NEXT loops, let us see what happens when a DATA Line is placed in the middle of a loop. Erase the old program with NEW and type in this program:

```
10 DATA 1,2,3,4,5
```

Y'KNOW SOMETHIN' FRIEND? YOU'RE NOT HALF AS SCARY AS IN THE BEGINNING.
RATS! MY COVER'S BLOWN!

```
20  FOR N = 1 TO 5
30   READ A
40   PRINT A;
50  NEXT N
```

...and RUN.

That DATA Line is outside the loop. Now move it to Line 25 and RUN. What happened?

Nothing different! It is important to absorb this fact or we wouldn't have gone to the trouble to prove it. We went through the N loop 5 times, READ the letter A 5 times, and the PRINT statement PRINTed A 5 times, but A's value was *different* each time. Its value was what it last READ from the DATA Line. The reason -- each piece of data in a DATA Line can only be read *once* each time the program is RUN. The next time a READ statement requests a piece of data, it will read the NEXT piece of data in the DATA Line, or, if that Line is all "used up", move on to the next DATA Line and begin READing it.

Change Line 20 in the program to read:

```
20 FOR N = 1 TO 6
```

...and RUN.

The READ statement was instructed to read 6 pieces of DATA, but there were only 5. An error statement caught it, as the screen shows.

```
 1 2 3 4 5
Out of DATA in 30
```

Change Line 20 so the number of READs is *less* than the DATA available.

```
20 FOR N = 1 TO 4
```

...and RUN.

No problem. It works just fine even if we don't use all the available data. The point is, each piece of data in a DATA statement can only be READ once during each RUN.

## Exceptions, Exceptions!

Because it is sometimes necessary to read the same DATA more than once without RUNning the complete program over, a statement called RESTORE is available. Whenever the program comes across a RESTORE, *all* DATA Lines are RESTOREd to their original "unread" condition, both those that have been READ and those that have not, and all are available for reading again. Change Line 20 back to:

```
20 FOR N = 1 TO 5
```

and insert:

```
35 RESTORE
```

...and RUN.

Oh-oh! The screen PRINTs five 1's instead of 1 2 3 4 5. Can you figure out why?

> Line 30 READ A as 1, but Line 35 immediately RESTOREd the DATA Line to its *original un*READ *condition*. When the FOR-NEXT loop brought the READ Line around for the next pass it again read the first piece of data, which was that same 1. Same thing happened with the remaining passes.

READ and DATA statements are extremely common. RESTORE is used less often.

> Do you begin to see some distant glimmer involving the storing of business or technical DATA in DATA Lines where it's easily changed or updated without affecting the rest of the program or its formulas?

## String Variables

Who knows where some of these seemingly unrelated words come from? If they weren't so important we could ignore them. We have been using the letters A through Z to hold number values. They are called *numeric variables*. We can use the same 26 letters to hold *string variables* by just adding a "$".

A$, for example is called "A String". String variables can be assigned to indicate *letters, words* and/or *combinations* of letters, numbers, spaces and other characters. Type NEW then type in:

```
10 INPUT "WHAT IS YOUR NAME";A$

20 PRINT "HELLO THERE ";A$
```

...and RUN.

Hey-hey! How's that for a grabber? If that, along with what we have learned in earlier Chapters doesn't make the creative juices flow, nothing will.

## That's Two....

We now know two ways to PRINT words. The first, learned long ago, is to imbed words in PRINT statements (and is called "PRINTing a string"). The second is to bring word(s) through an INPUT statement (called "INPUTting a string"). If you can't think of the third way, go back and check the title at the top of this Chapter.

Change the program to read:

```
10 READ A$

20 DATA IBM PERSONAL COMPUTER

30 PRINT "SEE MY FOXY ";A$
```

...and RUN.

```
SEE MY FOXY IBM PERSONAL COMPUTER
```

Let's use 2 string variables to accomplish the same thing, seeing how they work with each other. Reword the program to read:

```
10 READ A$

15 READ B$
```

```
20 DATA IBM, PERSONAL COMPUTER

30 PRINT "SEE MY FOXY ";A$;" ";B$
```

...and RUN.

Analyzing the program:

Line 20 contains two pieces of string Data, separated by a comma.

Line 10 READs the first one.

Line 15 READs the second one.

Line 30 contains 4 PRINT expressions.

The first one PRINTs "SEE MY FOXY", leaving a space behind the "Y" since, unlike numeric variables, string variables do *not* insert leading and trailing spaces. This gives excellent control over PRINT spacing.

The second PRINT is A$, and it prints "IBM".

The third PRINT inserts the space which is enclosed in quotes.

The fourth PRINT is "PERSONAL COMPUTER."

Together, they PRINT the entire message on the same line.

---

A semi-colon between STRING variables does *not* cause a space to be PRINTed between them. We have to insert a space using " " marks.

---

## Learned In Chapter 21

| Statements | Miscellaneous |
|---|---|
| READ | String Variables A$, B$,... |
| DATA | Numeric Variables |
| RESTORE | |

# PART 3
# STRINGS

# Intermediate BASIC

## Intermediate Features Of IBM BASIC

Now that we've learned the rudiments of "Elementary" BASIC we can get serious about "Intermediate" BASIC. The next Chapter is sort of a "catch up" and "catch all", explaining a lot of little unrelated features that didn't find convenient homes in the previous Chapters. Study each of them, do the sample programs and think about them. Each one is brief but important.

# Chapter 22

# Smorgasbörd

## Multiple Statement Lines : (Now he tells us!)

BASIC allows us to put more than one consecutive statement on each numbered Line, separating them by a colon (:). For example, a timer loop such as:

```
100 FOR N = 1 TO 500
110 NEXT N
```

can become...

```
100 FOR N = 1 TO 500 : NEXT N
```

**Caveat Emptor** *(Don't buy a used computer from a stranger.)*

Control yourself! It's easy to get carried away with this exciting feature. While we will use multiple statement Lines often from here on, you will quickly find that it's possible to pack the information so tightly it becomes hard to read, and also very hard to modify.

**More Caveat** *(or is it more Emptor?)*

Multiple statement Lines require careful understanding. Especially critical are statements of the IF-THEN variety.

Enter the following *incorrect* program:

```
10 INPUT "TYPE IN A NUMBER";X
20 IF X = 3 THEN 50 : GOTO 70
30 PRINT "HOW DID YOU GET HERE?"
40 END
50 PRINT "X=3"
60 END
70 PRINT "CAN'T GET FROM THERE TO HERE."
```

...and RUN it several times with different INPUT values, including 3.

**Line 20 has an error in logic**. If the IF-THEN test passes, control moves to Line 50. That's OK.

If the test fails, however, control drops to the next Line in the program -- Line 30, not to the 2nd statement in Line 20. **There is no way the 2nd statement in Line 20 (GOTO 70) can ever be executed.**

**The Message --** if you put an IF-THEN (or ON-GOTO) type-test in a multiple statement Line, it must be the *last* statement in that Line.

**Next Message --** we cannot send control TO any point in a multiple statement Line except to its FIRST statement. Look at Line 20. There is no way to address the GOTO 70 portion. It shares the same Line number as the first statement in the same Line. Only the first statement is addressable by a GOTO or IF-THEN. Other statements in a Line are accessed in sequence, IF each prior test is passed.

## New Numeric Variables

We know we can use the 26 letters of the alphabet as names for variables. We can also use the numbers 0 through 9 in conjunction with these letters:

```
A3 = 65
F9 = 37
```

etc.

Although the 26 letter variables are usually enough, addition of the numbers give us an additional 26*10 = 260. They can be very handy, particularly if we want to label a number of "sub" variables (D1,D2,D3,etc.) which combine to make a grand total which we can just call D.

```
PI = 3.14159
```

`C = PI*D`     Circumference = 3.14159 * Diameter

In addition, we can use any combination of upper case letters and numbers for a name, up to 40 characters long. For example:

```
LEARNINGIBMBASIC = 19.95
```

---

Now that really looks valuable.

---

If that doesn't provide enough variables to solve your problems, nothing will.

## New String Variables

So far we've used only A$ and B$ as string variables. We actually have *all* the letters of the alphabet available for strings. And the numbers 0 through 9 too, plus any letter-number combination. These are valid string names:

X$

D8$

Pi$

WHATAGREATBOOK$

etc.

As with numeric variables, string variables can have any combination of up to 40 upper case letters and numbers followed by the $ sign.

## Shorthand

There are several little "shorthand" tricks available.

The first is the use of ? in place of the very common word, PRINT. Type NEW, then this Line:

```
10 ?"QUESTION MARK"
```

...and LIST it.

Awwk! The pumpkin turned into a coach. The Computer rewrote it to read:

```
10 PRINT"QUESTION MARK"
```

It also works at the command level. Try:

`?3*4` and we get:

```
12
```

Try `?FRE(0)`

The ' is shorthand for REM, and is especially nice when documenting the purpose of a Line. It makes program Lines into multiple statement Lines. ' = :REM.

```
50 X = Z*C/4 + 33        'THE SECRET EQUATION
```

The only place ' can't be used unaided is in a DATA Line, and that problem can be overcome by actually adding a :

```
1000 DATA 102,3,9,105,10,1 : 'DATA IS IN
1010 DATA 108,7,3,111,6,1 : 'SEQUENCE
```

## The Enter Key

If you're the very observant type, you noticed that program execution begins when the [←┘] key is *pressed*, not when it's released.

## Use Of Quotes & Semicolons

Technically, it is not necessary to use quotes to close off many PRINT statements, or LOADs and SAVEs.

```
10 PRINT "WHERE IS THE END QUOTE?
```

Note lack of second ".

RUNs just fine. Leave it off at your own peril.

A BASIC interpreter that is "too forgiving" is like an airplane that is "too forgiving." It allows us to become sloppy, and when we need all the skill we can muster, it is gone from the lack of practice. You are strongly encouraged *not* to take these and other "cheap" short-cuts.

## INPUT

It's possible to INPUT several variables with a single INPUT statement. Type this program and respond with a cluster of 3 numbers separated by commas. It will "swallow" them all in one gulp.

```
10 INPUT A,B,C
```

...and RUN.

However, if we fail to INPUT them all, separated by commas, the error:

```
?Redo from start
?
```

points out that more DATA must be INPUT. To see the Error Message, RUN again, but only INPUT one number, then [↵], then [Break].

RUN again and try to INPUT letters instead of numbers. Same Error Message.

There is extensive information in Appendix E dealing with Error Messages. Most often, *Redo* reminds us that we can't INPUT a string variable into a request for a numeric variable.

HE JUST WORKED 3 HRS ON A PROGRAM and THE COMPUTER SAID:

## Optional NEXT

FOR-NEXT loops don't always have to specify which FOR we are NEXTing. This can be useful when dealing with nested loops.

Type this NEW program:

```
10 FOR A = 1 TO 2 : PRINT A
20   FOR B = 1 TO 3 : PRINT ,B
30      FOR C = 1 TO 4 : PRINT ,,C
40 NEXT : NEXT : NEXT
```

RUN it several times to get the flavor. (Note how commas were used to place PRINTing in different zones.

This method of NEXTing should not be used if the program contains tests which might allow a loop to be broken out of. Better then to be specific, or use this little short-cut.

```
40 NEXT C,B,A
```

## IF-THEN-ELSE

ELSE is an interesting addition to our stable of conditional branching statements. It allows an option other than dropping to the next Line if a test fails. Try this one:

```
10 INPUT "ENTER A NUMBER";N
20 IF N=0 THEN PRINT "0" ELSE PRINT "NOT 0"
30 PRINT : LIST
```

...and RUN.

See how smartly we can use LIST in a program so after the RUN it LISTs itself? Great for learning and troubleshooting.

## 254 Characters per Line

IBM BASIC permits up to 254 characters in a single program Line. (Don't ask **me** to debug such a Line!)

## Learned In Chapter 22

**Statements**

IF-THEN-ELSE

**Miscellaneous**

Multiple statement Lines
Variable Names
Some Shorthand
Quotes and Semi-colons
Multiple INPUTting
Optional NEXT
String Variables

# Chapter 23

# The ASCII Set

The purpose of this Chapter is to learn how to use ASC and CHR$. Before doing so, however, we must learn about something called "the ASCII set". (No, it's nothing like the "horsey set".)

ASCII is pronounced (ASK'-EE) and stands for American Standard Code for Information Interchange. Since a computer stores and processes only numbers, not letters or punctuation, it's important that there be some sort of uniform system to specify which numbers represent which letters and symbols. The ASCII Chart in Appendix B shows the relationship between the number system and symbols as used in the IBM. Take a minute to review the chart.

Type in this short program:

```
10 CLS
20 FOR N = 1 TO 255
30  IF N = 9 THEN = 14
40  PRINT "ASCII NUMBER";N;
50  PRINT "STANDS FOR";,CHR$(N)
60  FOR T = 1 TO 500 : NEXT T
70 NEXT N
```

SAVE as ASCII

...and RUN.

Observe that the characters between ASCII code numbers 97 and 122 are lower-case duplicates of ASCII numbers 65 to 90.

Numbers 128 to 168 are foreign language characters.

Code numbers 179 to 223 are special Graphics characters.

Codes 224-254 are special technical characters.

ASCII Codes 1-6 and 14-27 are special characters.

We bypass codes 9-13 because they do funny things with the video screen.

Codes 28-31 are cursor motion codes.

## ASCII Chart

Some of the ASCII numbers between 0 and 31 are used by the IBM for special control purposes:

| Code | Function |
|---|---|
| 7 | Bell |
| 9 | TAB(8,16,24,32,...) |
| 10 | Move cursor to beginning of next Line |
| 11 | Move cursor to upper left corner |
| 12 | Clear screen |
| 13 | Move cursor to beginning of next Line |
| 28 | Advance cursor without erasing |
| 29 | Backspace without erasing |
| 30 | Move cursor up |
| 31 | Move cursor down |

There is very little uniformity internationally (or even within the U.S.) in the assignment of ASCII code numbers, except those used for the "Roman" letters and numbers. Fortunately, they handle most of our everyday needs. If we contemplate the problems faced by the Japanese, Arabs and others who need special letters and characters, it's easy to see how good use can be found for the ASCII values between 127 and 255.

## Line Graphic Characters

While we are nosing around this region of the ASCII set, let's see what we can do with those Line Graphic characters IBM has bestowed on us.

Enter this NEW program:

```
10 REM  * LINE GRAPHIC CHARACTER PROGRAM *
20 CLS
30 FOR I=1 TO 4 : FOR J=1 TO 8
40  READ N : PRINT CHR$(N);
50  NEXT J : PRINT : NEXT I
70 DATA 218,196,196,191,218,196,196,191
80 DATA 179,218,191,179,179,218,191,179
90 DATA 179,192,193,193,180,195,217,179
100 DATA 192,196,194,194,180,195,196,217
```

...and RUN.

Line 30 starts two loops: one for the 4 rows and the other for the 8 characters per row.

Line 40 reads the code numbers from the DATA Lines and PRINTs the ASCII characters.

Line 50 closes both loops, adding a PRINT at the end of each row.

Now that our fingers are rested, change Line 30 to:

```
30 FOR I=1 TO 8 : FOR J=1 TO 8
```

and add the rest of the DATA:

```
110 DATA 218,196,180,195,193,193,196,191
120 DATA 179,218,180,195,194,194,191,179
130 DATA 179,192,217,179,179,192,217,179
140 DATA 192,196,196,217,192,196,196,217
```

*Truly amazing!*

Besides the Line graphic characters, there are lots of other weird characters between 128-255. IBM allows us to type these characters from the keyboard using the Alternate key. Referring to Appendix B, we see the ASCII chart and the codes of all the special characters.

Suppose we want to PRINT an English pound sign, code 156. Hold down the [Alt] key and type 156 with the numbers on the *numeric keypad*. Then release the [Alt] key and presto, the sign appears on the screen. This technique can sometimes be easier than using the PRINT CHR$(156) format. It can be used with all characters 32-255, although 32-126 can just as easily be entered directly from the regular keyboard.

Yup. We have control of these higher order ASCII codes. *Today the personal computer, tomorrow the world!*

## So What Is CHR$(N)

We have used CHR$ (pronounced Character String) without describing it, but you undoubtedly figured it out anyway. CHR$(N) produces the ASCII character (or control action) specified by the code number N. It is a one-way converter from the ASCII *code number* to the ASCII *character*, and allows us to throw characters around with the ease of throwing around numbers. The word "string" refers to any character or mixture of characters (letters, numbers or punctuation).

Enter this simple program:

```
10 INPUT "TYPE ANY NUMBER (33-126)";N
20 PRINT CHR$(N)
30 PRINT : RUN
```

...and RUN.

---

See how RUN can be used *inside* a BASIC program?

---

Almost all of our activity with ASCII numbers will be confined to this range.

**EXERCISE 23-1:** Using the ASCII chart (Appendix B) and the CHR$ function, create a program which will PRINT the name: IBM PC.

## ASCII Applications

If we end up in the Big House serving time for computer fraud, the following little program will make up our license plate combinations, putting CHR$ to good use.

Enter this NEW program:

```
10 REM * LICENSE PLATE NUMBER GENERATOR *
20 FOR N=1 TO 3 : PRINT INT(RND(1)*10);
30 NEXT N : PRINT "   ";
40 FOR N=1 TO 3
50  PRINT CHR$(INT(RND(1)*26+65));"   ";
60 NEXT N : PRINT : GOTO 20
```

SAVE as "LICPLATE"

...and RUN.

The RND generator in Line 20 PRINTs numbers between 0 and 9. Line 50 spits out numbers between 0 and 25. We add 65 to each number to make the sum fall in the range between 65 and 90. What do we see on the ASCII conversion chart between 65 and 90? Hmmmm???

## What Then Is ASC($)?

ASC is the exact opposite of CHR$(N). ASC is a one-way converter from the ASCII *character* to its corresponding ASCII *number*.

Type:

```
10 INPUT "TYPE NEARLY ANY CHARACTER";A$
20 PRINT "ITS ASCII NUMBER IS";ASC(A$)
```

```
30 PRINT : GOTO 10
```

...and RUN.

It will PRINT the ASCII number of almost all characters, too. It doesn't work with the comma (,), the quotation mark ("), the space bar, and some others, but then strings can be a real mystery at times, as we will see.

To get around this and other problems we use an advanced form of INPUT called LINE INPUT. LINE INPUT allows us to INPUT *any* character (that is assigned an ASCII code) as a string. Notice that the Computer will not insert a question mark when it asks for the text.

Change Line 10 to:

```
10 LINE INPUT "TYPE IN ANYTHING ";A$
```

...and RUN. Check comma, quote, space bar, etc.

An obscure way to use ASC is to imbed the character within quotes, thus:

but this latter method is rarely convenient.

## Home Base

So far we have talked exclusively about *decimal* numbers, since most of us have just 10 fingers. But the IBM has two intrinsic functions which convert decimal numbers to numbers with Hexadecimal and Octal Bases. Whereas the Decimal system is built on the base 10 (10 digits 0-9), Octal is base 8 (8 digits 0-7) and Hexadecimal is base 16 (16 digits 0-9 and A-F). We'll leave the mechanics of using other bases to other CompuSoft books, but just to be complete, change the resident program to read:

```
10 LINE INPUT "TYPE ANY LETTER, NUMBER OR
CHARACTER ";A$
20 PRINT "ITS ASCII VALUE IS";ASC(A$)
30 A = ASC(A$) : PRINT
40 PRINT,A,"DECIMAL"
```

NOW, WHAT'S ALL
THIS BABBLING ABOUT
"CHR$(N) and ASC($)?"

```
50 PRINT,HEX$(A),"HEXADECIMAL"
60 PRINT,OCT$(A),"OCTAL"
70 PRINT : GOTO 10
```

SAVE as BASECONV

...and RUN.

Before we can really understand the importance of CHR$ and ASC, we must learn a lot more about strings. Before we could learn about strings we had to learn something about ASCII. It's like "catch IBM".

**EXERCISE 23-2:** Input a single character from the keyboard and test its ASCII value to determine IF it is a number. If not, return program control to the INPUT statement. Hint: use two IF statements and ASC.

## Learned in Chapter 23

| Functions | Miscellaneous |
|---|---|
| CHR$ | ASCII Codes |
| ASC | |

## Chapter 24

# Strings In General

It was not our intention to "string you along" in the previous Chapter, but we really can't understand how strings work without first understanding the ASCII concept of numbers standing for letters, numbers and other characters and controls.

## Comparing Strings

One of the most powerful string handling capabilities is the ability to *compare* them. We compare the values of *numeric* variables all the time. How can we compare *strings* of letters or words? Well, why do you suppose we put the ASCII Chapter just before this one? **Right!** The Computer can compare the ASCII *code numbers* of letters and other characters. The net result is a comparison of what's in the corresponding strings.

Type in this NEW program:

```
1 CLS
10 INPUT"WHAT IS YOUR NAME";A$
20 IF A$ = "ISHKIBIBBLE" THEN 50
30 PRINT "SORRY, WRONG NAME!"
40 END
50 PRINT "FINALLY GOT IT!"
```

...and RUN.

If the Computer can compare A$ against *that* name it should be able to compare anything!

During the process of comparing what you enter as A$ in Line 10 to what's already in quotes in Line 20, the ASCII code numbers of each letter found in one string are compared, letter for letter, from left to right with those in the other. Every one must match, or the test fails.

Strings and "quotes" are inseparable. You know this from earlier Chapters where every PRINT "XXX" has its string enclosed in quotes.

PRINT "XXX" is called a string *constant*. A$ is a string *variable*.

RUN the above program again, this time answering the question with "ISHKIBIBBLE", but enclosed in quotes.

Sure -- it ran OK.

## READing Strings

A string can be INPUT with or without quotes. BASIC has become increasingly lenient about this matter, but every once in a while the rules come up from behind and bite us if we play fast and loose with them.

If we READ a string from a DATA Line, and it has no commas, semi-colons, leading or trailing spaces in it, we don't *have* to enclose it in quotes. We will never go wrong by *always* enclosing strings in quotes, but that can be a nuisance.

**EXERCISE 24-1:** Write a program that will compare two strings entered from the keyboard. PRINT them in alphabetical order.

Erase the resident program and type in this next one, which READs string data from a DATA Line.

```
10 CLS
20 READ A$,B$,C$
30 PRINT A$
40 PRINT B$
50 PRINT C$
```

SEE YOU'RE INTO STRINGS NOW, OL' BOY.

```
100 DATA COMPUSOFT, SAN DIEGO, CA, 92119
900 PRINT : LIST
```

...and RUN.

Look carefully at the results. The screen shows:

```
COMPUSOFT
SAN DIEGO
CA
```

That's nice, but where is the ZIP Code? And why weren't SAN DIEGO and CA PRINTed on the same Line? The answer, my friend, is blowing in the ... er, in the commas.

Because of the commas in the DATA Line, the READ statement sees 4 pieces of DATA, but only READs 3 of them. What do we have to do in order to PRINT a comma as part of a string? Right -- enclose it, or the string containing it, in quotes.

```
EDIT 100
```

and change Line 100 to read:

```
100 DATA COMPUSOFT, "SAN DIEGO, CA", 92119
```

...and RUN.

Aaaah! That's more like it. Notice that we didn't have to enclose *all* pieces of string DATA in separate quotes, but could have.

What would happen if we also enclosed the *entire* DATA Line in quotes, leaving the existing quotes in there? (Think about it, then try it. Every question raised has a specific purpose.)

Our EDITor is so easy to use, let's make it read:

```
100 DATA "COMPUSOFT, "SAN DIEGO, CA", 92119"
```

...and RUN.

Awwk! Disaster. A Syntax error in Line 100? Yes, there is no straightforward way to READ quotes as part of a string, even by enclosing them inside another pair of quotes. The Computer just isn't smart enough to figure out which quote mark is which. The usual way to overcome this BASIC language deficiency is to substitute ' for each " imbedded inside other quotes. Let's try it:

```
100 DATA "COMPUSOFT, 'SAN DIEGO, CA', 92119"
```

...and RUN.

Ooops, Out of DATA in 20? Of course. With quotes surrounding the whole works there is now just one piece of DATA and we are trying to read 3 pieces. Change Line 20 to just read one piece:

```
20 READ A$
```

...and RUN.

B$ and C$ are PRINTed as "blanks" since they are empty.

There we go. Might look a little strange, but it demonstrates the point and warns us a little about the "touchiness" of strings.

As we modify this program "over the cliff", that classic ballad from the hills is heard echoing:

> *"Ah-cigareets, and whuisky, and wild computers, they'll drive you crazy, they'll drive you insane!"*

But, undaunted by this high class philosophy, we steer our vessel towards the next Chapter.

... as the sun sinks slowly in the west, warm breezes fill our sails and waves slap the bow. Stars twinkle, and around the beach fires plaintive native chants are heard, calling ...

## Learned In Chapter 24

### Miscellaneous

String comparison
INPUTting strings
READing strings

# Chapter 25

# Measuring Strings

ne of the most frequently needed facts about a string is its length. Fortunately, the LEN function makes it easy to find. Type:

```
10 INPUT "ENTER A STRING OF CHARACTERS";A$
20 L = LEN(A$)
30 PRINT A$;" HAS";L;"CHARACTERS"
90 PRINT : RUN
```

RUN several times, entering your name and other combinations of letters and numbers. Try entering your name, last name first, with a comma after your last name.

AHA! Can't INPUT a comma. How about if we put it all in quotes? Try again.

Yep. Just like it said in the last Chapter.

LEN has only one significant variation, and it's not all that useful -- unless it's really needed. Change Lines 10-30 to read:

```
10 INPUT "ENTER A NUMBER";A
20 L = LEN(A)
30 PRINT A;" HAS";L;"CHARACTERS"
```

...and RUN.

Crash time again! "Type Mismatch" means we tried to INPUT a *number* into LEN -- but it requires a *string*.

Letters cause a "?Redo from start" since they need to be INPUT by an A$ or equivalent. RUN again, and INPUT a letter. Is there no justice here? OK, let's change LEN to make it a string:

```
20 L = LEN("A")
```

...and RUN, entering a Number. Then try bigger numbers.

Hmmm. Doesn't seem to matter what number we INPUT, it always comes back saying that we have only 1 character.

The answer is, LEN evaluates the LENgth of what is actually between its parentheses (or quotes). At first we brought in a string from the "outside" and measured its length. That worked fine. We are now measuring the length of what's actually between the quotes, and that *length* doesn't change with the *value* of A. We are using A as a "literal string constant", not a variable string.

Understand this?

Like we said, this second way to use LEN has its limitations, but don't lose any sleep over it. (Change the resident program back to the way it appears at the beginning of the Chapter.)

## DEFSTR -- For Thrill Seekers

Those among us who attract trouble will love this next one. As if handling strings isn't complex enough, this very powerful statement looks nice and clean but in long and complex programs can be the greatest source of heartburn since the horseradish pizza.

DEFSTR (pronounced "DEFine STRing") allows us to define *which* variables are to be *string* variables, so we don't have to use the $ any more. (Hmm ... Uncle Sam could put some of this DEFSTR business to good use.) Add this Line:

```
5 DEFSTR A
```

and use the EDITor to change Line 20 to:

```
20 L = LEN(A)
```

Then RUN.

Works fine, doesn't it. A was declared by Line 5 to be a string variable. So what's all the fuss about?

Well, this is a very simple program, but let's change 5 to read:

```
5 DEFSTR A-Z
```

which makes *all* letters string variables.

...and RUN.

Crasho again! **Too much** of a good thing. Because of Line 5, the L in Line 20 is now *also* a string. Since LEN gives us the length of a string as a number, it doesn't set at all well with L (really L string). Imagine the fun this can create in a long program.

---

Good thing we can learn by our errors!

---

DEFSTR is best used to define individual variables. For example:

```
DEFSTR A,N,Z
```

defines only A, N and Z as string variables. Rework Line 5 to read:

```
5 DEFSTR A
```

...and RUN.

That's a short course in what DEFSTR is all about.

## Concatenation

Concatenation? Concatenation??? Now what is that supposed to mean? Did you ever wonder who pays who to sit around and think up such nondescriptive words? It must have been done on a government grant. Wait till Senator Proxmire hears about it.

CONCATENATION?
CONCATENATION??
FORGET THE WEBSTER'S, PAL. IT MEANS, "ADD STRINGS TO-GETHER"

Concatenation (pronounced con-cat-uh-na'tion) is a national debt-sized word which means ADD, as in "add strings together". It's easier to do than to pronounce.

Type this NEW program:

```
10 CLS : FOR N = 1 TO 15
20  READ A$ : B$ = B$ + A$
30 PRINT B$ : NEXT N
100 DATA ALPHA,BRAVO,CHARLIE,DELTA
110 DATA ECHO,FOXTROT,GOLF,HOTEL
120 DATA INDIA,JULIETT,KILO,LIMA
130 DATA MIKE,NOVEMBER,OSCAR
```

Check it carefully but don't RUN it yet. The key Line is 20, which simply says B$ (a new variable) equals the old B$ (which starts out as nothing) plus whatever is in A$. The program cycles around and keeps adding what is in B$ to what is READ from DATA as A$. Now RUN.

Anyhoo, the point of all this is *concatenation*. Line 20 just did it, and that's about all there is to it. We added strings together.

**EXERCISE 25-1:** Use the LEN function to check the length of a string INPUTted from the keyboard. PRINT a message telling us if the string exceeded 10 characters.

**EXERCISE 25-2:** INPUT a word from the keyboard and compare it to a secret password. If there is a match, PRINT "CORRECT PASSWORD, ENTER". If not, PRINT "WRONG PASSWORD. GET LOST!". Store the ASCII number for each letter of the password in a DATA Line. READ each value and use CHR$ to build (concatenate) the password string.

## Learned In Chapter 25

| Statements | Functions | Miscellaneous |
|---|---|---|
| DEFSTR | LEN | Concatenation (+) |

# Chapter 26

# VAL and STR$

The "hassle factor" can be very high when converting back and forth between strings and numerics.

By definition, if we convert a *numeric* variable (can hold only a number) to a *string* variable (can hold almost anything), the *contents* of that new string is still the original number. No letters or other characters were converted (except for a leading space) since they weren't in the numeric variable to start with.

Conversely, if we change a *string* variable to a *numeric* variable, we can't change any letters or other characters to numbers. Only the *numbers* in a string can be converted to a numeric variable. (Don't confuse this with ASCII conversions.)

If you'll keep the two previous paragraphs in mind, it'll save an awful lot of grief in dealing with strings.

## VAL

Let's give string-to-numeric conversion a shot. The VAL function converts a *string* variable holding a *number* into a *number*, if the number is at the beginning of the string. Try this VAL program:

```
1 CLS : PRINT
10 INPUT"ENTER A STRING ";A$
20 A = VAL(A$)
```

```
30 PRINT"THE NUMERIC VALUE OF ";A$;" IS";A
90 PRINT : GOTO 10
```

...and RUN

Try lots of different INPUTs, such as:

```
12345
ASDF
123ASD
ASD123
1,2,3
A,B,C
```

and the same ones over again, but enclosed in quotes.

The screen tells all.

BREAK out of the program, then take the $ out of Lines 10, 20, and 30 and RUN, INPUTting both numbers and letters.

What you're seeing is typical of the frustrations that bedevil string users who don't follow the rules. VAL only evaluates STRINGs, and we've put A, a numeric value, in where a string belongs. Does this remind you of the problems in the last Chapter with LEN?

Let's put that A in quotes and see what happens.

```
20 A = VAL("A")
```

...and RUN.

No help at all! The rule remains unchanged.

*Properly used,* VAL converts a *string* holding a *number* into that *number*.

VAL ??
STR$(N)??
NOW HOW ABOUT
GIVING ME THAT
WEBSTER'S ?

Looking at the screen you can see all the other uses we are finding for VAL are just not in the cards. Remember this irritating frustration and "The Rule" when you get in the thick of debugging a nasty string-loaded program.

## STR$

Now let's try the opposite, converting a *numeric* variable to a *string* variable. Change the program to read:

```
1 CLS : PRINT
10 INPUT "NUMBER TO CONVERT TO STRING";A
20 A$ = STR$(A)
30 PRINT"THE STRING VALUE OF";A;"IS";A$
90 PRINT : GOTO 10
```

...and RUN, using the same INPUTs we used when wringing out VAL.

There it is. A short but very important Chapter. Spend as much time on this one as any other Chapter. The time spent learning to avoid the pitfalls surrounding these powerful two functions will come back manyfold in future debugging time. VAL and STR$ have very specific, but narrow abilities.

**EXERCISE 26-1:** INPUT your street address (e.g. 2423 LA PALMA). Use VAL to extract the street number. Add the number 4 to the street number and report this new number as your neighbor's street number.

**EXERCISE 26-2:** Write a program using STR$ to PRINT the following 20 store item stock numbers: 101WT, 102WT, 103WT,...120WT. Hint: Looks like a natural for a FOR-NEXT loop.

## Learned In Chapter 26

### Functions

VAL
STR$

# Chapter 27

# Having A Ball With String

## LEFT$, RIGHT$, MID$

Three different, yet very similar functions are used for playing powerful games with strings. They are LEFT$, RIGHT$ and MID$. Let's start with this program:

```
10 CLS : PRINT
20 S$ = "KILROY WAS HERE"
50 PRINT LEFT$(S$,6),
60 PRINT MID$(S$,8,3),
70 PRINT RIGHT$(S$,4)
90 PRINT : LIST
```

...and RUN.

The screen says:

```
KILROY          WAS             HERE
```

(How about that one, nostalgia buffs?)

Learning to use these string functions is exceedingly simple. Study the program slowly and carefully as we go thru what happened.

LEFT$ PRINTed the LEFTmost 6 characters in the string named S$.

MID$ PRINTed 3 characters in the string named S$, starting with the 8th character from the left. (Count 'em.)

RIGHT$ PRINTed the 4 RIGHTmost characters in the string named S$.

The commas after Lines 50 and 60 are to PRINT everything on the same Line.

SAVE this program as KILROY, then let's move some Lines around to exercise our new-found power. Move Line 60 to Line 40:

```
40 PRINT MID$(S$,8,3),
```

RUN ... and we get:

```
WAS             KILROY          HERE
```

Now move Line 70 to Line 30 and add a trailing comma.

```
30 PRINT RIGHT$(S$,4),
```

RUN ... and we get:

```
HERE            WAS             KILROY
```

These 3 functions can really do wonders with strings. Type in this NEW program and examine each one in more detail:

```
10 CLS
20 S$ = "KILROY WAS HERE"
```

```
30 FOR N = 1 TO 15
40  PRINT "N =";N,
50  PRINT LEFT$(S$,N)
90 NEXT : PRINT : LIST
```

...and RUN.

The picture tells it faster than words. LEFT$ picks off "N" letters from the LEFT side of S string. See how this string function could be used to strip off only the first 3 digits of a phone number, or the first letter of a name when searching and sorting?

Change Line 30 to read:

```
30 FOR N = 1 TO 20
```

SAVE as LEFT ... and RUN.

Even though there are only 15 characters in the string, the overRUN is ignored. Change Line 30 back to `N = 1 TO 15`.

RIGHT$ works the same way, but from the RIGHT:

Change Line 50 to read:

```
50 PRINT RIGHT$(S$,N)
```

SAVE as RIGHT ... and RUN.

It's the mirror image of LEFT$.

Now let's exercise MID$ and see where it goes. Change Line 50 to:

```
50 PRINT MID$(S$,N,1)
```

SAVE as MID ... and RUN.

It very methodically scanned the string, from left to right, picking out and

27 CHAPTERS and ALL YOU CAN DISPLAY IS: "KILROY WAS HERE"?
AW, WE WERE JUST FOOLIN' AROUND.

PRINTing one letter at a time. Slow it down with a delay loop if the action is too fast to follow.

With only a slight change, MID$ can act like LEFT$. Change Line 50 to:

```
50 PRINT MID$(S$,1,N)
```

...and RUN.

It PRINTed N characters, counting from number 1 on the left.

MID$ can also simulate RIGHT$. Change Line 50:

```
50 PRINT MID$(S$,16-N,N)
```

...and RUN.

Would you believe RIGHT$ backwards, one at a time?

```
50 PRINT MID$(S$,16-N,1)
```

...and RUN.

How about a sort of "histogram" type graph:

```
50 PRINT MID$(S$,N,N)
```

...and RUN.

---

Make notes below for future reference. If all these examples don't spark some ideas for your future use, I give up.

---

Suppose we want to PRINT the character in a specific position in the string. Make the program read:

```
1 CLS
10 S$ = "KILROY WAS HERE"
```

```
30 INPUT "CHARACTER # TO PRINT";N
40 PRINT MID$(S$,N,1)
90 PRINT : LIST
```

...and RUN.

If it's not obvious, we can assign any of these statements to a variable. That variable can in turn be used in tests against other variables. Change:

```
40 V$ = MID$(S$,N,1)
50 PRINT V$
```

...and RUN.

A short book could be written about these three powerful functions, but I think the point's been made. They are used *very* frequently in complex sort and select routines. If we dissect them into these simple components, they are easy to keep track of. The next section has some good examples.

**EXERCISE 27-1:** Write a program that asks the question "ISN'T THIS A SMART COMPUTER". Input a YES or NO answer. If the first character in the answer is a Y, PRINT "AFFIRMATIVE". If the first character is an N, PRINT "NEGATIVE". Otherwise PRINT "THIS IS A YES OR NO QUESTION" and send control back to the INPUT statement.

**EXERCISE 27-2:** READ in the following part numbers: N106WT, A208FM, AND Z154DX. Use MID$ to find the numbers. PRINT the number with the largest value.

## Searching With INSTR

INSTR (pronounced, "In-string") is a function that can be of value when searching for a needle in a haystack. It compares one string against another to see if they have anything in common.

Suppose we have a list of names and want to see if another name (or part of that name) is in our list. It's the "part of" which makes this operation very different from a straight comparison of name-against-name, which we already know how to do using ordinary string-against-string comparisons. Here we learn how to locate a name (and similar names) by asking for just a small part of it.

Start the NEW program by entering this list of Names:

```
10000 DATA SMITH, JONES, FAHRQUART, BROWN
10010 DATA JOHNSON, SCHWARTZ, FINKELSTEIN
10020 DATA BAILEY, SNOOPY, JOE BFTSPLK, *
```

That was the easy part.

How do we READ these names, one at a time, and compare them, or parts of them, with the name or part of a name which we INPUT? Add these Lines:

```
10 CLS
20 INPUT "WHAT LETTER(S) IS WANTED";N$
30 PRINT
40 READ D$
50 IF D$ = "*" THEN GOTO 99
60 IF INSTR(1,D$,N$) = 0 THEN 40
70 PRINT ,N$;" IS PART OF ";D$
80 GOTO 40
99 PRINT : PRINT "END OF SEARCH" : END
```

SAVE this program as "INSTR". We'll be needing it later.

Now this takes a bit of explaining:

Line 10 CLears the Screen.

Line 20 INPUTs the name, or part of the name we are trying to locate.

Line 30 PRINTs a blank space for easier reading to help give this book some class.

Line 40 READs a single name from the DATA file.

Line 50 tests to see if D$ is READing the last item in the DATA file, IF so, execution branches to Line 99.

Line 60 uses the INSTRing to do all the searching. INSTR looks at D$, starting with the 1st character, to see if the characters INPUT in N$ match characters in D$. If INSTR returns the value of 0, it means there is no "match", and the program should READ the next piece of DATA. If there is a match, INSTR returns a number which is the number of characters it counted in N$ before a match was found. Since this number is not 0, execution drops to:

Line 70 which PRINTs both what we're looking for and the match.

Line 80 starts the process over again.

RUN, trying various letters, names and parts of names to get the hang of what's going on. It's pretty impressive!

---

Now that wasn't too bad, was it? ('Twarnt nothin', really.) It doesn't matter how hard a program seems, when broken down to its individual parts it isn't very hard. Like we've pointed out before, "The BASICs Are Everything". A little time beside the pool reflecting on the logic will do wonders.

---

For those with only a silver fingerbowl, but no pool, these changes will show the inner machinations of INSTR.

```
60 L = INSTR(1,D$,N$)

65 IF L = 0 THEN 40

70 PRINT ,N$;" IS CHARACTER#";L;"IN ";D$
```

RUN it through a number of times trying different letters. It really does make sense!

To see the effect the starting number following INSTR has on our program, change Line 60 to:

```
60 L = INSTR(2,D$,N$)
```

INSTR now looks at D$, starting with the 2nd character.

RUN and type in the letter S. See how it skipped SMITH, SCHWARTZ and SNOOPY? Play around with the starting number in INSTR until you have a good handle on what it does.

**EXERCISE 27-3:** ReLOAD the "INSTR" program and change the DATA Lines to:

```
10000 DATA P-RUTH, OF-MANTLE, SB-MORGAN
10010 DATA SS-LEOTHELIP, P-KOUFAX
10020 DATA C-CAMPANELLA, P-FELLER,*
```

What string would we enter to LIST the pitchers only?

A. P
B. PITCHER
C. P-
D. None of the above

SAVE as BASEBALL and RUN. Practice sorting by team positions.

## Snarled STRING

In the last Chapter we learned about STR$, which lets us convert a numeric variable to a string variable. For the purpose of confusion (no doubt), there is another "string-string" that does something completely different. Fortunately, it is written differently.

STRING$(N,A) is a specialized PRINT *modifier* which allows us to PRINT a single ASCII character, represented by A, a total of N times. Quite simple, really, and very useful.

Type:

```
NEW
10 PRINT STRING$(32,42);
20 PRINT "STRING$ FUNCTION";
30 PRINT STRING$(32,42)
```

...and RUN.

Wow! That really moves. It PRINTed ASCII character 42, which is a *, 32 times, then PRINTed the phrase STRING$ FUNCTION, then PRINTed * 32 more times. This just has to have some good applications.

Suppose we need to type a "header" across the top of a report -- let's say the first Line of it is to be solid dashes. What is the ASCII code for a dash? Forgot? *Me too*. Everybody back to Appendix B to find the code number.

45 it is. We want to PRINT, 80 times, the character represented by ASCII code 45. That's the full width of a Line on our screen. The NEW program should look something like:

```
20 PRINT STRING$(80,45)
```

...RUN it.

An even easier way to use STRING$ is to replace the ASCII code of the character we wish to PRINT with the actual character itself. (It must be enclosed in quotes.) This works fine with characters that really PRINT, such as letters, numbers and punctuation marks. Change Line 20 so the program reads:

```
20 PRINT STRING$(80,"-")
```

...and RUN.

Works nice doesn't it, and we didn't have to look up the ASCII code.

We can bring in a single string character via a string variable. This simple NEW program shows a variation on the theme, and may trigger some ideas:

```
10 INPUT "ANY LETTER, NUMBER OR SYMBOL";A$
20 PRINT STRING$(80,A$)
30 PRINT : GOTO 10
```

Play around with STRING$ a while. It's really very helpful when needed, particularly for giving display PRINTouts some class. An obvious advantage is its ability to do a lot of PRINTing with very little programming.

**EXERCISE 27-4:** Print a string of 30 asterisks centered at the top of the screen.

## SPACE$ and SPC

The SPACE$ allows us to print from 0 to 255 blank spaces. For example:

```
PRINT "A";SPACE$(20);"B"
```

will print A and B with 20 spaces between them.

SPC is almost the same function as SPACE$, but it doesn't use string space. Example:

```
PRINT "A";SPC(25);"B"
```

prints 25 blank spaces between A and B.

## On The Lighter Side

The specialized string functions enable us to do all sorts of exotic things. Here is the beginning of a simple but fun NEW program which uses LEN and MID$. You can easily figure it out, especially after you've seen it RUN.

Enter:

```
10 REM  * TIMES SQUARE BILLBOARD *
20 CLS:N=0 : READ A$
30 L=LEN(A$) : F=1
40  IF L>N THEN L=N+2
50 B$ = MID$(A$,F,L)
60 PRINT TAB(78-N);B$
```

```
70 FOR T=1 TO 20 : NEXT T
80  IF N=75 GOTO 100
90 N=N+1 : IF N<75 GOTO 120
100 L=L-1 : F=F+1 : IF L<0 THEN L=0
110  IF L=30 GOTO 20
120 CLS : GOTO 40
500 DATA"LUCKY LINDY HAS LANDED IN PARIS . ." "
510 DATA". . MET BY CROWD AT LEBOURGET AIRPORT"
```

...and RUN.

Your assignment, if you choose to accept it, is to complete the program so it repeats, ends, or otherwise does not crash.
Good luck!.

.

.

.

.

.

....................Fsssss!

## Learned In Chapter 27

**Functions**

LEFT$
MID$
RIGHT$
INSTR
STRING$

**Miscellaneous**

INSTRing routine
Cursor OFF and ON

# Chapter 28

# TIME$ and DATE$

How about a short and simple Chapter?

Remember when we first turn on the Computer, and it asks us to type in the *date* and *time?* Wouldn't it be nice to be able to use this information in a BASIC program? We can, and it's as easy as A$, B$, C$,...

All we have to do is type:

```
PRINT TIME$
```

and TIME is displayed. The time shown is how long the Computer has run since it was last turned on.

The DATE is also stored as an 8 character string. Type:

```
PRINT DATE$
```

## Setting The Clock And Calendar

The DATE is set from BASIC by typing:

```
DATE$ = "12/12/85"
```

The Computer places the date into the Operating System. Verify it by typing:

AT THE TONE...

```
PRINT DATE$
```

```
12-12-1985
```

To set the time from BASIC, type:

```
TIME$ = "19:06:30"
```

All of the string operators we learned about in the previous Chapters can be used to manipulate these two strings. For example, to PRINT only the day and month from DATE$, use:

```
10 DAY$ = MID$(DATE$,4,2)
20 MONTH$ = LEFT$(DATE$,2)
30 PRINT "THIS IS DAY #";DAY$;
40 PRINT " IN MONTH #";MONTH$
```

SAVE as DATE

...and RUN.

Note carefully that DATE$ and TIME$ are built into the IBM, but DAY$ and MONTH$ are simply string variables we created.

Type in this NEW program:

```
10 PRINT DATE$, TIME$
20 GOTO 10
```

...and RUN.

How's that for cheap and dirty? There are an endless number of much more sophisticated ways to display time and date. Any ideas?

> **EXERCISE 28-1:** Write a program which continuously displays the time and date neatly on the screen.

## Keyboard Buffer

You may have noticed that the Computer seems to remember what we have typed on the keyboard even when it is busy performing some other task.

An area in memory is set aside to be a Keyboard Buffer. That buffer stores our keystrokes until the Computer is ready to accept them. We can easily "type ahead" of the Computer while it is busy performing such tasks as reading a Directory with the SYSTEM command, printing information on the screen or printer, performing large calculations, executing FOR-NEXT loops, backing up a diskette, etc.

The Keyboard Buffer can store up to 15 key strokes. The Computer beeps when we try to enter more than 16 characters before it's had a chance to clear the buffer. The buffer cannot store characters created by holding down the key as it does under normal keyboard repeat operation.

Enter this delay loop program.

```
10 CLS
20 FOR N = 1 TO 5000 : NEXT
```

As soon as you RUN the program, type:

```
LIST        [ENTER]
```

and wait. When the program execution is finished, the program is LISTed.

For fast typists this is a real time-saver.

## Learned In Chapter 28

| Statements | Miscellaneous |
|---|---|
| TIME$ | Keyboard buffer |
| DATE$ | |

# PART 4

# VARIABLE PRECISION AND MATH

# Chapter 29

# What Price Precision?

Unless told otherwise, IBM BASIC stores numeric variables with an accuracy of 7 digits, and PRINTs them out to 7, but only 6 will be accurate. This is called "single precision" accuracy and is more than adequate for most applications.

The old slide rule was only accurate to 3 digits.

For large businesses or special scientific applications, however, greater accuracy is needed and we have a capability called "double precision". By telling the Computer to go "double precision", it will store numbers accurate to 17 digits, and PRINT them out accurate to 16. However, we pay a price for this precision both in the additional memory it takes to store and process long numbers, and the extra time required to process them.

Type in this NEW program:

```
10 CLS : PRINT
20 X = 1234567890987654321          (check 'em)
30 Y = .000000000123456789          (check 'em)
40 Z = X * Y
50 PRINT X;"TIMES";Y;"EQUALS";Z
90 PRINT : LIST
```

...and RUN.

Ummm-hmmm. A very large number times a very small number, and the answer -- all expressed in Exponential notation. That's what the "E's" in the answer stand for, and it is clipped to 7 significant digits.

```
1.234568E+18 TIMES 1.234568E-10 EQUALS
1.524158E+08
```

The number values in Lines 20 and 30 have been converted to Exponential Double Precision. That's what the "D" in those lines stands for.

## DouBLe Precision

We can easily convert storage, processing and PRINTing of X, Y and Z to DouBLe precision. This is almost too easy:

```
15 DEFDBL A-Z
```

DEFDBL stands for "DEFine as DouBLe precision", and A-Z means "every variable from A through Z".

Add the Line and RUN.

```
1.2345678909876540D+18 TIMES 1.23456789D-10
EQUALS 152415787.6238379
```

Quite a difference, eh? Those lost digits in the answer came back from the hinterland, and expanded our PRINTout from 7 significant places to 16.

Such precision is usually wasteful of memory space and time, except in short programs; but fortunately only a few variables ever need to be so precise.

Since the letters X, Y and Z are in sequence, we could tell the Computer to process only those 3 variables in double precision, and leave all other variables (of which there are none, right now) in single precision. Change Line 15 to:

```
15 DEFDBL X-Z
```

...and RUN.

Same results.

## Overruled!

There is a way to *override* the DEFDBL declaration. Suppose we wanted Z to be PRINTed as just single precision. We can override part of the Line 15 declaration by changing each Line which contains Z, as follows:

```
40 Z! = X * Y
50 PRINT X;"TIMES";Y;"EQUALS";Z!
```

...and RUN.

```
1.23456789098765 4D+18 TIMES 1.23456789D-10
EQUALS 1.524158E+08
```

The "raw" data and the calculating were held at double precision, but the final answer is PRINTed with only single-precision accuracy. A *specific* declaration (like the !, which stands for "single precision"), always takes precedence over a *global* declaration like Line 15 DEFDBL X-Z. (Global means "valid for the entire program", not just one variable or one Line.)

## DouBLe Precision -- Simplified

There's another way to calculate with high precision but PRINT the answer in single precision. Since single precision is the "default" mode, we can simply not include Z in Line 15.

Change Lines 15, 40 and 50 and RUN.

```
15 DEFDBL X-Y          (or DEFDBL X,Y)
40 Z = X * Y
50 PRINT X;"TIMES";Y;"EQUALS";Z
```

...and RUN.

Same results, again.

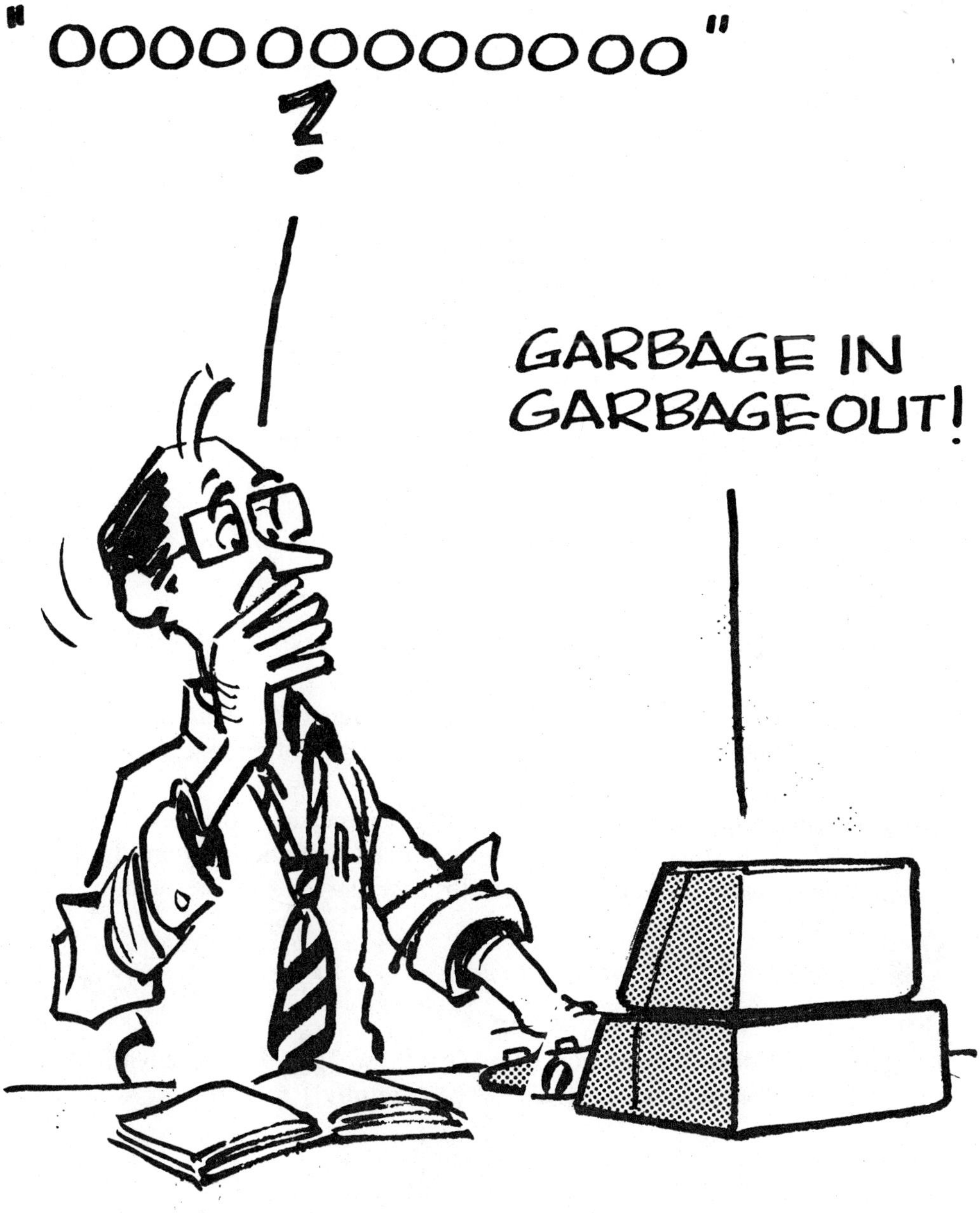

"OOOOOOOOOOOO"

?

GARBAGE IN
GARBAGE OUT!

## Global Override

It is also possible to override the global DEFDBL declaration with a global Single Precision declaration. **Single takes precedence over double!** DEFSNG changes all numbers back to single precision. Let's try it by adding:

```
60 DEFSNG X-Y
70 PRINT X;"TIMES";Y;"EQUALS";Z
```

...and RUN.

Good Grief -- our "redeclared" DEFSNG X and Y numbers turned to zeros but the Z answer is correct!

Well, it turns out that X *DouBLe precision* is a completely separate variable from X *SiNGle precision*. It's as different from X as is Y, or any other variable. If we want to use X and Y again as single-precision numbers, we have to go back and assign them values *after* declaring them to be single precision: Hmmmm. This is getting complicated.

A cheap and dirty way to show the point is to change Line 70 to:

```
70 GOTO 20
```

...and RUN very briefly -- hitting [Ctrl] [Break] after both DouBLe and SiNGle precision versions are PRINTed by Line 50. Compare the top 2 display lines.

> Line 60 reDEFined X and Y as SiNGle precision, then execution went back to Line 20 and performed the calculations again. (Fortunately, there is rarely reason to *redefine* a variable within a program.)

## DouBLe Precision, Another Way

Instead of a "global" declaration of accuracy, we can do it one variable at a time. Change the resident program (very carefully!) to read:

```
10 CLS : PRINT
20 X# = 12345678909876540+18
30 Y# = 1.23456789D-10
```

```
40 Z# = X# * Y#

50 PRINT X#;"TIMES";Y#;"EQUALS";Z#

90 PRINT : LIST
```

...and RUN.

Same results as before. The # sign declared that the variable letter preceding it was to be handled as DouBLe precision, overriding the normal presumption that it is SiNGle precision.

---

Shh! I'm not worried about that last "9" in the answer changing to an "8", are you?

---

Remember, X# is not the same as X -- it is an entirely different variable. Same with Y# and Z#. To nail this point down, add:

```
15 X = 4.321

60 PRINT "X =";X
```

...and RUN.

The values of X and X# stayed completely separate, didn't they?

## INTeger Precision

In those frequent cases where the numbers used are INTegers (and in the range between -32768 and +32767) execution can be speeded up by declaring them to be INTegers by using the % sign or the DEFINT statement. Enter this NEW program:

```
20 FOR N = 1 TO 8000

30 NEXT N

90 PRINT : LIST
```

Use a stopwatch or clock with a second hand and measure the time it takes for the 8000 passes thru the FOR-NEXT LOOP. Should be around 10 seconds.

...and RUN.

Now, let's declare N to be an INTeger, (which is all the accuracy we need) and time it again ... Add:

```
10 DEFINT N
```

...and RUN.

Aha! It took only about 7 seconds. A very significant difference.

We can accomplish the same thing using *specific* INTeger declarations. Delete Line 10 and change the program to read:

```
20 FOR N% = 1 TO 8000
30 NEXT N%
90 PRINT :LIST
```

RUN, and time.

## One More Way

The conversion functions CSNG(#), CDBL(#) and CINT(#) provide 3 additional ways to declare numbers as SiNGle, DouBLe or INTeger precision. Enter this NEW test program:

```
10 CLS
20 X = 12345.67898
30 PRINT X
40 PRINT CSNG(X)
50 PRINT CDBL(X)
60 PRINT CINT(X)
90 PRINT : LIST
```

...and RUN.

It tells the whole sordid story:

```
12345.68

12345.68

12345.6787109375

12346
```

Line 20 changed to 20 X = 12345.67898# indicating the number was so long that it could not be held in single precision.

Line 30 PRINTed the value of X accurate to 7 digits.

Line 40 PRINTed the SiNGle precision value of X -- the same value as printed by Line 30.

Line 50 PRINTed the DouBLe precision value of X, but it sure isn't a duplicate of what we specified as X in Line 20! The problem is, we only INPUT the number in Single Precision (by default). PRINTing it out in Double Precision requires the Computer to just "make up" numbers to fill out the places.

Don't try to be more accurate than what you begin with. It's the programmer who's supposed to be creative, not the Computer!

Line 60 PRINTed the INTeger value of X. This works slightly different than INT(X). CINT(X) "rounds off" the fractional part.

Make the value of X negative and see what happens. Change Line 20 to:

```
20 X = -12345.67890
```

...and RUN.

No surprises. CINT acted just like INT does, rounding downward to arrive at -12346.

## DouBLe The Trouble -- DouBLe The Fun

Now let's go back and declare the value of X to be *DouBle precision*, change it to a positive number, and do all our PRINTing in DouBLe precision. The EDITed program will read:

```
10 CLS
20 X# = 12345.67898
30 PRINT X#
40 PRINT CSNG(X#)
50 PRINT CDBL(X#)
60 PRINT CINT(X#)
90 PRINT : LIST
```

...then RUN.

and the display reads:

```
12345.67898
12345.68
12345.67898
12346
```

It makes sense, and was quite predictable, wasn't it? Even CDBL behaved.

What do you think will happen if we again change the value of X to a negative number? Think it through; then change it and RUN.

## Some Caveats

The Computer makes assumptions. When *any* double-precision number is used in a calculation, the entire calculation will be performed as though *all* numbers involved are double precision. This isn't necessarily bad, but an answer with lots of digits is no more precise than its least accurate ancestor.

Division follows suit. If we declare the numerator or the denominator (or both) to be double precision, that particular division is done in double precision. All other division is done in single precision. If an INTeger answer is needed, use Integer Division (with the backslash), or a plain old INTeger-defined variable.

## In Memoriam

This is really a very important Chapter. Most readers find it necessary to study it more than once. Degrees of precision may not be the most inspiring subject, but, if we have command of this Chapter we'll not be caught off guard nor be deceived by numbers that never were.

### Learned In Chapter 29

| Statements | Functions | Miscellaneous |
|---|---|---|
| DEFDBL | CDBL | DouBLe Precision (#) |
| DEFSNG | CSNG | SiNGle Precision (!) |
| DEFINT | CINT | INTeger Precision (%) |

# Chapter 30

# Intrinsic Math Functions

The BASIC language includes a number of **mathematical** functions. These math functions are all very straightforward and easy to use, but if your math skills are a bit rusty, you will want to refresh them to fully understand what we're doing. We'll keep everything here at the 9th-grade Algebra level so there's no need to panic (unless maybe you're in the 6th grade ... but even so, just hang on and you'll be OK).

## INT(N)

We have studied the INTeger function in some detail in earlier Chapters so we won't cover that ground again. INT stores and executes numbers in single precision.

## FIX(N)

FIX is just like INT, but instead of rounding negative numbers downward, it simply chops off everything to the right of the decimal point.

Try this simple test at the command level:

```
PRINT INT(-12345.67)
```

produces -12346

```
PRINT FIX(-12345.67)
```

produces -12345

The one we use depends on what we want.

## SQR(N)

The SQuare Root function is simple to use.

Type this:

```
10 INPUT "THE SQUARE ROOT OF";N
20 PRINT "IS";SQR(N)
30 PRINT : GOTO 10
```

...and RUN some familiar numbers.

Math types can add:

```
25 PRINT CHR$(251); N; "="; SQR(N)
```

to take advantage of some of our special characters.

Another way to find the square (or any) root of a number is by the use of the ^ (caret). It means "raised to the power". Finding the square root of a number is the same as raising it to the 1/2 power. Delete Line 25 and change Line 20 to:

```
20 PRINT "IS ";N^(1/2)
```

...and RUN some familiar numbers.

The same logic which allows us to find the *square* root with the ^ will let us find any *other* root. (Even the thought of doing that in pre-computer days drove men mad.) Out of the sheer arrogance of power, let's find the 21st root of any number. Change the first two lines:

```
10 INPUT "THE TWENTY-FIRST ROOT OF";N
20 PRINT "IS ";N^(1/21)
```

...and RUN.

Now there is real horsepower! Problem is, how are we sure that the answers are right? Well, it's easy enough to add a few lines that will take the root and raise it back to the 21st power to find out. Let's change the program to make it read:

```
10 INPUT "THE TWENTY-FIRST ROOT OF";N
20 R=N^(1/21)
30 PRINT "IS";R
40 PRINT
50 PRINT R;"TO THE 21ST POWER =";R^21
60 PRINT : GOTO 10
```

...and RUN.

The INPUT and output numbers check out pretty close, don't they? This "proof" process might not stand up under rigorous scrutiny, but the answers are correct.

**EXERCISE 30-1:** Pythagoras discovered that the sides of a right triangle always obey the rule:

$$C^2 = A^2 + B^2$$

where C is the longest side (hypotenuse). Stated another way: "The length of side C equals the square root of the sum of the squares of sides A and B" ($C = \sqrt{A^2 + B^2}$).

If side A = 5 and side B = 12, write a program to calculate the length of side C.

## ABS(N)

ABSolute value has a lot to do with signs, or without them. The absolute value of any number is the number *without* a sign. If you've forgotten, this program will quickly refresh the memory:

```
10 INPUT "ENTER ANY NUMBER";N
```

```
20 PRINT : A = ABS(N)
30 PRINT A
40 PRINT : GOTO 10
```

...and RUN.

Respond with various large and small, positive and negative numbers, and zero.

They all come out as they went in didn't they, except the sign is missing?

## MOD

No, not the Music. MOD isn't really a math Function, but more of a Math Operator. MOD returns the remainder when one number is divided into another number. For example:

```
PRINT 17 MOD 4
```

returns a 1 since 17/4 is 4 with a remainder of 1.

Other examples to try:

8 or 16 or 24 MOD 8 each equals 0 (There's 0 remainder when any of them are divided by 8.)

9 or 17 or 25 MOD 8 each equals 1 (There's 1 remainder after any of them are divided by 8.)

10 or 18 or 26 MOD 8 each equals 2 (There's 2 remainder after any of them are divided by 8.)

15 or 23 or 31 MOD 8 each equals 7 (There's 7 remainder after any of them are divided by 8.)

## LOG(N)

No, a LOG isn't what they build cabins with, but even the swiftest among us have to refresh their memory from time to time to keep the details straight.

A LOG (logarithm) is an *exponent*. Exponent of what? The exponent of a *base*. What's a *base?* A *base* is the number that a given number *system* is built on. Aren't all number systems built on 10? 'Fraid not.

$10^3 = 1000$

10 is the BASE.

3 is the LOG(exponent), and

1000 is the answer.

---

Think it has something to do with "new math", but I was too old to take it, too young to teach it, and grateful for not learning it from those who didn't understand it.

---

As if life isn't complicated enough, the LOGarithm system is centered around what are called *natural* logs. Exactly what that means is the subject of another discussion, but we're stuck with it anyway. Natural logs use the number 2.718282 as their base. (Really makes your day, doesn't it!) Some BASIC interpreters provide a second LOG option using 10 as the base, as in our decimal system, but making the conversion isn't too bad -- and we do have to live with it.

Type this NEW program:

```
10 INPUT "ENTER ANY POSITIVE NUMBER";N
20 PRINT : L = LOG(N)
30 PRINT ,"THE LOG OF";N;
40 PRINT "TO THE NATURAL BASE =";L
50 PRINT : GOTO 10
```

LET ME GUESS --
NEW COMPUTER?
New
Math

The LOG function is not valid for negative numbers or zero.

...and RUN.

Ummm Hmmm. Can't relate to the conclusion? Respond with the number 100 and you should get the answer 4.60517. What that means is, 2.718282 to the 4.60517 power = 100. Lay that one on them at the next meeting of the Audubon Society and they'll know you're a strange duck.

Let's jack this thing around to where the vast majority of us who have to work with LOGs can use it -- into the decimal system.

Decimal-based LOGs are called "common", or "base 10" Logs. Add these lines:

```
45 PRINT ,"THE LOG OF";N;
47 PRINT "TO THE BASE 10 =";L*.4342945
```

...and RUN, using 100 as the number.

Ahhh! That's more like it. We can all see that 10 to the 2nd power equals 100. It's good to be back on *relatively* solid ground.

The magic conversion rules are:

*To convert a natural log to a common log, multiply the natural log by .4342945.*

*To convert a common log to a natural log, multiply the common log by 2.3026.*

And that's the name of that tune.

This final NEW program scoops it up and spreads it out:

```
10 REM  * LOGARITHM DEMO *
20 CLS : PRINT
30 INPUT "ENTER A POSITIVE NUMBER";N
```

```
40 PRINT
50 PRINT "THE NUMBER","NATURAL LOG",
60 PRINT "COMMON LOG"
70 PRINT N,LOG(N),LOG(N)*.4342945
80 PRINT : GOTO 30
```

Wring it out until you're confortable with the concept.

## EXP(N)

EXP is sort of the opposite of LOG. EXP computes the value of the answer, given the EXPonent of a *natural* log. (Another winner.)

2.718282 raised to the EXP power = the answer.

Type in this NEW program:

```
10 INPUT "ENTER A NUMBER";N
20 A = EXP(N)
30 PRINT "2.718282 RAISED TO THE";N;
40 PRINT "POWER =";A
50 PRINT : GOTO 10
```

...and RUN.

We're entering the EXPonent now, so it's easy to INPUT a number that is too big for the Computer and will cause it to *overflow*.

As a benchmark against which tc test the program, enter this number:

```
4.60517
```

The BASE of the natural log system raised to this power should equal 100 (or very close).

Being this far into logs, you can create your own advanced test programs, and check the results against a LOG table. *And if you're not too comfortable with all this ... try making a log cabin with the remainders!*

> **EXERCISE 30-2: (For math fans only)** Convince yourself that LOG and EXP functions are inverses of each other (hint: LOG(EXP(N)) = N). Try putting the two functions together in the opposite order using both positive and negative values for N. Why do the negative values create havoc?

## Learned in Chapter 30

**Functions**

INT
FIX
SQR
ABS
MOD
LOG
EXP

**Miscellaneous**

Natural Logs
Common Logs

## Chapter 31

# The Trigonometric Functions

ince this is about as deep as we'll get into mathematics, I have to assume you know something about elementary trig.

Trigonometry, of course, deals with triangles, their angles, and the ratios between the lengths of their sides. In the triangle below, the Sine (abbreviated SIN) of angle A is defined as the *ratio* (what we get after dividing) of the *length* of side a to the *length* of side c. COSine and TANgent are defined similarly:

SIN A=a/c

COS A=b/c

TAN A=a/b

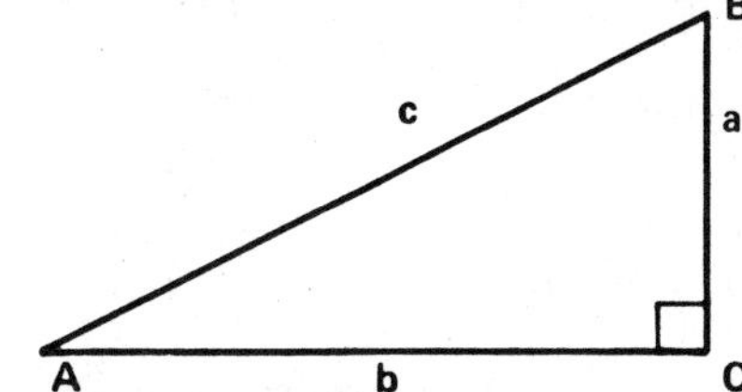


From these relationships, we can find any ratio if we know the corresponding angle. Let's try this simple NEW program:

```
10 INPUT "ENTER AN ANGLE (0-90 DEGREES)";A
20 S = SIN(A*.0174533)
30 PRINT "THE SIN OF A";A;"DEGREE ANGLE IS";S
40 PRINT : GOTO 10
```

...and RUN.

Ctrl Break to get out of the loop

It really works! Try the old "standard" angles like 45°, 30°, 60°, 90°, 0°, etc.

Unless you're right up to snuff on trig, Line 20 undoubtedly looks strange. Well, it turns out that most computers think in radians, not degrees (always has to be some nasty twist doesn't there...!) A radian is a unit of measurement equal to approximately 57 degrees. In order to convert from degrees (which most of us use) to radians, we changed the INPUT from degrees to radians. The SIN function will not work correctly without this conversion.

> To convert angles from degrees to radians, multiply the degrees by 0.0174533.
>
> To convert angles from radians to degrees, multiply the radians by 57.29578.

Failure to make these conversions correctly is by far the biggest source of computer users' problems with the trig functions.

COSine and TANgent work the same way. Change the resident program to:

```
10 INPUT "ENTER AN ANGLE (0-90 DEGREES)";A
20 C = COS(A*.0174533)
30 PRINT "THE COS OF A";A;"DEGREE ANGLE IS";C
40 PRINT : GOTO 10
```

...and RUN.

We know that COS(90°) should be 0. Unfortunately, the Computer is slightly off because it calculates these functions by approximation. It's doing the best that it can ... honest!

For TANgent, RUN this program:

```
10 INPUT "ENTER AN ANGLE (0-90 DEGREES)";A
20 T = TAN(A*.0174533)
30 PRINT "TAN OF A";A;"DEGREE ANGLE IS";T
40 PRINT : GOTO 10
```

NO, NO, NO! RADIANS HASN'T GOT ANYTHING TO DO WITH ATOMIC ENERGY!

The TAN function is not even defined for 90°, though the Computer will *try* to calculate it.

This next NEW program displays all 3 major trig functions at the same time. Note in Line 30 we *divide* our incoming angle by 57.29578 instead of multiplying it by 0.0174533. The results are the same.

```
10 CLS : PRINT
20 INPUT "ENTER AN ANGLE (0-90 DEGREES)";A
30 A = A/57.29578 : PRINT
40 PRINT "ANGLE","SIN","COS","TAN"
50 PRINT A*57.29578,SIN(A),COS(A),TAN(A)
```

When we try to find the TANgent of 90 degrees a "Division by zero" error occurs, because the Computer first finds the SIN of 90, which is 1, then divides into that the COS of 90, which is 0. 1/0 is a no-no as far as the Computer is concerned. However, the IBM thinks that Division by zero is an "unfatal" error, so execution doesn't stop there. It first prints out the highest number the Computer can handle, 1.701412E+38. It other words, the Computer's "Infinity".

## Inverse Trig Functions

The opposite of finding a *ratio* between two sides of a triangle when an *angle* is known, is finding an *angle* when the *ratio* of two sides is known. There are 3 trig functions available to do it, but most computers only make provision for one, called ATN (Arc of the TaNgent).

The following simple program takes the angle we INPUT, converts it to radians, computes and PRINTs its TANgent. Then, as a "proof check", takes that TANgent value and reverses the process by computing its arc (angle). The letter "I" is used in the program since the arctangent is also known as the "Inverse" (sort of the "opposite") of the TANgent.

```
10 REM  * ATN DEMO *
20 CLS : PRINT
30 INPUT "ENTER AN ANGLE (0-90 DEGREES)";A
```

```
40 T = TAN(A/57.29578) : PRINT
50 PRINT "TANGENT =";T,
60 I = ATN(T) * 57.29578
70 PRINT "ARC OF THE TANGENT =";I
```

If you're one of those rare types who is very familiar with trig, you can probably throw numbers around in such a fashion that the other 2 "inverse" trig functions, ARCSIN and ARCCOS are not needed. But for those of us who get confused when we run out of fingers, the last 2 functions are built into this simple NEW program by way of special routines. The accuracy is close enough for "government" work. Give it a try:

```
10 REM  * INVERSE FUNCTION ROUTINES DEMO *
20 INPUT "ENTER THE RATIO OF 2 SIDES";R
30 CLS : PRINT
40 AS=2*ATN(R/(1+SQR(ABS(1-R*R)))) * 57.29578
50 AC=90 - AS : PRINT
60 PRINT "RATIO","ARCSIN","ARCCOS","ARCTAN"
70 PRINT "(NUMBER)","(DEGREES)","(DEGREES)",
80 PRINT "(DEGREES)" : IF ABS(R)>1 THEN 110
90 PRINT R,AS,AC,ATN(R)*57.29578
100 PRINT : GOTO 20
110 PRINT R,"U","U",ATN(R)*57.29578
120 PRINT : GOTO 20
```

Remember, while the TANgent can be any number, when our ratio moves outside the range of $-1$ to 1, SIN and COS are both mathematically "Undefined." Also, ARCTAN and ARCSIN produce angle measures between $-90$ and 90 degrees, but ARCCOS has a range between 0 and 180 degrees.

## Learned In Chapter 31

**Functions**

SIN
COS
TAN
ATN

**Miscellaneous**

Degrees
Radians

# Chapter 32

# DEFined FuNctions

This Chapter is for advanced math types. If that isn't your bag, skim it lightly, and move on down the road.

In addition to the *intrinsic* (built-in) Functions, IBM BASIC allows us to define *our own* Functions.

In what kind of situation would we want to do that? Repetition of formulas and simple operations that are used repeatedly can be greatly shortened by building a custom Function. They won't operate as fast as other factory built-in Functions, but, like subroutines, they greatly simplify BASIC programming.

The Format for defining a Function is:

```
DEF FN name(v1,v2,...) = formula
```

where:

> *name* is the Function name, and
>
> *v1, v2, ...* are dummy variables that represent the values the Function will act on. *Name* and *v1, v2 ...* can be any valid variable names.
>
> *Formula* is the expression where the calculations are carried out.

Let's create a Function to do MODular arithmetic. MOD is one of our math operators, but we'll use it to demonstrate the technique DEFined FuNction.

I DUNNO, YOU MIGHT GIVE THE CHAPTER A SHOT...
DIPLOMA
ADVANCED MATH

Try this on for size:

```
10 CLS : PRINT
20 INPUT "ENTER X";X
30 INPUT "ENTER Y";Y
40 DEF FNC(X,Y) = INT(X-Y * INT(X/Y))
50 REM C = FUNCTION NAME/X,Y = THE NUMBERS
60 PRINT X;"MOD";Y;"=";FNC(X,Y)
```

...and RUN.

The variables X and Y used in defining the Function in Line 40 are really "dummy arguments". They only show the Computer *how* to perform the calculations. Change Line 40 to:

```
40 DEF FNC(A,B) = INT(A - B*INT(A/B))
```

...and RUN.

Same results? You betcha. In fact, we could even use A and B elsewhere in the program; Line 40 won't effect their values at all.

The FuNction variable can be INTeger, Single, or Double precision or even as a string variable. The value returned to the program is determined by the type of variable. Try this NEW sample with a string:

```
10 DEF FNZ$(A$) = "-" + A$ + "-"
20 PRINT FNZ$("FUNCTION")
```

...and RUN.

*Functions* are very powerful when used for repetitive calculations. How about the distance between two coordinate points in a plane, (X1,Y1) and (X2,Y2)? Use:

```
10 DEF FND#(X1,Y1,X2,Y2) = SQR((X1-X2)*(X1-X2)
   + (Y1-Y2)*(Y1-Y2))
```

```
20 PRINT "DISTANCE IS"; FND#(-1,3,2,7)
```

Note: Line 10 is shown on two Lines to fit the book. The Computer displays it on one Line.

...and RUN.

NOTE that D# is a double precision variable.

And it is even possible to come up with a Function that uses no variables at all:

```
10 DEF FNA = 1 + INT(RND*5)
20 PRINT FNA
```

## Learned In Chapter 32

**Statement**

DEF FN

# PART 5

# DISPLAY FORMATTING

# Chapter 33

# Formatting With LOCATE

he LOCATE statement allows PRINTing to *begin* anywhere on the screen by first positioning the cursor. Type:

```
10 CLS
20 LOCATE 12,30
30 PRINT "HELLO THERE 12,30!"
```

...and RUN.

See the Video Display Worksheet.

The LOCATE locations start at 1,1 in the upper-left hand corner and go through 1,80 in the first line. They pick up on the second line with 2,1 and continue through 25,80 (the lower-right hand corner).

LOCATE can directly address any of the 2000 PRINT locations.

If we want to PRINT on Line 25, we must first turn off the Soft key display by typing:

```
KEY OFF
```

or else we'll get an "Illegal Function Call" error notice.

## It's That Time Already?

Let's create a 24-hour clock. That sounds like more fun than digging through this obscure PRINT Statement mapping. Type:

```
10 CLS
20 LOCATE 12,35
30 PRINT "H    M    S"
40 FOR H = 0 TO 23
50   FOR M = 0 TO 59
60    FOR S = 0 TO 59
70      LOCATE 13,34
80      PRINT H;":";M;":";S
90       FOR N = 1 TO 800 : NEXT N
100    NEXT S
110  NEXT M
120 NEXT H
130 GOTO 10
```

SAVE as TIMER ... and RUN.

Nothing to it. Ahem!

## "Hello? Bureau Of Standards?"

Of course, the accuracy of this timer depends on how closely we calibrate it. We earlier discussed that the IBM will execute somewhere around 800 simple FOR-NEXT loops per second when written as shown in Line 90 -- a multiple statement Line. If we really get carried away with this program, it can be calibrated against a precision timepiece, increasing or decreasing the "800" as needed, or better yet, just use our TIME$ statement along with LOCATE. Over the short RUN, it is quite a good timer. Note that we are not triggering this with the power line frequency or a crystal oscillator, but relying solely on the amount of time required to execute FOR-NEXT loops. (It's not nearly as accurate as the Real Time Clock built into the Computer).

## Oh, Yes ... The LOCATE

Anyway -- let's not lose sight of the forest for the trees (or is it trees for the forest). The purpose of this little program is to demonstrate the LOCATE statement. We used it twice. With blazing speed, the HMS (no, no, not Her Majesty's Service -- it stands for Hours, Minutes and Seconds), are PRINTed -- and the HM&S are updated each second.

The real clock nut should see Section C for a better clock program. It only needs closer calibration to be an acceptable sundial. The Computer becomes the most expensive clock in the house!

## LOCATEing the Cursor

The LOCATE statement has 3 more variable parts which determine the characteristics of the cursor. Type:

```
NEW

10 CLS
20 LOCATE 5,40,1,11,12
30 PRINT "THIS IS 5,40"
60 PRINT : LIST
```

...and RUN.

The cursor looks just like it always did, right? The first 2 numbers determine the position on the screen. The 1 means "make the cursor visible". A 1 in this third posiiton means make it visible, 0 makes it invisible.

The last two numbers, 11 and 12, determine the start and end *Scan Lines* for the cursor, in other words, how big the cursor will be. When the display PRINTs something on the screen, it doesn't do it in one shot. It has to continuously update 25 * 14 = 350 scan lines. The IBM monochrome display has 14 horizontal scan lines per row of text. They are numbered 0 through 13, 0 being at the top. (If you're using the Color/Graphics adapter, there are 8 scan lines.)

DID WE LOSE OUR CURSOR ?
NAW, A LENS OUTTA MY GLASSES!

Change Line 20 to:

```
20 LOCATE 5,40,1,0,6
```

...and RUN.

Now the cursor is a solid block, at the top of a Line. The 0,6 did it. We "turn on" the cursor starting at its top Line (Line 0), and "turn it off" on Line 6. The cursor is, therefore, 7 scan lines tall, which is half the size of a character.

Pretty hard to see which Line it's on, isn't it? To find out, type EDIT 20 [←┘], then hit [Ins]. The cursor appears as a small block in the middle of the scan!

Hit [Ins] to leave Insert mode, and hit [End] (1 on the keypad).

Let's make the cursor a full block. Change the last number in Line 20 to a 13 and RUN.

What if we wanted to make the cursor a single Line? Change Line 20 to:

```
20 LOCATE 5,40,1,13
```

Since we don't specify a number for where to end the scan, the last number is assumed to be the same as the start Line.

## Special Effects Dept.

Now let's try for some special effects. If we start the cursor scan towards the bottom, and end it at the top, it will "wrap around" and create a 2 part cursor. How about if we try surrounding a Line of type with the cursor. Change Line 20 to:

```
20 LOCATE 5,40,1,11,1
```

This will make the cursor have three Lines on the bottom (11, 12 and 13) and two Lines on the top (0 and 1). Move the cursor up a couple Lines and then to the right. We really know what letter is inside.

We can only make the cursor invisible at certain times. For example we can't during an INPUT. To prove it, type:

```
50 INPUT "INPUT HERE"; A$
```

and change the 3rd number in Line 20 to a 0:

```
20 LOCATE 5,40,0,0,13
```

...and RUN.

Nope. The cursor won't disappear. Now try:

```
40 FOR X=1 TO 5000 : NEXT X
```

and during the loop, the cursor is nowhere to be seen.

Now change the 3rd number to a 1 and RUN it to see that the cursor is there.

But let's say that we want to make the cursor invisible all the time. How about we start and end the scan on (nonexistent) Line 14. Change:

```
20 LOCATE 5,40,1,14,14
```

...and RUN.

First type KEY OFF and then [Ctrl] [Home] to completely clear the screen. Looks dead, doesn't it? Now type in your name. It looks a little different with no cursor.

In order to get our cursor back, we have to perform some fancy footwork. Hit [Esc] to erase what you just typed, and then LIST your program. Type EDIT 20 to change the Line. Hit [End] then hit the left arrow (4 on the keypad) 4 times. Now type a 2 and it should put a 2 over the 4. Hit the right arrow twice and type a 3, then hit [↵]. The Line should now read:

```
20 LOCATE 5,40,1,12,13
```

If any of the quantities are deleted, they take on their previous values. For example, to get the cursor back to normal, type:

```
LOCATE ,,,11,12
```

To summarize, the LOCATE statement looks like this:

```
LOCATE A, B, C, D, E
```

A is the ROW, 1-25

B is the COLUMN, 1-80

C determines if the cursor is ON or OFF. Valid numbers are 0 and 1. Zero means cursor OFF, one means cursor ON. The default value is 0 (OFF).

D is the starting scan Line for the cursor, 0-13. The default is 11.

E is the end Line for the cursor, 0-13. The default value is 12.

## POS(N) and CSRLIN

An additional and sometimes useful statement allows the Computer to report back the horizontal POSition of the cursor. This simple NEW program exercises the POS function.

```
10 CLS : PRINT
20 INPUT "A NUMBER BETWEEN -9 AND 70";A
30 PRINT TAB(10 + A)
40 PRINT POS(0);
50 PRINT " WAS NUMBER OF NEXT PRINT
POSITION"
60 PRINT : LIST
```

...and RUN.

Line 40, containing POS, is the key.

The 0 inside the brackets is just a "dummy". Most any other number or variable would work as well -- but something has to be placed there. POS reports back any cursor POSition on the screen up thru 80 on any 80 column Line. Numbers above 80 start over again with 1.

To help locate the cursor, we can add these Lines to the resident program:

```
45 L = CSRLIN

55 PRINT "AND IS LOCATED IN LINE";L
```

CSRLIN tells us the CuRSor LINe (Row) number from 1-24 that the cursor was on at the time CSRLIN is encountered.

Remember, CSRLIN returns the CuRSor LINe (Row), 1-24, and POS(0) returns the column, 1-80.

## WRITEing to the Screen

The WRITE statement allows us to PRINT on the screen. It is similar to PRINT, but the WRITE statement automatically *inserts a comma* between each item the Computer WRITEs on the screen. It also places quotes around all strings. Try this NEW program:

```
10 CLS : PRINT

20 READ A,B,C,D$

30  WRITE A;B;C;D$

40 DATA 100,200,300, ...ETC

50 PRINT : LIST
```

Variables in Line 30 can be separated by semicolons or commas. The Computer will treat them the same.

RUN, and see:

```
100,200,300," ...ETC"
```

We already know that BASIC is unable to READ a string from the DATA Line if it contains quotes within quotes. By using WRITE, we can READ a string and let the Computer insert the quotes.

## Screen WIDTH Control

When the Computer enters BASIC, the screen width is set at 80 column width. This "normal" screen width can be changed to 40 column by typing:

```
WIDTH 40        [↵]
```

Try it and type a Line containing more than 40 characters. Notice how the Computer refuses to display a Line longer than 40 columns. Reset the WIDTH to 80 column by typing:

```
WIDTH 80        [↵]
```

## Learned In Chapter 33

### Statements

LOCATE
POS(N)
KEY OFF/ON
CSRLIN
WRITE
WIDTH

# Chapter 34

# INKEY$ & INPUT$

The INKEY$ (pronounced Inkey-string) function is a powerful one which enables us to INPUT information from the keyboard without having to use the [↵] key.

Enter this NEW program:

```
10 CLS : PRINT
20 IF INKEY$="T" THEN 40
30 GOTO 20
40 PRINT "YOU HIT THE LETTER 'T'"
50 GOTO 20
```

...and RUN.

Press a variety of individual alpha and numeric keys, but not [Break].

The keyboard seems to be dead, until we hit the "T" key. Why?

Aha! The test in Line 20 then passes, execution moves to Line 40 and a message is PRINTed. Then the process starts over. Hit T again. Hold it down.

The way INKEY$ works is clever if somewhat subtle, so pay close attention.

The IBM keyboard is constantly scanned by the Computer, checking to see if any key is pressed. If a key was pressed before the Computer encounters

INKEY$, the character that key represents was stored in the INKEY$ storage, or buffer area. The buffer can hold only one character at a time so when a new key is pressed, that new character replaces whatever preceeded it in the buffer, if anything. INKEY$ automatically assumes the String Value of whatever character is in its buffer.

Since INKEY$ can only "photograph" one letter or number at a time, if we want to test for more than one character we have to write the program to test for each one in sequence. In so doing, however, we must be careful or INKEY$ will trip us up.

Add these Lines to the program:

```
25 IF INKEY$="P" THEN 60

60 PRINT "YOU HIT THE LETTER 'P'"

70 GOTO 20
```

...and RUN again.

As you can see, we no longer get an "instant" response each time T or P are pressed. This distressing condition exists because the INKEY$ buffer is cleared and reset to a null string *each* time INKEY$ is hit. Aaawk! Just when it was starting to make sense. BREAK and LIST so we can take a good look at the program and see how this clearing of the buffer results in the "loss" of a keystroke.

Suppose the operator presses the T key just as Line 25 begins execution. Where does the T go? Into the INKEY$ buffer, of course. There it sits until another key is pressed, or INKEY$ is "called".

When Line 25 is executed, INKEY$ "reads" the buffer. The buffer's current value ("T") is compared to Line 25's "P". Since the two strings are not equal, control passes to the next Line, then back to Line 20. In Line 20, INKEY$ is called again, but when it checks the buffer this time, "T" is gone. What happened to the T?

Let's replay that last sequence and zoom in for a closeup on the INKEY$ buffer. As the operator hits the T key, we see the T stored in the buffer. As the INKEY$ Function in Line 25 is executed, the buffer suddenly goes blank. Ahhhhh! Thank heavens for instant replay. It's now obvious that each time INKEY$ is called, its buffer is cleared, whether or not it meets the string test

WAKE UP HARRY! JUST WHO IS THIS "INKEY$" YOU KEEP MUMBLING ABOUT?

in the Line calling it. If we want to preserve the value of T, we'll need to store it elsewhere, maybe in a temporary string variable.

Change Lines 20 and 25 to:

```
20 A$=INKEY$ : IF A$="T" THEN 40
25 IF A$="P" THEN 60
30 GOTO 20
40 PRINT "YOU HIT THE LETTER'T'"
50 GOTO 20
60 PRINT "YOU HIT THE LETTER 'P'" : GOTO 20
```

...and RUN.

Aha! Now we're getting somewhere. Give it the ultimate test -- alternate pressing "T" and "P" as quickly as possible.

By setting a "regular" string variable equal to INKEY$, and having T and P checked against the variable instead of against the INKEY$ buffer, we store its value for as long as needed and process it much more efficiently and predictably.

## Rapid Scanner

If INKEY$ scans the buffer and does not find a key pressed (the usual case), it is said to read a "null string". INKEY$ is a string Function, and null means *nothing*. A null string is represented by two quote marks with nothing between them, thus:

```
""
```

The ASCII code for null is 0.

To see how fast we can scan for INPUT with INKEY$, try this NEW program:

```
10 K$ = INKEY$
```

```
20 IF K$ ="" THEN PRINT "NO KEYBOARD INPUT"
30 PRINT ,,K$ : GOTO 10
```

...and RUN.

Type in random characters and words and see them break the scan.

Get the general idea how to use INKEY$? So simple, yet the possibilities are enormous. Only a lot of experimenting will make you comfortable with it, but INKEY$ will keep you awake nights staring at the ceiling thinking of ways to put it to work.

## Out Of The Blue Of The Western Sky...

While chasing the solitude needed to write Computer books, your author piloted a heavily loaded private plane, packed with computers, ham radio and other goodies, into a medium sized city airport. Transferring this freight to a rental car turned out to be a big deal since security wouldn't let a car on the apron to unload the plane. (You're supposed to drop it by parachute?)

After some cajoling (and a gratuity) it was agreed that my car could be driven up *near* the apron, and an "officially approved" car would haul the goodies from the plane to the car. It seemed a bit officious, but elections were far away...

Anyway, to get my car thru the security fence it was necessary to drive to an electrically-operated gate. A secret code was punched into a numeric keypad for some sort of computer to analyze, and it controlled the motorized gate. *The secret code number was 1930.*

Needless to say, as soon as the computer was set up I wrote a BASIC program to do everything but actually open the gate. It provides a good example of a real-life application of INKEY$, and is offered here for your amusement, amazement and careful study.

```
10 CLS : LOCATE 17,30 : PRINT "TYPE THE COMBINATION"
20 LOCATE 18,30 : PRINT "FOLLOWED BY AN ASTERISK"
30 LOCATE 2,27 : PRINT "THE ELECTRIC GATE IS CLOSED"
40 K$ = INKEY$ : IF K$ = "" GOTO 40
```

```
50 READ D$ : IF D$ = "*" GOTO 80
60 IF D$ = K$ THEN 40
70 RESTORE : GOTO 40
80 CLS : LOCATE 2,31 : PRINT "YOU MAY ENTER NOW";
90 LOCATE 4,27 : PRINT "WAIT FOR THE GATE TO OPEN"
100 FOR T=1 TO 3000 : NEXT T
110 RESTORE : GOTO 10
1000 DATA 1,9,3,0,*
```

SAVE as GATE and RUN. Try the combination.

The password (1930 followed by an asterisk) is imbedded, a character at a time, in DATA Line #1000. The commas only separate the characters and should not be typed in as part of the password.

Line 40 holds the magic. It stores the buffer contents in K$ and checks K$ for something besides a null string. If it finds a key was pressed, execution drops to Line 50.

Line 50 READs a piece of DATA. If it happens to be an asterisk (which can only be READ from DATA after all of the other code characters have been READ), execution moves to Line 80 where the gate is OPENed.

If, however, the test in Line 50 does not find an asterisk, execution defaults to the next test, in Line 60.

Line 60 checks to see if the keyboard character matches up with the character READ from DATA. If so, the first hurdle has been passed and execution returns back to Line 40 for INKEY$ to await another keyboard character. If the keyboard and DATA characters don't match, the test fails and execution drops to Line 70.

Line 70 RESTOREs the DATA pointer back to its beginning, and returns execution to Line 40 to start scanning all over again. The keypad puncher sees none of this and has no idea if he is making progress towards cracking the code.

Line 100 merely allows the gate a brief time to open and close (and us to read the screen), then

Line 110 RESTOREs the DATA and starts the program over from the beginning.

The password can be changed to any combination of characters by changing Line 1000. If we wanted it to be 'IBM' for example:

```
1000 DATA I,B,M,*
```

Or, 'OPENSESAME'

```
1000 DATA O,P,E,N,S,E,S,A,M,E,*
```

Don't forget that last piece of DATA, the asterisk. By changing Line 50, of course, we could change the asterisk to any other character we wanted.

Happy gate crashing!

## INPUT$

INPUT$ can be thought of as a *multi-character* INKEY$. It allows us to INPUT a certain number of characters from the keyboard without printing them on the screen. It's great for entering passwords.

Delete Line 20 and make the following changes:

```
40 RESTORE : READ PASSWORD$
50 L = LEN(PASSWORD$)
60 K$ = INPUT$(L)
70 IF K$ = PASSWORD$ THEN 80 ELSE 40
1000 DATA IBM
```

...and RUN.

Very carefully, type IBM (no [↵]).

This change has a disadvantage in that once you start typing there's no way to start over if you make a mistake. With more elaborate programming, a "reset" could automatically take place after a period of time.

I hope you enjoyed this Chapter as much as I did creating it.

## Learned In Chapter 34

**Functions**

INKEY$
INPUT$

**Miscellaneous**

INKEY$ Buffer

# Chapter 35

# PRINT USING

f all the ways we have to PRINT, the most powerful (and most complex) is one called PRINT USING. The name PRINT USING implies that we PRINT by USING something else. That implication is correct.

As originally developed for use on large computers, PRINT USING consists of two parts -- PRINT and USING. PRINT prints, USING the format (called the "image") found in *another* Line. The IBM PRINT USING feature is similar, but does not always require a second Line for the "image" ... as we will see.

## PRINT USING With Numbers

Type in this NEW program:

```
10 CLS : PRINT
20 A = 123.456789
50 U$ = "###.##"
60 PRINT USING U$;A
90 PRINT : LIST
```

...and RUN.

The answer is:

```
123.46
```

It was rounded UP and PRINTed to an accuracy of 2 *decimal* places, following the same format as Line 50, the *image Line*.

Add:

```
30 B = 1.6
70 PRINT USING U$;B
```

...and RUN.

The Display shows:

```
123.46
  1.60
```

Notice that we called upon Line 50, the *image Line*, twice -- once in Line 60 and again in Line 70. Also, note that the answers appear with their decimal points lined up. Last, see that a 0 has been added to the 1.6 to make it read 1.60. These latter 2 points are important when PRINTing out financial reports.

One more addition:

```
40 C = 9876.54321
80 PRINT USING U$;C
```

... and RUN, produces:

```
123.46
  1.60
%9876.54
```

Oh-oh! Vas ist los?

Well, the % sign means we have overrun our *image Line's* capacity to PRINT digits *left* of the decimal point, but it PRINTs them anyway. Better to lose the decimal point lineup than important numbers, but it does call our attention to a programming problem.

Let's add another # sign to make room for that extra digit left of the decimal point. (We are adding another *element* to the *field* in the *image Line*. Got that?)

```
50 U$ = "####.##"
```

Line 50 now has 4 elements in "left field" and 2 in "right field". The decimal point is the dividing point.

...and RUN.

That's better -- but the overRUN message would appear again if we tried to PRINT a number with more than 4 digits on the left.

This PRINT USING business looks like it might have some potential, lining up decimal points like it does. We don't have any other reasonable, straightforward way to accomplish that, and it's essential for PRINTing dollars and cents. Wonder how we can PRINT a dollar sign?

Change the *image Line* to:

```
50 U$ = "$####.##"
```

(check 'em carefully)

...and RUN.

Nice, eh? The dollar signs all line up in a row:

```
$ 123.46
$    1.60
$9876.54
```

But suppose we want the dollar signs to snug right up against each dollar amount? Make 50 read:

```
50 U$ = "$$###.##"
```

...and RUN.

and shure enuf:

```
  $123.46
    $1.60
 $9876.54
```

Not an especially attractive format, but taken singly, as when writing checks, it's almost essential.

The lessons so far are:

1. PRINT USING with # lines up the decimal points.
2. It rounds off the cents (the numbers to the right of the decimal point) to the number of elements specified. It does not round off dollars (left of the decimal point), but sends up an error flag %, PRINTs all dollars, and slips the printout to the right if the field isn't large enough.
3. If a single $ is added to left field, dollar signs are PRINTed and lined up in a column like decimal points. This single $ does not expand the field.
4. If two $ are placed on the left, one $ will be PRINTed on each Line immediately in front of the first dollar digit. One of these $'s can be used to replace one # in the field, thereby not expanding it.

We've covered a lot in a very small program, but have a long ways to go.

## Printing Checks

When using a printer for writing checks, it's usually wise to take extra precautions against "alterations". This is easily accomplished by changing Line 50 to read:

```
50 U$ = "*****.##"
```

(count 'em)

...and RUN.

The Display reads:

```
**123.46
****1.60
*9876.54
```

That's swell. It fills up the unused space alright, but there's no dollar sign. Okay, replace the first # sign with a dollar sign, like so:

```
50 U$ = "**$##.##"
```

---

Aren't you glad we have an Editor for all these changes?

---

See it Now:

```
*$123.46
***$1.60
$9876.54
```

just like they do it uptown! Only 1 $ was needed why using leading *'s, compared to $$ without them.

If we really want to impress others with the size numbers we usually deal in at our local lemonade stand, add lots more # signs to the *image Line*, thus:

```
50 U$ = "**$################.##"
```

and our checks read:

```
***************$123.46
*****************$1.60
**************$9876.54
```

...very impressive.

An Illegal funcion call error will occur if more than 24 characters are assigned to a PRINT USING variable.

Since we're obviously big time operators, having now franchised the lemonade stands, it's getting hard to keep track of the big numbers. How about some commas to break them apart? (Knock out those extra #'s first. Too hard to count them.)

```
50 U$ = "**$,##.##"
```

(look closely)

...and RUN.

```
**$123.46
****$1.60
$9,876.54
```

Only one of our numbers has more than 3 digits in left field, but a comma separated its 9 and 8 for easier readability. In the image field, the comma can be placed *anywhere* between the $ and the decimal point, and only *one* comma is required to automatically insert commas to the left of every 3rd digit left of the decimal point. (You really big-time operators who deal in the millions will have to wait 'til the next chapter to see how to go "double precision" to avoid losing the loose change.)

NOTE: The comma does *not* serve as a field element.

## Stringing It Out

Let's rework the resident program to show some other PRINT USING capabilities:

```
10 CLS : PRINT
20 A = 123.456789
30 B = 1.6
40 C = 9876.54321
                          5 spaces          5 spaces
50 U$ = "####.##     ####.##     ####.##"
```

YOU PRINTED A CHECK FOR -$001.50?
DON'T NAG!

```
60 PRINT USING U$;A,B,C

90 PRINT : LIST
```

...and RUN.

The PRINT USING statement will reuse its image Line until all the fields are PRINTed.

Shorten Line 50 to:

```
                       5 spaces
50 U$ = "####.##        "
```

...and RUN again, with the same effect.

See how numbers can be displayed horizontally instead of vertically? Line 60 determines *where* the fields are PRINTed.

```
123.46   9 spaces   1.60  6 spaces  9876.54
```

**EXERCISE 35-1:** Write the various forms Line 50 must take to PRINT these formats:

```
123.46         1.60           9876.54

$ 123.46       $    1.60      $9876.54

$123.46        $1.60          $9876.54

$123.46        $1.60          $9,876.54
```

and finally

```
***$123.46     *****$1.60     *$9,876.54
```

## PRINT USING With Strings

Change the program to read:

```
10 CLS : PRINT

20 A$ = "IT'S"
```

```
30 B$ = "HOWDY"
40 C$ = "DOODY"
50 D$ = "TIME"
60 U$ = "\\"
70 PRINT USING U$;A$
90 PRINT : LIST
```

...and RUN.

The only thing unique about this program are the back slashes in Line 60. \ is a symbol in IBM PRINT USING which is to strings something like what the # is to numbers.

The \\ reserved 2 spaces for strings. Only IT was PRINTed. Unlike #, however, to reserve more spaces in a *string* field, we add spaces between the \ signs. Change Line 60 to:

```
60 U$ ="\ 2 \"       (the small 2 is just for us)
```

...and RUN.

4 spaces are set aside and IT'S is PRINTed without clipping.

Let's make room for PRINTing another string on the same Line.

```
60 U$ = "\2 \\ 3 \"
70 PRINT USING U$;A$,B$
```

...and RUN.

Oops! We ran:

```
IT'SHOWDY
```

together.

To space them apart we have to put an actual space in the image field just as we did earlier when PRINTing numbers.

```
60 U$ = "\ 2 \1\ 3 \"
```

...and RUN.

That's more like it.

Now it's your turn. Complete Lines 60 and 70 to print `IT'S HOWDY DOODY TIME` all on one line.

---

**Answer:**

```
60 U$ = "\ 2 \1\ 3 \1\ 3 \1\ 2 \
70 PRINT USING U$;A$,B$,C$,D$
```

If you have trouble counting the spaces in PRINT USING, add an adjacent "measuring" line like this, to help in both the LISTing and PRINTout.

```
59 PRINT "123456789012345678901234567890"
```

It's time to quit doodling around and get down to business! Change our HOWDY DOODY to some typical report headings.

```
10 CLS : PRINT
20 A$ = "PART NUMBER"
30 B$ = "DATE PURCHASED"
40 C$ = "DESCRIPTION"
50 D$ = "COST"
60     (Figure out this one yourself)
70 PRINT USING U$;A$,B$,C$,D$
90 PRINT : LIST
```

Assignment: Design the *image* needed in Line 60.

**Answer:**

```
60 U$ = "\   9 spaces   \  4  \        12        \  4  \
         9  \  4  \ 2 \"
```

**EXERCISE 35-2:** Duplicate the following statement. Use PRINT USING for all but the column headings.

```
                            CREDITS      TAX       TOTAL
Astral Computer              18.30       .70       19.00
Biofeedback adapter           1.80       .00        1.80
Personality module            7.20       .30        7.50
                                        DUE:       28.30
```

## Learned In Chapter 35

**Statements**

PRINT USING

**Miscellaneous**

Image Line
PRINT USING
Symbols
# . $ * , \

# Chapter 36

# PRINT USING -- Round 2

In the previous Chapter we learned almost everything really needed to put PRINT USING to work. Here are a few other "tricks" that some will find helpful.

When PRINTing big bucks (over 9,999,999 dollars) it is necessary to use double precision or we lose the loose change. Type in this NEW program:

```
10 CLS : PRINT
20 A$ = "$$#######,###.##"          (count 'em)
30 D = 123456789.01
40 PRINT USING A$;D
90 PRINT : LIST
```

...and RUN.

Sure enough, it rounds to $123,456,800.00. Granted, it's only a few seconds interest on the national debt, but for businesses doing the tax*paying*, the accuracy can be easily improved by simply switching to double-precision.

Change Lines 30 and 40 to:

```
30 D# = 123456789.01
```

```
40 PRINT USING A$;D#
```

...and RUN.

There it is -- $123,456,789.01 -- even the change to tip the porter who hides the public baggage carts. Notice that the *image Line* didn't have to change? All we did was use the double-precision techniques we learned earlier.

If the 17-place accuracy of double precision isn't adequate to keep track of the Krugerrands in your mattress, you and Scrooge McDuck can probably afford to spring for a bigger computer.

## Profit, Or Loss?

Was that last number this quarter's PROFIT from the lemonade stand, or was it a LOSS? We can make the *image Line* PRINT either one. Change it to read:

```
20 A$ = "+$$######,###.##"
```

...and RUN.

Very nice. Wonder what would happen if D was a negative number?

```
30 D# = -123456789.01
```

...and RUN.

So far, so good. Suppose we take the + out of the image Line. Wonder if it will PRINT the minus sign anyway? Use the EDITor and remove it from Line 2Ø.

Then RUN.

Oh, Pshaw! It goofed it up. Negative numbers require one more field element than positive numbers, and the extra $ doesn't do the job. The + did count as an element, so let's put the + sign back in, this time at the *end* of the image.

```
20 A$ = "$$#######,###.##+"
```

...and RUN.

Mmmmm. That's nice. The sign is PRINTed at the end. Let's change D back to a *positive* number and see what happens.

```
30 D# = 123456789.01
```

...and RUN.

Very nice. Looks better to have the signs at the end, not interfering with the dollar sign, don't you think?

Most printers don't PRINT deficits in red. How can we tag them so it's harder for the project manager to slip them by us? (We'll just take all + numbers for granted.) Let's try changing the image + to a minus and see what happens.

```
20 A$ = "$$#######,###.##-"
```

...and RUN.

Seems normal. How about when it's hit with a negative number.

```
30 D# = -123456789.01
```

...and RUN.

AHA! Sticks out like a sore thumb. Now about this little deficit here, Smythe...

**EXERCISE 36-1:** Duplicate this simplified ledger by use of PRINT USING:

```
REVENUES            EXPENSES   ASSETS

1,203,104.22            0.00   1,203,104.22

        0.00      560,143.80     560,143.80-
```

## More On Strings

There are two more PRINT USING characters that have real value. Like so many exotic "upgrades" of BASIC, it does nothing that can't be achieved using other BASIC words, but does it easier. Enter this NEW program:

```
10 CLS : PRINT
20 X$ = "ALEXANDER"
30 Y$ = "GRAHAM"
40 Z$ = "BELL"
50 A$ = "!1!1\2 \"
60 PRINT USING A$;X$,Y$,Z$
90 PRINT : LIST
```

...and RUN.

Who should appear before our very eyes but:

```
A G BELL
```

Each ! reserves an element in the field for the *first letter* of the string assigned to it. Very handy when we want to PRINT the initials and last names of a list of people.

## Another Short Cut

An area of PRINT USING worthy of examination is incorporation of the *image Line* into the PRINT USING Line. It requires some care, and has value primarily when only a few variables are to be PRINTed, or only PRINTed once. In most practical applications, the *image Line* is referenced many times during a RUN, frequently by different PRINT USING Lines.

Make a few changes in the resident program so it looks like this:

```
10 CLS : PRINT
20 X$ = "ALEXANDER"
30 Y$ = "GRAHAM"
40 Z$ = "BELL"
60 PRINT USING "!1!1\ 2 \";X$,Y$,Z$
90 PRINT : LIST
```

...and RUN.

We simply did away with A$ and incorporated its elements into a combination PRINT and *image Line*, separated by a semicolon. It does save space, and for short and uncomplicated PRINT USING applications, has great value. For the long and complicated ones, it's better to keep the *image* and PRINT USING Lines separate.

## INPUTting The Image

We move deeper into the woods as we make BASIC's PRINT formatting capabilities resemble the superior (and far more complicated) ones of the FORTRAN language from which it is derived. We can even INPUT the *image Line*, since it is a string. An easy way to see this is by using our resident program, but change:

```
50 INPUT A$
60 PRINT USING A$;X$,Y$,Z$
```

...and RUN.

We now have to respond by typing in the *image Line*. (Seems like they're hard *enough* to create without INPUTting.) The safest one to use is old Line 50, so respond to the question mark with:

```
? !1!1\ 2 \
```

and see:

```
A G BELL
```

appear again.

RUN again, this time responding with something like:

```
? \   7   \1\  4  \1\ 2 \
```

and we should see something like:

```
ALEXANDER GRAHAM BELL
```

Try some other INPUTs and see how fast we get into trouble with "Illegal Function Call" errors. The down-to-earth value of this particular capability is a little elusive.

Let's experiment with a new PRINT USING character. RUN the program again, and when it asks for an INPUT type:

```
&
```

This new character allows the use of variable length strings. The three names are concatenated and PRINTed. This is a little strange because it defeats the purpose of PRINT USING since there's no way to control column placement. However, when the right application pops up, it's there to use.

## Scientific Forms Of PRINT USING

Would you believe a double-precision number, clipped and expressed via PRINT USING in double-precision Exponential notation? The technical types among us with mismatched socks and rope for a belt will salivate at that one. We aren't going to bore the business types with gory details except for a quick intro.

WOULD YOU BELIEVE A DOUBLE-PRECISION NUMBER, CLIPPED and EXPRESSED IN DOUBLE-PRECISION EXPONENTIAL NOTATION, IN PRINT USING?...
Z

Change or add these Lines:

```
10 CLS : PRINT
20 A$ = "##################^^^^"          (18 + 4)
30 D# = 1234567890987654321
40 D = 1234567890987654321
50 PRINT USING A$;D#
60 PRINT USING A$;D
90 PRINT : LIST
```

...and RUN.

What we see is what we get, both in double and single precision. Using the Editor, move the block of 4 up-arrows to the left, one position at a time, filling in with #'s. Have fun!

## Bring On The Money Changers

Here is a straightforward user program which uses PRINT USING in a practical way. One would be hard pressed to get the same results in so short a program without USING it.

If you're not in the international currency biz, just type in the first half-dozen or so DATA Lines, plus Line 1500 to get a feel for what PRINT USING can do. See how \ and # can be mixed with blank spaces on the same image Line?

Count spaces in Line 90 *very carefully!* Add a "measuring Line" 89 if necessary.

```
1 CLS
10 REM  * INTERNATIONAL MONEY CHANGER *
20 REM  * RATES AS OF FEBRUARY 1984 *
30 KEY OFF : RESTORE : LOCATE 25,15
40 PRINT "HOW MANY U.S. DOLLARS";
50 INPUT" DO YOU WISH TO EXCHANGE ";D: CLS
```

```
60 PRINT TAB(26); "AT TODAY'S RATE YOU WILL GET"
70 PRINT
80 READ A$,A,B$,B : IF A$ = "END" THEN 30
90 P$ = "\      (16 spaces)      \    ########.##"
100 PRINT USING P$; A$; D/A; B$; D/B
110  GOTO 80
1000 DATA ARGENTINE PESO, .03821
1010 DATA AUSTRALIAN DOLLAR, .9224
1020 DATA AUSTRIAN SCHILLING, .05125
1030 DATA BELGIAN FRANC, .01782
1040 DATA BRAZILIAN CRUZEIRO, .0009411
1050 DATA BRITISH POUND, 1.4125
1060 DATA CANADIAN DOLLAR, .8017
1070 DATA CHINESE YUAN, .4839
1080 DATA COLOMBIAN PESO, .01108
1090 DATA DANISH KRONE, .09945
1100 DATA ECUADORIAN SUCRE, .01780
1110 DATA FINNISH MARKKA, .1702
1120 DATA FRENCH FRANC, .1179
1130 DATA GREEK DRACHMA. .009735
1140 DATA DUTCH GUILDER, .3210
1150 DATA HONG KONG DOLLAR, .1282
1160 DATA INDIAN RUPEE, .0929
1170 DATA INDONESIAN RUPIAH, .001004
1180 DATA IRISH PUNT, 1.116
1190 DATA ISRAELI SHEKEL, .008083
1200 DATA ITALIAN LIRA, .0005885
1210 DATA JAPANESE YEN, .004267
1220 DATA LEBANESE POUND, .1715
1230 DATA MALAYSIAN RINGGIT, .4277
```

```
1240 DATA MEXICAN PESO, .005997
1250 DATA NEW ZEALAND DOLLAR, .6526
1260 DATA NORWEGIAN KRONE, .1280
1270 DATA PAKISTANI RUPEE, .07490
1280 DATA PERUVIAN SOL, .0004223
1290 DATA PHILLIPPINE PESO, .07132
1300 DATA PORTUGUESE ESCUDO, .007259
1310 DATA SAUDI ARABIAN RIYAL, .2849
1320 DATA SINGAPORE DOLLAR, .4694
1330 DATA SOUTH AFRICAN RAND, .7955
1340 DATA SPANISH PESETA,.006363
1350 DATA SWEDISH KRONA, .1228
1360 DATA SWISS FRANC, .4480
1370 DATA TAIWANESE DOLLAR, .02488
1380 DATA THAI BAHT, .04350
1390 DATA URUGUAY NEW PESO, .02148
1400 DATA VENEZUELAN BOLIVAR, .1941
1410 DATA WEST GERMAN MARK, .3619
1500 DATA END, 0, END, 0
```

As we've seen, PRINT USING is the most complex of our PRINT statements but by far the most powerful. If you're a serious programmer you should master PRINT USING completely. Then you can take our many simple learning examples and expand them into large, useful routines.

## Learned In Chapter 36

### Miscellaneous

PRINT USING symbols
+ − ^ !

# Chapter 37

# Coloring In Text Mode

Color statement? I thought we couldn't use COLOR with the Monochrome Display? Well you're *right*. COLOR is mostly used with the Color/Graphics Adapter to choose the COLOR we want to draw in. However, we *can* use the COLOR statement on the "Green Screen" for some nice effects. You *do not* need a color monitor or any other special hardware to use this Chapter. We can get different "Shades" of green.

Back in Chapter 33, when we talked about LOCATE, we said that to print on the bottom line of the video display, the Soft Key display has to be turned off. What if we turn OFF the Keys, set a *new* color, and then turn the Keys back ON? I don't know, let's try it. Type in and RUN this NEW program:

```
10 CLS
20 KEY OFF
30 COLOR 25
40 KEY ON
50 COLOR 7
```

Turn the top knob on the video display counterclockwise. The normal intensity characters will disappear, but the high intensity ones will stay on the screen. Press [Ctrl] [Home] to bring the display back to normal.

Color 25 means high intensity, underlined, and blinking. Here's what the rest of the numbers mean:

| NUMBER | RESULT |
|---|---|
| 1 | Underline |
| 7 | Normal |
| 9 | High intensity Underlined |
| 15 | High intensity |
| 17 | Underline Blinking |
| 23 | Blinking |
| 25 | High intensity Underlined Blinking |
| 26 | High intensity Blinking |

All of these color code numbers can be used with the COLOR statement. In these special modes, the characters are printed white on black, or green on black. We also have a reverse mode that can print black on green.

The COLOR statement can really have 2 numbers after it, controlling the foreground color and the background color.

Let's try doing a screen "White Out". If we put the screen in reverse mode, and then clear everything with CLS, the screen will fill with the background color which will be "white" (looks green to me). Try this:

```
COLOR Ø,7 : CLS
```

and the screen changes COLOR. Type:

```
COLOR 7,Ø : CLS
```

to go back to normal.

Let's set the foreground to black and the background to "white" in the Command mode.

```
COLOR Ø,7 : PRINT "REVERSE MODE" : COLOR 7,Ø
```

After REVERSE MODE is PRINTed, `COLOR 7,0` restores things back to normal.

The following program completely demonstrates the "COLOR" capabilities of the IBM Personal Computer when using the Monochrome Display. Study the program and result carefully.

Enter this NEW program:

```
10 CLS
20 COLOR 7                'NORMAL DISPLAY
30 PRINT "C";
40 COLOR 1                'UNDERLINED NORMAL
50 PRINT "O";
60 COLOR 15               'HIGH INTENSITY
70 PRINT "M";
80 COLOR 9                'HIGH INTENSITY UNDERLINED
90 PRINT "P";
100 COLOR 7 + 16          'NORMAL BLINKING
110 PRINT "U";
120 COLOR 1 + 16          'UNDERLINED BLINKING
130 PRINT "T";
140 COLOR 15 + 16         'HIGH INTENSITY BLINKING
150 PRINT "E";
160 COLOR 9 + 16          'HIGH INTENSITY UNDERLINED BLINKING
170 PRINT "R";
200 COLOR 7,0             'BACK TO NORMAL
220 LIST
```

SAVE as COLOR1.

...and RUN.

Now we'll PRINT the word in reverse mode. Unfortunately, this is the only way to PRINT reversed. We can't do flashing or high intensity reversed. Add the following Lines:

```
180 COLOR 0,7
190 PRINT "COMPUTER"
```

Be *sure* to save this program as COLOR1 since we will be adding on to it in a later Chapter.

The use of reverse letters adds considerable impact to visual displays. Type in this NEW program:

```
10 REM  * ON BASE OF STATUE OF LIBERTY *
20 REM  * LARGEST STATUE EVER ERECTED *
30 CLS : KEY OFF : COLOR 0,7
40 LOCATE 10,10 : PRINT "KEEP, ANCIENT LANDS,"
50 LOCATE 12,12 : PRINT "YOUR STORIED POMP!"
60 FOR T = 1 TO 3000 : NEXT
70 COLOR 7,0 : CLS : COLOR 0,7
80 LOCATE 3,1 : PRINT "GIVE ME YOUR TIRED, YOUR POOR,"
90 FOR T = 1 TO 2000 : NEXT
100 LOCATE 7,1 : PRINT "YOUR HUDDLED MASSES YEARNING TO"
110 LOCATE 8,5 : PRINT "BREATHE FREE,"
120 FOR T = 1 TO 2700 : NEXT
130 LOCATE 12,1 : PRINT "THE WRETCHED REFUSE OF YOUR"
140 LOCATE 13,5 : PRINT "TEEMING SHORE."
150 FOR T = 1 TO 3000 : NEXT
160 LOCATE 17,1 : PRINT "SEND THESE, THE HOMELESS,"
170 LOCATE 18,5 : PRINT "TEMPEST-TOST TO ME,"
180 FOR T = 1 TO 3200 : NEXT
```

```
190 LOCATE 22,1 : PRINT "I LIFT MY LAMP BESIDE THE GOLDEN"
200 LOCATE 23,5 : PRINT "DOOR!"
210 FOR X=1 TO 8000 : NEXT
220 COLOR 7,0 : KEY ON : END
```

...and RUN.

Since we only use the left half of the screen, let's create something on the right side of the display.

Add the following Lines on the resident program:

```
35 GOSUB 1000
75 GOSUB 1000
1000 REM  * SUBROUTINE TO PRINT GRAPHICS CHARACTERS *
1010 RESTORE : COLOR 7,0
1020 FOR I = 1 TO 3              ' 3 LETTERS
1030  PRINT : PRINT
1040  FOR J = 1 TO 5             ' 5 LINES PER LETTER
1050   PRINT : PRINT TAB(72)
1060   FOR K = 1 TO 4            ' 4 CHARACTERS PER LINE
1070    READ Y
1080    PRINT CHR$(Y);
1090   NEXT K
1100  NEXT J
1110 NEXT I
1120 COLOR 0,7
1130 RETURN
1200 DATA 186,32,32,186,186,32,32,186,186,32,32,186
1210 DATA 186,32,32,186,200,205,205,188
1220 DATA 201,205,205,205,186,32,32,32,200,205,205,187
```

WITHOUT NUMBERS, ..AMAZING!
EAT YOUR HEART OUT, PICASSO!

```
1230 DATA 32,32,32,186,205,205,205,188
1240 DATA 201,205,205,187,186,32,32,186,204,205,205,185
1250 DATA 186,32,32,186,186,32,32,186
```

...and RUN.

This one gives us a chance to flex our muscles with the *Line graphics* characters.

My country 'tis of thee...

## Learned In Chapter 37

### Statements

COLOR

Chapter 38

# Using A Printer

**R**eady for a break to learn something that's very simple?

## LPRINT And LLIST

These BASIC Commands/Statements are almost too easy.

We have learned a lot of ways to PRINT, but they have all been on the video screen. Now we'll learn how to PRINT-out to a Computer Printer. If you don't have a printer yet, at least skim this Chapter before proceeding.

Hook up and turn on the printer and type this new one-Line program:

```
10 LPRINT "THE PRINTER WORKS!!!"
```

Notice that the first word is LPRINT, not PRINT. RUN the program.

Did it print? If your printer did nothing, check the connections again. Make sure the printer is *on* and *on-line.* Try RUNning the one-Line program again.

NOTE: There is much widespread misuse of the language when it comes to naming printers. Here are some definitions:

PRINTer = a device which converts computer talk to "hard copy".

Dot Matrix Printer = A printer such as the EPSON MX-80 which creates characters by printing clusters of dots which resemble letters and numbers.

DON'T YELL AT ME!
YOU ORDERED A
LINE PRINTER.

Character Printer = A printer which, like most typewriters, prints complete pre-formed characters.

Line Printer = A very large "hi-speed" printer which literally "sets" and then prints an entire LINE of print at one time.

There is much misnaming of printers. Very few are true "Line Printers", though many are sold under that name. True Line Printers are very expensive, and can print over 1000 Lines of type per minute.

It is from the Line Printer name that the "L" in LPRINT was derived.

## LLISTing The Program

LLIST is typed at the command level when we want a LISTing of a program sent to the PRINTer.

Both LPRINT and LLIST can be used either as statements or commands. If you want to PRINT both on the screen and on paper, use duplicate program Lines, with PRINT for the screen, and LPRINT for the PRINTer.

Enter any program of your choice and convert it to LPRINT the results on your PRINTer. Make a "hard copy" LLISTing of it.

To LIST a program on the printer, you can also use:

```
LIST, "LPT1:"
```

The program will be LISTed on printer #1.

Notice that we can do this very easily with the function keys. Just press [F1] and then [F6] (no need to hit [↵]).

If we accidentally precede either PRINT or LIST with the letter L and don't have a PRINTer connected, there may be trouble. It's especially easy to have a simple LIST turn into LLIST. If there is no PRINTer hooked up or it's turned OFF, we will get an "Out of Paper" error. If the PRINTer is hooked up, but it's Off Line, after about 8 seconds we will get a "Device Fault" error.

To stop an LLIST with IBM DOS 1.10, hit [Break] ( [Ctrl] [Scr Lock] )

The IBM Personal Computer has a special Screen Dump key directly below the [↵] key. Type ⇧ [PrtSc] to send all the characters on the screen to the PRINTer. Unprintable characters are printed as blanks.

## LPRINT TAB

The TAB function can handle numbers up through 32767. This has little value in displays PRINTed on the Computer, but on big PRINTers it is common to PRINT Lines up to 132 characters long.

We recall that PRINT STRING$ is used to repeat a number of characters or actions. We can use it to sneak around the above rule by having it repeat a number of spaces. For example:

```
10 LPRINT STRING$(95,32);X
```

will "PRINT" 95 blank spaces before PRINTing the value of X. "32" is the ASCII code for a space.

The WIDTH statement can be used to tell the Computer that the PRINTer is wider than 80 columns. Use:

```
WIDTH "LPT1:",255
```

at the beginning of programs that need to use more than 80-column width.

## Formatting

Now, let's see how to PRINT with a nice format. Type:

```
10 FOR X=1 TO 100
20 LPRINT X,
30 NEXT X
```

...RUN it.

See how the printer will format the PRINTing into neat little columns? The comma with LPRINT works the same as it does with PRINT, except there may be a different number of columns on your printer. (The number of columns depends on which PRINTer you have.)

Try using a semi-colon in Line 20 rather than a comma. Type:

```
20 LPRINT X;
```

...and RUN. The semi-colon works the same on the PRINTer as it does on the video screen. Let's see how TAB works. Type this simple NEW program:

```
10 LPRINT TAB(25); "TELEPHONE LIST"
20 LPRINT
30 LPRINT TAB(15); "NAME";
40 LPRINT TAB(45); "TELEPHONE NUMBER"
50 LPRINT
60 INPUT "TYPE A FRIENDS NAME";A$
70 INPUT "PHONE NUMBER";B$
80 PRINT "THANK YOU"
90 LPRINT TAB(15); A$;TAB(45); B$
100 INPUT "IS THERE ANOTHER FRIEND (Y/N)";Q$
110 IF Q$="Y" THEN 60
```

...and RUN.

If the paper size is larger or smaller than 8 1/2 by 11 inches, you'll want to use different TAB settings.

## LPRINT USING

In the last Chapter we saw how PRINT USING can format our PRINT outputs on the screen. Those same features can be applied to the printer by using LPRINT USING. Incorporate LPRINT USING in one of the simple programs from the last Chapter.

```
10 X$ = "ALEXANDER"
20 Y$ = "GRAHAM"
30 Z$ = "BELL"
```

```
60 LPRINT USING "! 2 !1\1\";X$;Y$;Z$
```

...and RUN.

## Advanced LPRINT Capabilities

6 different ASCII codes are set aside for use with PRINTers. Since different PRINTers respond differently, we can only talk here in general terms, and learn how to test our own PRINTer to see how it responds. The 6 codes are:

| | |
|---|---|
| 6 | Beep |
| 10 | Line feed and carriage return |
| 11 | Line feed and carriage return |
| 12 | roll paper to top of next sheet |
| 13 | Line feed and carriage return |
| 138 | carriage return and Line feed |

To see what this all means, enter this program:

```
10 CLS : PRINT
20 INPUT "ENTER A CODE NUMBER";N
30 LPRINT CHR$(N)
90 PRINT : LIST
```

...and RUN.

Try each of the codes and see what happens. Some codes may do nothing. Your PRINTer's manual may have additional (or replacement) codes.

*There are no universal rules. Keep your test program simple and be aware that LPRINT with CHR$ is not always predictable when mixed on the same program Line.*

The "top of form" or "top of next sheet" feature is a necessary one for preparing PRINTed statements, or PRINTing information which must always start at the top of a page.

When your Computer is turned on, if it is going to do any PRINTing, it automatically assumes it will be PRINTing 6 Lines per inch on sheets of paper 11 inches long, 66 Lines per page.

With a little experimenting, your PRINTer will be doing what you paid to have it do.

## Learned In Chapter 38

| Statements | Miscellaneous |
|---|---|
| LPRINT | Trailing semi-colon |
| LLIST | |

# PART 6
# ARRAYS

## Chapter 39

# Arrays

We know we can use combinations of the 26 letters of the alphabet and digits 0-9 to create variable names. We've also discovered that very few of our programs have required anywhere near that many variables. There are times, however, when we need more variables -- sometimes *hundreds* or even *thousands* of them.

The way we control and keep track of that many variables is by holding them in an ARRAY. Array is just another word for "lineup", "arrangement" or "series of things".

Let's organize a collection, arrangement or lineup (array) of autos, each of which has a different I.D. (address) number.

We line up 10 cars, as in an *array*. They are all the same except for their engine size -- and each has a different I.D. or license number. Let's say the I.D. numbers range from 1 to 10, and we want to use the Computer to quickly spit out the engine size when we identify a car by its I.D. number. This might not seem like a real heavyweight problem -- but, as before, we discover the full potential of these things by learning little steps at a time.

The I.D. numbers and engine sizes are as follows:

| CAR # | ENGINE |
|---|---|
| 1 | 300 |
| 2 | 200 |
| 3 | 500 |
| 4 | 300 |
| 5 | 200 |
| 6 | 300 |
| 7 | 400 |
| 8 | 400 |
| 9 | 300 |
| 10 | 500 |

Now, we could give each of these cars a different letter name, using the variables A through J, but what a waste -- and what will we do when there are a thousand cars, not just ten?

## Setting Up Arrays

IBM BASIC allows any valid variable name to be used as an array name. An *Array* named "A" is not the same as the *Numeric* variable "A", and neither is it the same as *string* variable A$. It is a totally separate "A" used to identify a *Numeric array*. We call it A-sub(something) and it can only hold numbers. We will name the cars A(1) through A(10), pronounced "A sub 1" through "A sub 10". Get the idea?

What's that -- you don't believe there can be 3 separate variables all named "A"? Ok, in immediate mode type:

```
A = 12                [↵]
A$ = "(YOUR NAME)"        [↵]
A(1) = 999            [↵]
```

then: `PRINT A,A$,A(1)` [ENTER]

Does that make you a believer?

Let's store the car engine sizes in DATA statements. Type in:

```
500 DATA 300,200,500,300,200
510 DATA 300,400,400,300,500
```

Notice how carefully we kept the DATA elements in order from 1 to 10 so the first car's engine size is found in the first DATA Location, and the 10th one's in the 10th location?

We now have to "spin up" an array inside the Computer's memory to make these data elements *immediately addressable.*

---

Big words meaning "so we can find a car fast."

---

Think how difficult it would be to try to address the 7th engine (or the 7 thousandth!) for example, using only what we've learned so far. It *can* be done using only DATA, READ and RESTORE statements but that would be very messy and slow.

The easy way to create the array is to type in:

```
30 FOR L = 1 TO 10
40   READ A(L)
50 NEXT L
```

...and RUN.

Nothing happen? Yes, it did. We simply didn't display what happened.

The FOR-NEXT loop READ 10 pieces of DATA, and named the elements (or "cells") in which they're stored A(1) through A(10). To PRINT out the values in those array elements, type:

```
105 FOR N = 1 TO 10
```

```
110   PRINT A(N)
120 NEXT N
```

...and RUN.

Aha! It works, but how? We READ the DATA elements into an array called A(L), but PRINTed them out of an array called A(N). Why the difference? Nothing significant.

The array's NAME is "A". The *location* of each data element within that array is identified by the number we place inside the parentheses. That number can be brought inside the parentheses by using any numeric variable, and can even do some simple arithmetic inside the parentheses, if necessary. We arbitrarily used N to READ them in, and L to PRINT them out.

Remember, the array we are using is named "A". Its elements are numbered, and called A-sub(number).

---

Some pure mathematicians might insist on calling A(X) A "OF" X. We don't need that added confusion. Best you know, just in case.

---

Let's work some more on the program.

Type:

```
10 CLS
90 PRINT
100 PRINT "CAR#","ENGINE SIZE"
110 PRINT N,A(N)
```

...and RUN.

Now that's more like it. We have every I.D. number, every engine size, and are not "using up" any of the "regular" alphabetic variables to store them. Having demonstrated that point, Delete Lines 105 and 120, and type:

```
20 INPUT "WHICH CAR'S ENGINE SIZE";W
110 PRINT W,A(W)
```

```
990 PRINT : LIST
```

...and RUN, answering with a car #.

Get the idea? Can you see the crude beginning of a simple inventory system for a small business?

Let's go one small step (for mankind) further. Suppose we know the color of each of the 10 cars, and for simplicity, suppose the colors are coded 1, 2, 3 and 4. We might then have a master chart that looks like this:

| CAR# | ENG. SIZE | COLOR |
|---|---|---|
| 1 | 300 | 3 |
| 2 | 200 | 1 |
| 3 | 500 | 4 |
| 4 | 300 | 3 |
| 5 | 200 | 2 |
| 6 | 300 | 4 |
| 7 | 400 | 3 |
| 8 | 400 | 2 |
| 9 | 300 | 1 |
| 10 | 500 | 3 |

In the language of professional computer types, this is called a *matrix*. A *matrix* is just an array that has more than one dimension. Our first array had the dimension of 1 by 10 -- 1 *column* by 10 *rows*.) This new array has a horizontal dimension of 2 and a vertical dimension of 10.

If we wanted to be terribly inefficient about the matter, we *could* say that this is a 3 by 10 array, counting the I.D. number. If so, our first example would be called a 2 by 10 array -- but who needs it? As long as we keep the I.D. numbers in a simple 1 to 10 FOR-NEXT loop, and the DATA in proper sequence, the arrays will be simple and easier to handle.

---

Since we do not store the car number in the Computer it is a "pointer" or an "index". That's why we don't consider it as another "DIMension" to the matrix.

---

How then can we label this 2 by 10 *matrix*? We have already used up our A array elements numbered 1 through 10. Oh, you want to know how many elements we have to work with? Very good!

Let's arbitrarily assign array locations 101 through 110 to hold the color code. We also have to put the color code info in the program using a DATA statement. From the table, type:

```
520 DATA 3,1,4,3,2,4,3,2,1,3
```

and:

```
60 FOR S = 101 TO 110
70  READ A(S)
80 NEXT S
```

These last Lines load the color code DATA into the array. Array element numbers 11 through 100 are not used, nor are those from 111 to the end of memory since they have not been formally assigned any values.

...RUN, and select any car number.

Awwk!! What is this "Subscript out of range" business? Well, since arrays take up a lot of memory space, the Computer automatically allows us to use up to only 11 array elements without question. (They can be numbered from 0 to 10.) Then our credit runs out. We earlier used elements numbered from 1 to 10 without any problem.

If we'd wanted to, we could have put at the beginning of our program:

```
5 OPTION BASE 1
```

This OPTION changes the lowest array element number to 1, instead of 0. 1 or 0 are the only numbers that can be used with the OPTION BASE statement.

To use array elements numbered beyond 10 in the array called "A", we have to "reDIMension" the available array space. Our highest number in Array "A" needs to be 110, so we'll add a program DIMension statement:

```
10 DIM A(110) : CLS
```

HEH, HEH. ALL I ASKED FOR WAS ARRAYS.

...and RUN again. That's better, but it's not PRINTing the color code.

To display all the information, change these Lines:

```
20 INPUT "WHICH CAR TO EXAMINE";W
100 PRINT "CAR#","ENG. SIZE","COLOR"
110 PRINT W,A(W),A(W+100)
```

...then RUN.

Check your answers against the earlier master matrix chart. SAVE the program as "CARARRAY".

Let your imagination go. Can you envision entire charts and "look-up" tables stored in this way? Entire inventory lists? How about trying to *find* the car which has a certain size engine *and* a certain color? Hmmm. We will come back to the Logic needed for that last one.

**EXERCISE 39-1:** Assume that your inventory of 10 cars includes 3 different body styles, coded 10, 20 and 30, as follows:

| CAR# | BODY |
|---|---|
| 1 | 20 |
| 2 | 20 |
| 3 | 10 |
| 4 | 20 |
| 5 | 30 |
| 6 | 20 |
| 7 | 30 |
| 8 | 10 |
| 9 | 20 |
| 10 | 20 |

Modify the resident program to PRINT the body style information along with the rest when the car is identified by I.D. number.

## A Smith & Wesson Beats 4 Aces

If we want to create a computerized card game (they make good examples to show so many things), how can we program it so it draws the 52 or so (watch the dealer at all times) cards in a totally random way? **ANSWER:** Spin up the deck into a single-dimension array, pick array elements using a random number generator, as each card is "drawn" set its array element value equal to zero, then test each card drawn to be sure it isn't zero. Now that is *really* simple! (Might want to read it once again, more slowly.)

We will now, a step at a time, write a program which will draw, at random, all 52 cards numbered from 1 through 52, and PRINT the card numbers on the screen as they are drawn. No card will be drawn more than once. When all cards have been drawn, it will PRINT "END OF DECK!"

You do a step first, then check against my example. Then change yours to match mine -- otherwise we might not end up at the same place at the same time.

---

STEP 1: Spin up all 52 cards into an array.

```
20 DIM A(52) : CLS
30 FOR C=1 TO 52 : READ A(C) : NEXT C
500 DATA 1,2,3,4,5,6,7,8,9,10,11,12,13
510 DATA 14,15,16,17,18,19,20,21,22,23
520 DATA 24,25,26,27,28,29,30,31,32,33
530 DATA 34,35,36,37,38,39,40,41,42,43
540 DATA 44,45,46,47,48,49,50,51,52
```

At this point, all we can tell when RUNning is that processing time is required since the Ok doesn't come back right away.

---

Shhhh! I know there's a shorter way to program this special case, but it doesn't teach what's needed.

---

STEP 2: Draw 52 cards at random, PRINTing their values.

```
40 FOR N = 1 TO 52
50   V = RND(52)
60   PRINT A(V);
70 NEXT N
990 PRINT : LIST
```

...and RUN.

True, 52 card values are PRINTed on the screen, but if we look carefully, the same number appears more than once. This means that some "cells" are not being READ and some READ more than once.

---

STEP 3: When a card is drawn, set its array value equal to 0. Test each card drawn to be sure it is not 0. When 52 cards have been drawn and PRINTed, PRINT "END OF DECK!".

```
40 P = 52
55 IF A(V) = 0 GOTO 50
70 A(V) = 0 : P = P - 1
80 IF P<>0 GOTO 50
90 PRINT : PRINT "END OF DECK!"
```

...and RUN.

Line 70 sets the value in cell A(V) equal to 0 only if Line 55 finds it *not* equal to 0 already, letting the program pointer fall through.

When a "fall through" occurs:

1. The card's value is PRINTed (Line 60)
2. The number stored in that cell is set to 0 (Line 70)
3. The second statement in Line 70 counts down the number of cards PRINTed. Line 40 initialized the number of PRINTs at 52.

4. The number of PRINTs is tested (Line 80). When there are no more PRINTs to go, "END OF DECK!" is PRINTed (Line 90).

Pretty slick -- and we don't have to watch the dealer (just the programmer).

But how do we really know that every card has been dealt? Write a quick addition to the program to "interrogate" each array cell and PRINT its contents.

```
100 FOR T = 1 TO 52
110 PRINT A(T);
120 NEXT T
```

RUN ... and every cell comes up zero. If you don't really trust all this, change Line 40 to read:

```
40 P = 50
```

...RUN and see what happens.

AHA! It flushed out those 2 cards up the sleeve, didn't it?

To add a final tough of "randomness" to the deal, add:

```
10 RANDOMIZE
```

Change P back to 52, Delete test program Lines 100, 110, and 120, and we end up with a good card-drawing routine. You might want to clean it up to your satisfaction and SAVE it as "CARDDRAW" for future projects.

**Question:** Why does the PRINTing of card numbers slow down to a near halt as those last few cards are being drawn. Is the dealer reluctant?

**Answer:** The random number generator has to keep drawing numbers until it hits one that is the array address of an element which has *not* been set to zero. Near the end of the deck, almost all elements have been set to zero. The random number generator has to draw numbers as fast as it can to find a "live" one.

Look again at the card numbers PRINTed. There will not be any duplication. No stray aces.

**EXERCISE 39-2:** Change the program so the original array can be loaded with the card numbers without having to READ them in from DATA Lines.

## New Dimensions

We have already done some DIMensioning with single dimension *numeric* arrays. *String* arrays must also be DIMensioned.

Suppose we have a program like this: (Type it in)

```
10 FOR N = 1 TO 15
20  READ A$(N)
30  PRINT A$(N),
40 NEXT N
90 PRINT : LIST
100 DATA ALPHA,BRAVO,CHARLIE,DELTA
110 DATA ECHO,FOXTROT,GOLF,HOTEL
120 DATA INDIA,JULIETTE,KILO,LIMA
130 DATA MIKE,NOVEMBER,OSCAR
```

...and RUN.

Oops. There's that same problem. "Subscript out of range in 20" means "not enough space set aside for an array". Recall that only 11 elements *per array* (from 0-10) are set aside on power-up. We are trying to read in 15 of them, starting with 1. The solution:

```
5 DIM A$(15)
```

...and RUN.

DIMensioning a string array is just like dimensioning a numeric one -- simply call it by its name. In this case, its name is A$. You "high speed" types will want to know that to do "dynamic redimensioning" (that's doing it while a program is running) the program must first encounter a CLEAR. Oh.

## All CLEAR

The CLEAR statement simply CLEARs the memory of all meaningful information except the actual program. It makes *all* string variables and arrays contain nothing and sets *all* numeric variables to 0. And anything we DEFined with a DEF FN statement will be forgotten.

For example type:

```
CLEAR
```

and then:

```
PRINT A$(3)
```

Nothing. RUN the program again to reload the Array, then PRINT A$(3).

ERASE will null out the contents of a *specific* array variable.

For example, type:

```
ERASE B$
```

By telling the Computer to ERASE all data in the B$ array (even tho we don't have a B$ array in our program) we have not removed the data in A$ array. To prove this point type:

```
PRINT A$(3)
```

Now type:

```
ERASE A$
```

and

```
PRINT A$(3)
```

Try PRINTing other elements in A$ array. They have *all* been ERASEd.

## Array Names

```
A(N)

BC(N)

D3(N)

E4$(N)

XY$(N)
```

are examples of legal array names. The last 2 are for "string arrays."

> **EXERCISE 39-3:** Study the User programs in Section C to better understand the use of arrays for storage and access purposes. Time spent studying programs written by others is wisely invested.

## Learned In Chapter 39

| Statements | Miscellaneous |
|---|---|
| DIM | Arrays |
| CLEAR | |
| ERASE | |

# Chapter 40

# Search And Sort

One of the Computer's most powerful features is its ability to *search* through a pile of DATA and *sort* the findings into some order. Alphabetical, reverse alphabetical, numerical from smallest to largest, or the reverse are all common sorts. The *search/sort* feature is so important we will spend this entire Chapter learning how to use it.

Typical applications of *search* and *sort* include:

1. Arranging a list of customers' or prospects' names in *alphabetical* order.

2. Sorting names in *ZIP-Code* order for lower-cost mailing.

3. Sorting the names of clients in telephone *area code* order.

While not really all that complicated, the sorting process is sufficiently rigorous that we are going to take it *very slowly* and examine each step. Once we get the hang of it, the Computer can blaze away without our considering the staggering number of steps it's going through.

## A Problem of Sorts

Let's start with a problem. We have the names of 10 customers. (If that doesn't grab you, make it 10 million -- the process is identical.) We wish to arrange them in alphabetical order.

Start by storing their names in a DATA Line. Type in:

```
1000 DATA BRAVO,XRAY,ALPHA,ZULU,FOXTROT,TANGO,
     HOTEL,SIERRA,MIKE,JULIETTE
```

Since we are sorting by *name* rather than by number, we have to use *string* variables, *string* arrays, etc. They work equally well with numbers such as zip codes, while numeric variables and arrays work *only* with numbers.

The backbone of a *sort* routine is the array. Each name is to be READ from DATA into an array. So add:

```
10 REM  * ALPHA SORT OF STRINGS FROM DATA *
20 CLS : FOR D=1 TO 10 : READ A$(D) : N=N+1 :
   NEXT D
```

Line 10 is, of course, just the title.

Line 20 clears the screen, then "loads the array" by READing the 10 names into storage slots A$(1) to A$(10). N is simply a counter which will follow through the rest of the program. In this simple program we could have made N=10 since we know how many names we have. In the next sample program we won't know how many names there are, so let's leave N the way it's usually used.

Important to the *sort* routine are 2 nested FOR-NEXT loops.

1. The first one, F, controls the First name.

2. S, the second one, controls the name to be compared against the first.

---

Names and words are compared as we learned in the Chapter on ASCII set, remember?

---

Let's establish the loops first, and fill in the guts later:

```
30 FOR F = 1 TO N-1        (F=First word to be compared)
40    FOR S = F+1 TO N     (S=Second word to be compared)
90    NEXT S                           (Makes 9 passes)
100 NEXT F                             (Makes 9 passes)
```

It may seem puzzling that F and S only have to make 9 passes when there are 10 names. Think of it this way. Whatever word *isn't* smaller (ASCII #) than the rest, just ends up last. No need to test again to prove that.

The F loop READs array elements 1 through 9 (N - 1 = 9). The S loop READs array elements 2 through 10. This always provides *different* array elements to compare.

Now we'll jump to the end of the program and prepare it to PRINT out what will happen. Type:

```
110 FOR D = 1 TO N : PRINT A$(D), : NEXT D
990 PRINT : LIST
```

When the *sort*ing is done, the contents of A$(1) to A$(10) will be the same names READ from DATA, but they will be in alphabetical order. We'll PRINT the array contents on the screen.

```
50    IF A$(F) <= A$(S) THEN 90   (Tests for smaller ASCII#)
60    T$ = A$(F)           (First word to Temp storage)
70    A$(F) = A$(S)        (Copy Second word to First place)
80    A$(S) = T$           (Copy Temp word to Second place)
```

And there is the biggie! If you can understand the last 4 Lines the rest is duck soup.

> Line 50 says, "If the First word is smaller than (or equal to) the Second word, leave well enough alone and bail out of this routine by going to Line 90, which will end this pass and READ another word to compare against F. If it is larger, drop to the next Line.

Line 6Ø says, "Oh, they weren't in the right order, eh? We'll just copy the First word in a Temporary storage location called T$ and store it there for future use. I'm sure we'll need it again."

Line 7Ø copies the name held in the Second cell into the First array cell. If the Second one had an earlier starting letter than the First one, we do want to do this, don't we?

Line 8Ø completes the switch by copying the name Temporarily stored in T$ into the Second array cell. A$(1) and A$(2) contents have now been exchanged with the aid of the Temporary holding pen, T$.

---

Us simple country boys find this one easy: *There are two brahma bulls in separate pens, A$(1) & A$(2), and we want to switch them around. Ain't no way we're going to put them in the same pen at the same time. (Not with me in there anyway. Already broken too many 2 by 4's between their horns, and have some scars on the wrong end from escapes that were a hair too slow.) That's why we built a temporary holding pen called T$.* Got it?

---

If we did everything right, the program should:

RUN

and in a flash the names appear on the screen in alphabetical order:

```
ALPHA    BRAVO    FOXTROT   HOTEL    JULIETTE
MIKE     SIERRA   TANGO     XRAY     ZULU
```

---

Printing will be in standard 14 space tab zone format.

---

IBM wanted to let us have 6 PRINT zones on one Line. So they squeezed a 6th 10 column zone in columns 71-80. But in order to keep the last zone 14 characters, they stole 4 characters from the next Line. So your PRINTout looks like:

```
ALPHA         BRAVO         FOXTROT       HOTEL         JULIETTE      MIKE
    SIERRA    TANGO         XRAY          ZULU
```

HEY, DOC, WHAT'S 2 PENS WITH BULLS IN 'EM GOT TO DO WITH "SEARCH and SORT"?
IT'S A TRICK QUESTION

In order to get around this small "quirk" change Line 11Ø to:

```
110 FOR D = 1 TO N : PRINT A$(D), :
    IF D = 5 THEN PRINT
```

This will make your display look like everyone else's.

SAVE as "SORT" and RUN it to your heart's delight. This is one of the most powerful things a Computer can do, and it does it so well. The identical procedure is used to sort very long lists of names (or zip codes, or whatever) but we would, of course, have to reDIMension for a larger array.

To get a really good look at what's happening, it's necessary to slow the beast *way* down, and insert a few extra PRINT Lines. They allow us to peer inside the program by watching the tube.

Add these temporaries:

```
45      PRINT F;A$(F),,S;A$(S)
55      PRINT TAB(10); "<<--<<   SWITCHEROO"
85      PRINT F;A$(F),,S;A$(S)
```

(Allow three spaces after the arrow -- that way it will look nice on the screen when you RUN it.)

...and RUN.

*Aw c'mon horse -- Whoa!*

If that wasn't slow enough, add Line 47 and make the delay long enough so there is time to completely think through each step. Pretend you're the Computer, and make the decision that Line 5Ø has to make. Take it from the top -- very slowly!

```
47      FOR Z = 1 TO 1000 : NEXT Z
```

## The Diagnosis

```
    1 BRAVO                                    2 XRAY
```

Means "in cell #1 is the word BRAVO. In cell #2 is the word XRAY" just like they came from the DATA Line. Of those two words, BRAVO is the "smallest" (ASCII#), so it stays in number 1 place. On to the next pass of S.

```
    1 BRAVO                                    3 ALPHA
```

Oops. BRAVO is in #1 and ALPHA is in #3, but ALPHA is smaller than BRAVO. We better switch them around. So

‹‹--‹‹ SWITCHEROO

```
    1 ALPHA                                    3 BRAVO
```

Don't worry too much about what is happening in the second column. S is scanning through the array and its contents are always changing, testing against what's in the first. It's what *ends up* in the *first* column that counts -- and that list must be in increasing alphabetical order.

As the program RUNs, watch new words appear in S, loop and column, and compare them against what's in F. Try to guess what the Computer's going to do. Also keep an eye on the increasing numbers on the left. The *final word* assigned to a given number in the first column is what will appear in the final PRINTout.

RUN the program as many times as it takes (and at as many sessions as it takes) to completely understand what's happening. It's awfully clever, very important, and absolutely fundamental. We carry this technique over to many useful programs in the future, but only if we *really* understand it.

When you feel it's under control, add one more little item to the screen. What T$ is holding while all this *sort*ing is going on is interesting. Add and change these Lines so they read:

```
45   PRINT F;A$(F),,S;A$(S),"T$ = ";T$
85   PRINT F;A$(F),,S;A$(S),"T$ = ";T$
```

...and RUN.

"T$ = " starts off empty since there is nothing in the holding pen. BRAVO is replaced by ALPHA in the switching process, however, T$ holds it. When BRAVO replaces XRAY in the #2 position, T$ holds XRAY, etc.

On a clear head it's not hard to follow what's happening. If you're tired, it's hopeless. SAVE this program and review it as often as necessary for a deep understanding of the process.

## SORTing From The Outside

We don't really have to keep all our names, numbers or other information in DATA Lines. It can be INPUT from the keyboard or from disk. The following program is quite similar to the resident one, and the logic is identical. Change and add these Lines:

```
10 REM  * ALPHA SORT OF NAMES VIA INPUT *
20 INPUT"NEXT NAME";N$ : IF N$="END" GOTO 30
25 N=N+1 : A$(N) = N$ : GOTO 20
```

Delete Line 1000.

...and RUN.

INPUT 6 or 8 random names, and when finished, INPUT the word "END". The sort process is identical to what we used before.

*Can you see the potential for all this?*

> **EXERCISE 40-1:** Change Line 50 of the *sort* program to list the names in reverse alphabetical order.

## Learned In Chapter 40

### Miscellaneous

Sorting

# Chapter 41

# Multi-DIMension Arrays

We have learned that an array is nothing more than a temporary parking area for lots of numbers, or characters, or both. In addition, we learned that it is a straight-forward procedure to compare values of variables outside the matrix (or array) with those inside it.

An array which only has one DIMension, that is, just one long line-up of parking places is sometimes called a *vector*. We can take that one-dimensional array and cut it into perhaps four equal chunks, and position those chunks side by side. We then call it a two-dimensional array -- since the parking places are lined up in *rows* and *columns* (or *streets* and *avenues*). Its DATA holding or processing abilities are not changed. Only the *addresses* of the parking places (or elements or memory cells) has changed.

Type in this NEW program:

```
10 DIM M(50)
20 FOR V = 1 TO 50
30  PRINT V,M(V)
40 NEXT V
```

---

Remember, any array with more than 11 elements (counting 0) must be DIMensioned.

---

...and RUN.

The RUN simply shows the addresses (numbers) of 50 storage positions, and their contents. Since they are all lined up in a single row, it is a vector array.

Why are the cell contents always 0? Because every cell value is initialized at zero upon entering BASIC, and whenever we RUN, just like all other numeric and string variables. Line 30 shows how easy it is to specify the *address* and read the *contents* of each memory cell.

## Side by Side

Let's cut our 50 cell array into 5 equal strips and line them up side by side. That would make 10 *rows* each containing 5 cells ... right? Or 5 *columns* each containing 10 cells. "Multi-dimensional arrays" always have *rows* and *columns*.

Start over with this NEW program:

```
10 DIM M(10,5)          (10 rows by 5 columns)
20 FOR R = 1 TO 10
30  FOR C = 1 TO 5
40   PRINT R;C,
50  NEXT C : PRINT
60 NEXT R
```

SAVE as MATADR and RUN.

The *addresses* of all 50 cells displayed on the screen at the same time, but not their contents. Nothing was changed from the earlier vector array containing the same 50 cells. We just rearranged the furniture and gave it different addresses. They read:

1 1 means "first ROW, first COLUMN"

8 3 means "8th ROW, 3rd COLUMN"

etc.

ARRAY'S
PARKING
VECTOR
I'LL TAKE 'ER NEXT DOOR
MULTI-
LOT FULL
NUMBERS

To view the *contents* of each of these cells, change Line 40:

```
40    PRINT M(R,C),
```

...and RUN.

See, the contents remain unchanged. They are still at their initialized value of 0, since we made no arrangement to store information in them. (The *addresses* are no longer displayed) Isn't this easy (...so far)?

Memory cells, like any other variables have to be "loaded" with values to be useful. This can be done by READing in DATA from DATA Lines, by INPUTting it via the keyboard or from a previously recorded DATA disk. We will load our Matrix from DATA Lines imbedded in the program.

Add these Lines:

```
100 DATA 1,2,3,4,5,6,7,8,9,10,11 etc. to 26
110 DATA 27,28,29,30,31,32,33,34,35 etc. to 50
```

and this Line to READ the DATA into matrix cells:

```
35   READ M(R,C)
```

SAVE or MATCONT and RUN.

The DATA is nicely arranged in the matrix, and each matrix position has its original specific address. Again, that address is not displayed -- just the contents. Let's stay in the command mode for a minute and "poll" or "interrogate" several matrix positions and see what they are holding. Ask:

```
PRINT M(2,3)        [ENTER]
```

Write down 8, the answer. We'll RUN the program again later and check it.

```
PRINT M(9,4)        [ENTER]
```

Says *that* cell holds the number 44.

```
PRINT M(3,6)
```

Subscript out of range? Why did we get that? Oh, there is no column 6? No wonder.

RUN the program again and check the screen, counting down the Rows and over the Columns to see if the answers match up.

Mine did -- how about yours?

---

Row 2 Col. 3 = 8
Row 9 Col. 4 = 44

---

As an aside, type:

```
ERASE M
```

then, at the command level, check any matrix memory spot again.

```
PRINT M(2,2)
```

and get 0. ERASE M re-initialized *all* cells of array M to zero. We can, of course, reload them by:

...RUN

and verify the results by:

```
PRINT M(2,2)
```

---

Row 2 Col. 2 = 7

---

We must ERASE an array before reDIMensioning it, or will get a "Duplicate Definition" error. It isn't often necessary to reDIMension.

## Okay, Now What Do We Do With It?

Good question. Everything we learned in the last Chapter on Arrays applies. We've only rearranged the deck chairs on this Titanic -- the end result is unaffected.

At this point, what we've learned is best utilized for calling up and loading relatively unchanging DATA. It is placed in a matrix so it can be accessed and compared, processed or otherwise put to work. Typical applications are:

1. Technical Tables: Instead of looking up the same information in tables, store the tables in DATA Lines and let the Computer look them up and do any needed calculations. The time saved may quickly pay for the Computer.

2. Price Quotes: I saw this approach used by a lumber yard to furnish fast quotes on building materials, and by a printing shop for fast quoting of all sorts of printed matter. The programs are written so simply that customers just belly up to the counter, answered the computer's questions, and get their quote right on the screen and printer.

The latest prices on paper products and printing costs are held in DATA Lines and "spun up" into the Matrix at the beginning of the day. The customer responds to a "Menu" on the screen, and answers some questions on quantity and quality. The quote is calculated, and PRINTed.

When DATA is loaded in externally, either via the keyboard or disk, we obviously don't want to have to go through that loading process *each time* we want an answer. It's important therefore, to never let execution END. Always have it come back to a screen "Menu" of choices, or at least a simple INPUT statement. If an END is hit, the matrix crashes and the DATA has to be reRUN to reload it.

## String Matrices

So far we have concentrated on *numeric* arrays. They can also be used to hold letters or words, using the same rules learned in the Chapters on Strings, including CLEARing enough String space.

String matrices need String names. Make these subtle changes in the resident program.

```
10 DIM M$(10,5)

35   READ M$(R,C)

40   PRINT M$(R,C),
```

...and RUN.

Absolutely no difference! We changed to a string matrix but the data is all numeric. Strings handle numbers as well as letters, but not vice-versa.

Let's change the DATA to words and try it again. Change:

```
10 CLS : DIM M$(5,5)
20 FOR R=1 TO 5
90 PRINT : LIST
100 DATA ALPHA,BRAVO,CHARLIE,DELTA,ECHO,FOXTROT,
    GOLF,HOTEL
110 DATA INDIA,JULIETTE,KILO,LIMA,MIKE,NOVEMBER,
    OSCAR,PAPA,QUEBEC
120 DATA ROMEO,SIERRA,TANGO,UNIFORM,VICTOR,
    WHISKEY,XRAY,YANKEE
```

SAVE as STRMAT and RUN.

Stop for a moment and contemplate the string-comparing and string-handling techniques we learned a few Chapters ago. Your mind should be running flat out at this point, considering the possibilities.

## How About Mixing Strings And Numerics?

Oh! Funny you should ask. That's why we ran all numbers in a string matrix, then all words with that same program. They mix very well, as long as the mixer is a string matrix and not a numeric one.

We have one final program. It is designed for demonstration only, but could be expanded to INPUT the DATA from disk and be quite usable. It demonstrates some important possibilities and programming techniques.

## The Objective

The objective of this demo program is to allow a church treasurer to keep track of who gave what, when. Could use the same program with a service club, bowling league, or any organization that has a membership and dues. We want to be able to access every member's record by name, and get a readout on his status.

Let's start with the DATA. Type this in the NEW program:

```
1000 REM  * DATA FILE *
1010 DATA 07.0185,JONES,15
1020 DATA 07.0185,SMITH,87
1030 DATA 07.0185,BROWN,24
1040 DATA 07.0185,JOHNSON,53
1050 DATA 07.0185,ANDERSON,42
```

The first number in each DATA Line employs "data compression", that is, "encoding" several pieces of information into one number. This number contains the Month, Date and Year in one 6 digit number. (Using string techniques, we could easily strip them apart again if we wished, for special reports.) Single precision will hold the 6 digits accurately.

The second thing we've done with this first number is protect the leading 0. Since months below October are identified by only one digit, the leading 0 would be lost in these months and the number changed to only 5 digits. There are other ways to get around that problem, but we put in a decimal point just to act as an unmovable reference.

The second element in each DATA Line is the *name*. We could put in the full name, and if we used a comma would of course have to enclose the name in quotes.

The third element in each DATA Line holds the amount of money tendered on that date.

Obviously, a full DATA set would contain many entries for each week, and many weeks in a row. We don't need to enter that much DATA to demonstrate the principles involved, and want to keep it short and to the point.

This DATA must now be READ into a string matrix (displaying it as we go).

```
10 CLS : PRINT
20 FOR E = 1 TO 5 : PRINT E,  'LOAD 5 ENTRIES
30  FOR D = 1 TO 3            'LOAD DATE, NAME AMT
40   READ R$(E,D)
50   PRINT R$(E,D),           'TEMP ARRAY PRINTOUT
```

```
60   NEXT D
70   PRINT
80 NEXT E
100 PRINT : "ENTRY #","DATE","NAME","AMT $"
```

SAVE as RECORDS1 and RUN.

Very good. The Matrix is loaded, and its accuracy confirmed on the screen. We see the first 5 bookkeeping entries from July 1, 1985.

Now that we know it loads OK, we can remove some of the test software. Change these Lines:

```
20 FOR E = 1 TO 5                    'LOAD 5 ENTRIES
```

Delete Lines 50 and 70

...and RUN.

Good. We still get the heading, but the matrix contents display is gone. Now, how can we interrogate the Matrix to pull an individual member's record? Guess we first have to ask a question. Type:

```
90 INPUT "WHOSE RECORD ARE YOU SEEKING";N$
```

Then we have to write the program to scan the matrix and compare N$, the name we INPUT, with each element, R$(E,D), until we find a match. This means setting up the FOR-NEXT loops again and scanning every element. Add:

```
110 FOR E = 1 TO 5
120   IF R$(E,2) = N$ THEN 160
130 NEXT E
140 PRINT N$; "IS NOT IN THE FILE."
150    PRINT : GOTO 90
```

```
160 PRINT E,R$(E,1),R$(E,2),R$(E,3)

170   PRINT : GOTO 90
```

SAVE as RECORDS2 and RUN.

Answer with names that are in the DATA Lines, and those that are not. Lines 150 and 170 have built-in defaults back to the question.

The key Line is #160. It PRINTs 4 things:

E The entry Number on that date

R$(E,1) The Date in the memory cell just *preceding* the one containing the member's name

R$(E,2) The Name

R$(E,3) The Amount

If you have trouble visualizing what Line 160 is doing, add this temporary Line. It PRINTs the *address* of each DATA element just below it, and is very helpful:

```
165 PRINT E, E;1, E;2, E;3
```

...and RUN.

Again, the preceding program was not written to be a model of programming style and efficiency -- but to teach the basics of loading and retrieving "record-keeping" type information from a Matrix.

**EXERCISE 41-1:** Write a program that fills a two dimension string array with:

```
JONES, C.       10439       100.00
ROTH,J.         10023        87.24
BAKER,H.        12936       398.34
HARMON,D.       10422        23.17
```

**EXERCISE 41-2:** Sort the names of the array in Exercise 41-1 alphabetically. Don't forget to keep the rest of the information on each row with the original name. This Exercise will be a challenge. Think it through carefully.

**EXERCISE 41-3:** If you survived Exercise 41-2, try sorting the array in increasing order by the numbers in Column 3.

## Learned In Chapter 41

| Statements | Miscellaneous |
|---|---|
| ERASE | Multi-Dimension Arrays |
| | String Arrays |
| | Data compression |

# PART 7
# SOUND

## Chapter 42

# A Cheap Buzz

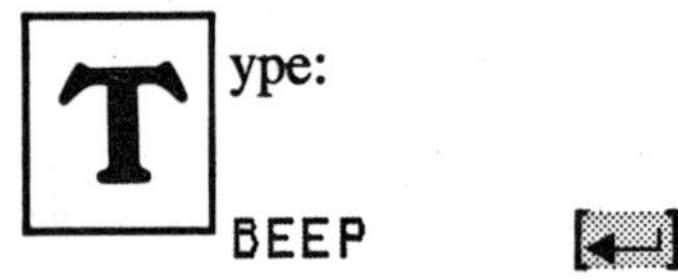

Type:

```
BEEP          ↵
```

Sorry if that scared the dog! Just couldn't resist it. It is widely incorporated in programs as an alarm to indicate something.

Sure...do it again. We'll wait.

Since our Computer has a "Real Time Clock", we can use it as a "time is up" alarm. Just include BEEP in the program. It also makes a great audio prompter, telling the operator it's time to do something. The applications are virtually endless.

The BEEP is just a simplified form of:

```
PRINT CHR$(7)          ↵
```

Try it.

Technically, what we heard is called The BELL, and ASCII 7 makes it ring. Buzzers have pretty well replaced bells, so we'll usually refer to it as a buzzer, alarm, or something more contemporary.

Type in this NEW program:

```
10 CLS : PRINT
```

```
20 INPUT "ENTER A NUMBER TO DIVIDE INTO 100";X
30 IF X <> 0 THEN 60
40 BEEP : PRINT "I CAN'T DIVIDE BY ZERO!"
50 GOTO 20
60 PRINT "100 /";X;"="100/X
70 PRINT : GOTO 20
```

...and RUN.

SAVE as ERROR0

Enter some familiar numbers and try 0. The Computer tells all. The noise can be interpreted as a chastisement for trying to divide by 0. Your imagination can take it from there.

Here's another program using BEEP, LOCATE, POS, CSRLIN, and the Print Screen button (only if you have a printer).

```
10 CLS : KEY OFF
20 READ A$
30 X=POS(0) : Y=CSRLIN
40 LOCATE 25,1
50 IF A$ = "END" THEN 120
60 BEEP
70 PRINT " INSERT ";A$;" DISK AND STRIKE A KEY       ";
80 IF INKEY$=""THEN 80
90 LOCATE Y,X
100 PRINT TAB(32)A$
110 FILES : PRINT : PRINT : GOTO 20
120 PRINT "THAT'S ALL THE DISKS, ";
130 PRINT " PRESS <"CHR$(24)"><PrtSc> ";
140 PRINT "WHEN PRINTER IS READY";
150 IF INKEY$<>"F" THEN 150
```

NOW, FOR MY NEXT NUMBER...
OH NO! NOT TOCCATA and FUGUE AGAIN!

```
160 KEY ON : CLS : END
170 DATA GAMES,SYSTEM MASTER,VISICALC,GRAPHICS
180 DATA END
```

SAVE as DIRS.

Change the DATA Line 170 to suit your own needs.

This one allows us to get a hard copy LISTing of the DIRectories of our disks. In Line 20 we READ the name of a disk. The Computer then instructs us, with the help of BEEP, to insert that disk in the default drive and uses FILES to put the directory on the screen. We then loop back to READ another DATA item. After all the disks have been READ, the Computer tells us to press ⇧ [Prt Sc]. After the dump is finished, hit **F** to end. We can really do the screen dump anytime the screen is full.

The point of this is that the BEEP statement is used mostly to alert the user about something. It may tell us to do something, or alert us we've made an error or we just zapped a Klingon.

However, (as we segway into the next Chapter), BEEP is pretty limited as far as Music is concerned...

## Learned In Chapter 42

### Functions

BEEP

# Chapter 43

# The SOUND Of Music

Fortunately, our use of sound isn't limited to the single tone of the BEEP statement. The full range of frequencies useable by most human ears is available to create our concertos with. Move over Beethoven!

For example type:

```
SOUND 440,18        [↵]
```

We hear a perfect concert pitch A of 440 cycles per second, for about 1 second.

In the last Chapter we used BEEP as a prompt. Now type:

```
SOUND 800,4
```

Sound familiar? It is the frequency used by the BEEP statement, and sounded for 4 internal "clock ticks", or about 4/18 = .22 seconds.

The SOUND statement plays a specific frequency for a specific duration, and we do the specifying. The first number is the frequency in cycles per second or Hz. The second number is the duration in clock ticks. The clock ticks about 18 times per second.

Now try:

```
SOUND 550, 0.01
```

"This is a test of the Emergency Broadcast System..."

For some reason a duration of .01 makes the note play forever. Now for our next project ... Wait! How do I turn the fool thing OFF!? Just hit [Ctrl] [Break].

If we happen to have an acoustic Modem for communicating over the phone line, put it in originate Mode and type:

```
SOUND 2100, 25
```

We must use the chart shown below to determine the frequency of the note we want to play. Let's listen to the range of sounds we can do. Type in this program:

```
10 FOR X=37 TO 2000 STEP 10
20  SOUND X, 65
30  PRINT X,
40 NEXT X
50 CLS : PRINT "SECOND LOOP"
60 FOR X=2000 TO 20000 STEP 250
70  SOUND X,5
80  PRINT X,
90 NEXT X
```

SAVE as RANGE

...and RUN.

It sounds terrible because we're going up the musical scale without regard to musical "intervals". We must choose the notes more "chromatically". Try this NEW program:

```
10 SOUND 523,7
20 SOUND 880,7
30 SOUND 698,7
```

...and RUN.

| Note | Freq | Note | Freq | Note | Freq | Note | Freq |
|---|---|---|---|---|---|---|---|
| C2 | 65 | A3 | 220 | F#5 | 740 | C7 | 2489 |
| C#2 | 69 | A#3 | 233 | G5 | 784 | C#7 | 2637 |
| D2 | 73 | B3 | 247 | G#5 | 831 | D7 | 2794 |
| D#2 | 78 | C4 | 262 | A5 | 880 | D#7 | 2960 |
| E2 | 82 | C#4 | 277 | A#5 | 932 | E7 | 3136 |
| F2 | 87 | D4 | 294 | B5 | 988 | F7 | 3322 |
| F#2 | 93 | D#4 | 311 | C6 | 1047 | F#7 | 3520 |
| G2 | 98 | E4 | 330 | C#6 | 1109 | G7 | 3729 |
| G#2 | 104 | F4 | 349 | D6 | 1175 | G#7 | 3951 |
| A2 | 110 | F#4 | 370 | D#6 | 1245 | A7 | 4186 |
| A#2 | 116 | G4 | 392 | E6 | 1319 | A#7 | 4435 |
| B2 | 123 | G#4 | 415 | F6 | 1397 | B7 | 4699 |
| C3 | 131 | A4 | **440** | F#6 | 1480 | C8 | 4978 |
| C#3 | 139 | A#4 | 466 | G6 | 1568 | C#8 | 5274 |
| D3 | 147 | B4 | 494 | G#6 | 1661 | D8 | 5587 |
| D#3 | 156 | C5 | 523 | A6 | 1760 | F#8 | 5919 |
| E3 | 165 | C#5 | 554 | A#6 | 1865 | G8 | 6271 |
| F3 | 175 | D5 | 587 | B6 | 1976 | G#8 | 6645 |
| F#3 | 185 | D#5 | 622 | D#8 | 2093 | A8 | 7040 |
| G3 | 196 | E5 | 659 | E8 | 2217 | A#8 | 7459 |
| G#3 | 208 | F5 | 698 | F8 | 2349 | B8 | 7902 |

We could use a different statement for each note, as above, but we're into advanced stuff now so let's cut down the programming by using READ-DATA statements. Type NEW and then we'll start over again:

```
10 CLS
20 READ N,L
30 IF N = 0 THEN END
40 PRINT N;L,
50 SOUND N,L
60 SOUND 32767,2
70 GOTO 20
500 DATA 523,7,523,7,784,7,784,7,880,7,880,7,784,16
599 DATA 0,0
```

...and RUN.

Yes, yes, I'm sick of Twinkle Twinkle too, but now that we have it started, we might as well finish it:

```
510 DATA 698,7,698,7,659,7,659,7,587,7,587,7,523,16
```

```
520 DATA 784,7,784,7,698,7,698,7,659,7,659,7,587,16
530 DATA 784,7,784,7,698,7,698,7,659,7,659,7,587,16
540 DATA 523,7,523,7,784,7,784,7,880,7,880,7,784,16
550 DATA 698,7,698,7,659,7,659,7,587,7,784,7,1047,16
```

SAVE as TWINKLE

...and RUN.

We simply READ in a pair of numbers, the frequency and duration, and PLAY them in Line 50. A rest is needed between notes in our masterpiece. By selecting 32767 as the frequency in Line 60, the SOUND is out of the audible range, giving a note that only the dog will enjoy.

Now let's try for a song with a little more programming built in. Since we don't think in clock ticks, let's use timing numbers that make more sense, and let the program do the converting for us. How about 1 divided by the actual note length? Quarter notes would be 4, eighth notes would be 8, and whole notes would be 1.

Delete Lines 500-550 and change Line 50 to:

```
50 SOUND N,(1/L)*18
```

and let's put in some DATA:

```
500 DATA 659,1,587,4,523,8,659,4,587,8,523,2,1047,2,880,
    4,1047,1
```

...and RUN.

SAVE as SWANEE

...and RUN.

Hey, that doesn't SOUND too bad. Since this phrase is repeated, we can use the same DATA Line. We could retype them, but why not use the EDITor and change Line numbers? Type EDIT 500 and then type 520. Hit [←] and do a LIST. Both Lines 500 and 520 are exactly the same.

NOW, FOR MY NEXT NUMBER...

We must be careful when doing this. It's very easy to get GOTOs or GOSUBs mixed up when just changing individual Line numbers like this. When we use the RENUM statement, all of that is taken care of for us.

Now add Lines 510 and 530:

```
510 DATA 784,1,659,2,523,2,587,.5
530 DATA 784,2,659,4,523,8,587,2,587,2,523,1
```

SAVE as "SWANEE"

...and RUN.

*(Hey man, where's the gig?)*

## Learned In Chapter 43

### Statements

SOUND

# Chapter 44

# A Tune Or Two

(Non-Disk users should skip this chapter)

dvanced BASIC users (BASICA) have the added capability of a musical "language" to make PLAYing songs much easier. By just saying PLAY "A" the Computer will PLAY the note A. For example type:

```
PLAY "CEG"
```

(Major Key)

and those 3 notes C, E, & G are PLAYed. We'll use the upper registers now, and come back down later. Isn't that how Maynard started out? If we want to PLAY sharp or flat notes we insert a # or - after the name of the notes. For example:

```
PLAY "CE-G"
```

(Minor Key)

will PLAY the notes C, E flat, and G. Also:

```
PLAY "CEG#"
```

(Augmented)

will PLAY the notes C, E and G sharp. Now you don't have to be a Bach or Beethoven to use Music with your IBM. A good ear helps, however, and *real* talent is always in short supply.

In addition to the names of the notes, we can also specify the Length of a Note, Octave, Tempo, and style.

We have a full 7 octaves, numbered 0-6. For example type:

```
10 REM  * CLOSE ENCOUNTERS  *
```

```
20 PLAY "MST120O3"

30 PLAY "L4CDO2B-O1B-O2L1F"
```

SAVE as ENCOUNTR

...and RUN.

Here's how it works.

Line 10: The MS says PLAY every note "stacatto", (3/4 of the Length specified later). T120 specifies the Tempo as 120 beats per second. O3 means use the notes in the 3rd Octave.

Line 20: L4 says make the note Length 1/4 notes. The actual note length is 1/n. Sixteenth notes are L16, half notes are L2, and a whole note is be L1. We then start PLAYing the notes. First a C and a D, then we jump down to O2 with a B flat, drop one more octave to O1 and PLAY another B flat, then back up to Octave 2 to PLAY a whole note F.

We also have 5 Music string modifiers to change the way all the notes are PLAYed. We already talked about MS, Music Stacatto.

MN is Music Normal. Every note will be PLAYed 7/8 of the time specified by the Length statement.

ML is Music Legato. Every note will be PLAYed the full Length of what's specified.

MF is Music Foreground. The Computer waits until each note is played before continuing. This is the normal default mode.

MB is Music Background. This places the string in a buffer so our program can continue execution while the music is being PLAYed. For example:

```
PLAY "MBO2CDEFGABO3CDEFGABO4CDEFGABL1O5C"
```

PLAYs 3 octaves of the musical scale.

There are also 3 more commands that are used by the PLAY statement. To

THAT STACCATO GOTCHA, HUH?

PLAY a specific note (0 through 84) we can use:

```
PLAY "N20"
```

To PLAY the 20th note, or G in Octave 1 (the second octave). N0 is a rest.

If we want a pause we can use P in our music string:

```
PLAY "L4CP4DP4EP4FP4G"
```

The length of the pause is determined by the current value of L.

The X command eXecutes a certain string to be PLAYed:

```
10 LAMB$ = "EDCDEEE"
30 PLAY "XLAMB$;"
```

...and RUN.

To PLAY it low and slow add:

```
20 PLAY "O1T60"
```

For a high and fast etude, try:

```
20 PLAY "O5T240"
```

Now let's try a whole song. An old college fight song:

```
10 REM  * SAN DIEGO STATE FIGHT SONG  *
20 CLS : PRINT
30 INPUT"ENTER TEMPO (32-255)";Z
40 PLAY "T=Z;O3"
50 A$ = "B-2P4F4A2P4F4G2F2D1"
```

```
60 B$ = "D4D4C#4D4F4F4C#4D4A2A-4G1P4"
70 C$ = "C4C4O2B4O3C4E-2D4C4O2B-2O3D2F1E4E4F4F#4G4G4F#
        4G4A4P4G#4P4A4F4G4A4"
80 D$ = "D4D4C#4D4F2F#2G1P4G4F#4G4O4C2O3B-2F#2E-2D2F2A2G2B
        4G4B-4G4B-2O4C2O3B-1"
90 REM *  BEGIN PLAYING  *
100 PLAY "MSMBF2"
110 PLAY "XA$;XB$;XC$;XA$;XD$;"
130 COLOR 7 : CLS
140 END
```

SAVE as FIGHT

...and RUN.

The four parts of the song are assigned to strings A$, B$, C$ and D$ in Lines 50-80. We then play the parts in Line 110. Notice section A is repeated after PLAYing section C.

We can execute a display subroutine while PLAYing background music. Type in the remainder of the program.

```
120 GOSUB 1000
1000 REM  * SUBROUTINE TO PRINT CHARACTERS  *
1010 COLOR 23
1020 FOR V = 1 TO 300
1030   E$ = CHR$(INT(RND*241+14))
1040   X = INT(RND*79)+1
1050   Y = INT(RND*24)+1
1060   LOCATE Y,X
1070   PRINT E$;
```

```
1080 NEXT V
1090 RETURN
```

SAVE again as FIGHT.

...and RUN.

The entire song is played staccato in the background.

Hooray for our team!

## Learned In Chapter 44

**Statement**

PLAY

# PART 8
# MISCELLANEOUS

# Chapter 45

# PEEK and POKE

PEEK and POKE are BASIC words that allow us to do "non-BASIC" things. They provide the means whereby we can PEEK into the innards of the Computer's memory, and if we wish, POKE in new information.

It is not our purpose here to become an expert in machine language programming, nor on how the Computer works. We have to approach this and related topics a little gingerly lest we fall over the edge into a Computer abyss (or is it an abysmal Computer?).

We do know, however, that computers do their thing entirely by the manipulation of numbers. Therefore, when we PEEK at the contents of memory, guess what we'll find? Numbers? Very good! (Ummmyass).

**MEMORY MAP**

| Decimal Address | Hex Address | Function |
|---|---|---|
| 0 | 00000 | UP TO 64K READ/WRITE |
| 65535 | 0FFFF | MEMORY ON SYSTEM BOARD |
| 65536 | 10000 | UP TO 192K MEMORY |
| 262143 | 3FFFF | IN I/O CHANNEL |
| 262144 | 40000 | 384K FUTURE MEMORY |
| 655359 | 9FFFF | IN I/O CHANNEL |
| 655360 | A0000 | RESERVED |
| 671743 | A3FFF | |

## MEMORY MAP

| Decimal Address | Hex Address | Function |
|---|---|---|
| 671744 | A4000 | GRAPHICS/DISPLAY |
| 720896 | B0000 | MONOCHROME DISPLAY BUFFER |
| 753664 | B8000 | COLOR/GRAPHICS |
| 786431 | BFFFF | |
| 786432 | C0000 | 192K MEMORY EXPANSION |
| 983039 | EFFFF | |
| 983040 | F0000 | RESERVED |
| 999423 | F3FFF | |
| 999424 | F4000 | 48K SYSTEM ROM |
| 1048575 | FFFFF | |

**Figure 45-1**

The Memory Map in Figure 45-1 shows that large chunks of the Computer's memory are reserved or "mapped" for very specific uses. The BASIC ROM for example, uses byte addresses 999424 through 1032192 (commonly referred to as 1 MEGAbyte). All numbers we talk about here are decimals, not hex, octal, binary or Sanskrit.

The range of the numbers we can PEEK or POKE is 0 to 65535 (64K). But that's just our Read/Write user memory. We obviously have *many* more addresses than 0-65535. Our 16 bit IBM Computer allows us to use up to 256K of memory (if we have it installed), beyond the range of our usual PEEK and POKE. In order to access these additional memory addresses, we use the DEF SEG statement. This statement DEFines the SEGment of memory that we will PEEK or POKE at a given time.

But it isn't as easy as it sounds. We must give the DEF SEG statement the address of the segment we want, *divided* by 16. When the DEF SEG statement gets an address, *it* automatically multiplies it by 16.

Turn the Computer off to clear out memory, wait a minute, turn it back on, bring up BASICA and type in this NEW program:

```
10 DEF SEG = 62464

20 N = 8200

30 PRINT N, PEEK(N), CHR$(PEEK(N))
```

```
40 N = N + 1

50 GOTO 30
```

Let's analyze the program before RUNning it.

Line 10 sets the SEGment of memory to the beginning of ROM. The actual highest absolute address is 62464 * 16 = 999424 (F4000 Hex).

Line 20 sets the *beginning* address where we want to start PEEK-ing. As Figure 45-1 shows, there are lots of good places to go spelunking, and we can change Line 20 to start wherever we want.

Line 30 PRINTs three things:

1. The address -- that is, the number of the byte, the contents of which we are PEEKing.

2. The contents of that byte, expressed as a decimal number between 0 and 255.

3. The contents of that address converted to its ASCII character. (Many of the ASCII characters are not PRINTable. Go back to the Chapter on ASCII if *your* memory has grown dim.)

OK, now. RUN the program, being ready to freeze it with [Ctrl] [Num Lock] if you see something interesting. It can also be STOPped at any time with [Ctrl] [Break], and restarted with CONT [←] without having to start all over again with N at 8200.

Didn't see anything interesting? What did you find starting at address 9141? You have to be able to read vertically as the letters swish by.

Change N to start at different places in memory and PEEK to your heart's delight. You can't goof up anything by just PEEKing. It's indiscriminate POKEing that gets one into trouble.

The command level is very handy for resetting the starting address. Change the value of N by just typing:

[Ctrl] [Break]

```
N = 15000        [↵]
```

for example, then:

```
CONT        [↵]        (or [F5])
```

instead of RUN.

When done PEEKing, and having seen far more information than can possibly be absorbed, rework Line 30 to read simply:

```
30 PRINT CHR$(PEEK(N));
```

...and RUN.

It PRINTs only the ASCII characters, horizontally, and is the ideal program to RUN when friends visit. Just act casual about the whole display and avoid any direct questions. Makes a great background piece for a science fiction movie.

When you find an interesting spot, hit [Break], then:

```
PRINT N        [↵]
```

at the command level to find out where in memory we are PEEKing. (Don't you wish we could explore the corners of our minds as easily?)

CONTinue on when ready.

Having degenerated from PEEKing to leering, we'd better move on.

## Careless POKEing Can Leave Holes...

Before POKEing, we'd better see that we're not POKEing a stick into a hornets' nest. It's with the greatest of ease that we destroy a program in memory by POKEing around where we shouldn't.

Obviously there is no use POKEing the ROM area since ROM stands for Read Only Memory. It's not changeable. The rest of the "Memory mapped" area, from 12288 thru 17384 is reserved for specific things, so best not to POKE in there while we're just bungling around. Anything above 17384 should be available memory, unless taken up with our BASIC program or required for processing. With such a short program as ours we surely can't goof anything up? Can we?

Let's PEEK around 10000 and see if anything is going on there. Change these 3 program Lines to:

```
10 DEF SEG
20 N = 10000
30 PRINT N; PEEK(N),
```

...and RUN.

```
10000  0   10001  0   10002  0   10003  0   10004  0
10005  0   10006  0   10007  0   10008  0   10009  0
10010  0   10011  0   10012  0   10013  0   10014  0
10015  0   10016  0   10017  0   10018  0   10019  0
```

etc.

This default value of DEF SEG means set the segment to the beginning of where BASIC stores its programs. This may be as high as 25000 in Disk BASICs.

What we see are the address numbers and their contents, in easy-to-read parallel rows. Unless you've been messing around with other programs since power-up, you should just see nice rows of 0's. The memory at these locations is in "neutral", waiting to be used.

Great! Write a NEW program, POKE in some information and do something with it. Make it read:

```
10 REM  * POKE PROGRAM *
20 DEF SEG
30 N = 10000
40 READ D
```

HEE HEE HEE
HO HO HA
HEE HEE HEE
THAT TICKLES!
JES' POKIN', BUDDY!

```
50 POKE N,D
60 N = N + 1
70 IF N = 10011 THEN END
80 GOTO 40
100 DATA 80,69,69,75,45,65,45,66,79,79,33
```

Before RUNning, let's analyze it.

Line 20 sets the SEGment to the beginning of program storage.

Line 30 initializes the starting address at 10000.

Line 40 READs a number from the DATA Line.

Line 50 POKEs the DATA "D" into address "N".

Line 60 increments the address number by one.

Line 70 ENDs execution after we've POKEd in all 11 pieces of DATA.

Line 80 sends us back for more DATA.

Line 100 holds the DATA we are going to POKE into memory.

...now RUN.

Well, that was sure fast. I wonder what it did? How can we find out? Should we PEEK at it? Yes, but let's leave the old program in and just start a new one at 200.

```
200 REM * PEEK PROGRAM *
210 FOR N = 10000 TO 10010
220  PRINT N, PEEK(N)
230 NEXT N
```

...and RUN 200.

```
10000   80
10001   69
10002   69
10003   75
10004   45
10005   65
10006   45
10007   66
10008   79
10009   79
10010   33
```

How about that? We really *did* change the contents of those memory locations. We shot the numbers from our DATA Line right into memory. Now if we only knew what those numbers stood for. Wonder ... if we changed them to ASCII characters, would they tell us anything?

Add:

```
205 CLS
220 LOCATE 13,30 + N-10000
225 PRINT CHR$(PEEK(N));
```

to PRINT at a certain location on the screen

...and RUN 200.

That's how PEEK and POKE work.

## Learned In Chapter 45

| Statements | Miscellanous |
|---|---|
| PEEK | Memory Map |
| POKE | |
| DEF SEG | |

## Chapter 46

# Special POKE Addresses

### Function Keys

Let's take one more look at our 10 special function keys. We'll leave Keys 2-5, 7 and 8 alone since they seem to be pretty useful, but why don't we change the others? After all, this *is* a *personal* computer. Enter this NEW program:

```
10 KEY 1, "LIST" + CHR$(13)
20 KEY 6, "EDIT "
30 KEY 9, "AUTO" + CHR$(13)
40 KEY 10, "CLS" + CHR$(13)
50 DEF SEG : POKE 106,0
```

...and RUN.

SAVE this program as "KEYS". Notice the bottom row on the display, with our new creations. We perform the POKE in Line 50 to avoid complications on the INPUT buffer. This is a good idea when ever we program any of the "soft" keys, or after INKEY$ has received the last character from a Soft Key string.

Perhaps the most used of these keys will be [F10]. When we get in the habit, it's so convenient to just hit a single key to CLear the Screen. To use [F10] there can't be anything on the screen on the same Line as the cursor, or we'll get a Syntax error. Best in that case to use [Ctrl] [Home] instead.

Suppose we like this new "soft key" arrangement so much that we want the Computer to automatically power-up with it, instead of what comes with the Computer. Disk users have a beautiful feature called AUTOEXEC.BAT that bypasses typing in the DATE and TIME and AUTOmatically EXECutes a command, such as LOAD BASIC. So, let's add one more line before we go back to DOS:

```
60 KEY ON : NEW
```

Be sure to SAVE the program as "KEYS" *before* you RUN it.

We put in the NEW command so the program will erase itself after the Keys are reprogrammed.

We include here the process without explanation for the thrill seekers among us who can't leave well enough alone. If you aren't a thrill seeker (or don't own a disk system) skip ahead to the Video Display Buffer section.

First return to DOS (SYSTEM) and make the prompt read:

```
A>_
```

Now (temporarily) take the write-protect tab off the **COPY** of your System Master disk you've been using, and type:

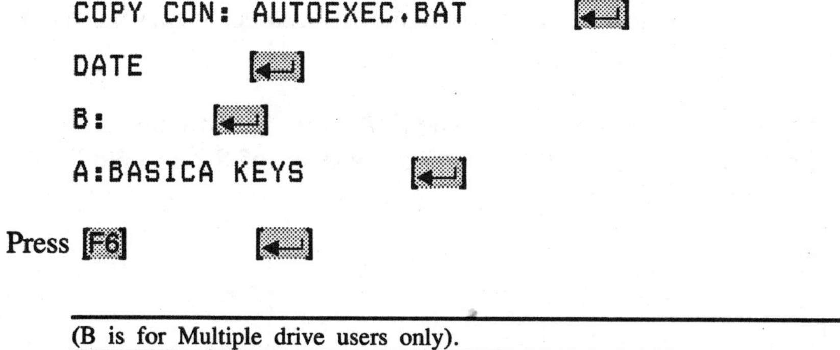

```
COPY CON: AUTOEXEC.BAT
DATE
B:
A:BASICA KEYS
```

Press F6

(B is for Multiple drive users only).

And the Display reads:

```
1 file(s) copied
```

The first instruction copies from the CONsole (keyboard) into the file AUTOEXEC.BAT. After we type in the DATE, the rest of the routine takes care of the startup process we have to go through. We could also make the last Line simply:

```
A:BASICA
```

That way we wouldn't have to RUN a program, just load BASICA. Replace the write-protect tab on the System Master disk. Reset the Computer by simultaneously pressing the [Alt] [Ctrl] and [Del] keys.

The Computer will AUTOmatically power-up with the soft keys programmed as before, and will continue each time the Computer is Reset or turned on, as long as we use the same System Master disk. Other disks could be prepared for other automatic soft key programming, or a variety of BASIC programs held on 1 disk and called up for different purposes as needed.

## Video Display Buffers

Beginning at absolute address B0000 hex (720896 decimal (704K)) is a 4K memory buffer on the monochrome display card. Since there are 2000 print positions on the screen, we need 2 memory locations for each screen position.

The first location holds the actual ASCII code for the character (an even numbered address). The second is the "attribute" for the corresponding character (odd address). The attribute tells us what mode the character was printed in, such as high intensity, underlined, blinking, etc.

We already know about ASCII codes. The code for the attribute is a little harder to understand. Each byte of address is made up of 8 bits. We'll label the bits as follows:

128 - □
064 - □
032 - □
016 - □
008 - □
004 - □
002 - □
001 - □

Why not label the bits 1,2,3,4,...8? Well, the numbers shown are the actual ASCII numbers that activate the respective bits. CHR$(128) activates or "sets" the top one, and CHR$(1) sets the bottom one. CHR$(7) sets the bottom three (4 + 2 + 1).

It all goes back to binary math. (Oh, great!) If we send a decimal 1 (0000 0001 binary), the bottom bit is set. A decimal 2 (0000 0010 binary) sets bit 2. A decimal 3 (0000 0011 binary) sets bits 1 and 2 and so on.

So what does all this mean? It means that when we PEEK at an odd address in the buffer, we see a coded attribute of the ASCII character in the memory location just *preceding* it.

Let's look at the chart again and find out what the different bits mean:

128 - ☐ Flash
064 - ☐
032 - ☐ Background
016 - ☐
008 - ☐ Intensity
004 - ☐
002 - ☐ Foreground
001 - ☐ Underline

If the bottom 3 bits are set (1+2+4) the character is normal white on black.

If the 5th, 6th, and 7th bits are set (16+32+64=112) the *character* is *reversed* (black on green, *background* is ON, *foreground* is OFF).

If we take a normal character and set the top "flash" bit, the attribute changes from 7 (1+2+4) to 135 (1+2+4+128). If we then set the 4th "Intensity" bit, we will have a high intensity flashing character with attribute 143 (1+2+4+8+128).

If we set the bottom underline bit only, we will have a normal underline character. If we then set the Top bit our character will flash with an underline (attribute 129). Etc. Do you follow the grand plan?

To get a better feeling for all this LOAD in the COLOR1 program from Chapter 37 and make the following changes:

```
210 DEF SEG = &HB000
```

```
220 REM  SEGMENT IS MONOCHROME DISPLAY BUFFER
230 PRINT
240 FOR X=0 TO 30 STEP 2
250    IF X=16 THEN PRINT
260    PRINT PEEK(X); PEEK(X+1),
270 NEXT X
```

SAVE as COLOR2.

...and RUN.

We immediately recognize the numbers 67,79,77,80, etc. as the ASCII codes for the letters of the word "COMPUTER". The other numbers are the attributes we just learned. For example the first "M" is high intensity so its attribute is 15 (1+2+4+8), and the bottom 4 bits are set.

## POKEing Characters

Now that we have done some PEEKing, let's do some POKEing to the video screen. ENTER this short NEW program:

```
10 DEF SEG = &HB000
20 REM  45056 DECIMAL = 720896 ABSOLUTE
30 CLS
40 FOR X =0 TO 255
50    POKE 2*X, X
60 NEXT X
70 LOCATE 6,1
```

...and RUN.

Nothing new here. But look carefully at positions 8-13 and 28-31. We discovered some new characters! We can use these fancy new characters only by POKEing to the video memory. For example, let's see some of these codes in action. Type from the command level:

```
PRINT CHR$(30);
```

THE GUY YOU WANT LIVES NEXT DOOR!
29½
MOM

the cursor jumps up and partly erases what we typed. 30 is the code for cursor up. Now type:

```
CLS
POKE 1500,30
```

a triangle appears to the right. In both cases we used code 30, although CHR$ treats it as a control code.

**EXERCISE 46-1:** Write a program which displays the word POKE centered in the top line of the video display, using the POKE statement instead of PRINT.

## Learned In Chapter 46

### Miscellaneous

AUTOEXEC.BAT
Video Display Buffers
Character Attributes

# Chapter 47

# Logical Operators

In classical mathematics (fancy words for simple ideas), there exist what are known as the "logical AND", the "logical OR", and the "logical NOT".

## So The One Cow Said to the Other Cow...

In Figure 47-1, if gate A AND gate B AND gate C are open, the cow can move from pasture #1 to pasture #2. If any gate is closed, the cow's path is blocked.

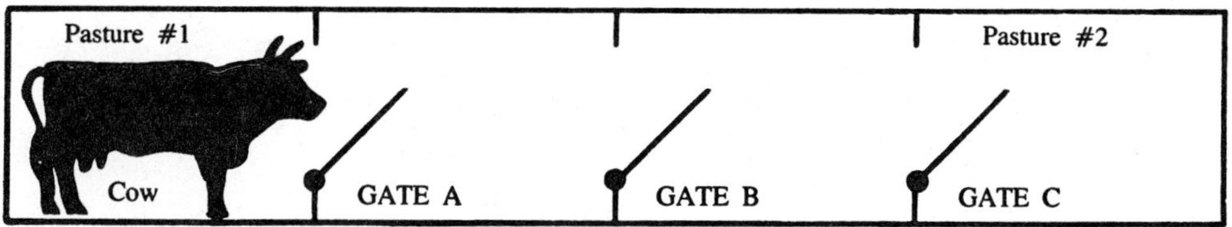


**Figure 47-1**

The principle is called "logical AND".

In Figure 47-2, if gate X OR gate Y OR gate Z are open, then old Bess can move from pasture #3 to #4. That principle is called "logical OR". These ideas are both pretty logical. If the cow can figure them out surely we can!

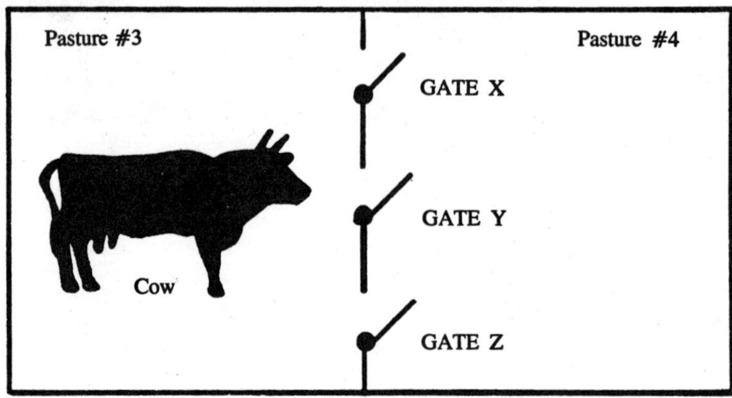


**Figure 47-2**

Using these ideas is very simple. Type this NEW program:

```
10 INPUT "IS GATE 'A' OPEN";A$
20 INPUT "IS GATE 'B' OPEN";B$
30 INPUT "IS GATE 'C' OPEN";C$
40 PRINT
50 IF A$="Y" AND B$="Y" AND C$="Y" THEN 80
60 PRINT "OLD BESSIE IS SECURE."
70 END
80 PRINT "ALL GATES ARE OPEN."
90 PRINT "OLD BESSIE IS FREE TO ROAM."
```

...and RUN.

Answer (Y/N) the questions differently during different RUNs to see how the logical AND works in Line 50.

## Where Is the Logic in All This?

You should by now understand every part in the program, except perhaps Line 50.

> Lines 10, 20, and 30 INPUT the gate positions as *open* (which we defined as equal to "Y"), or *closed* (defined as "N"). We could have defined them the other way around and rewritten Line 50 to match, if we'd wanted to.

JEEPERS! HOW DID YOU GET IN HERE?
THE NAME'S BESSIE and GATE C WAS OPEN-

Line 50 is the key. It reads, literally, "If gate A is *open*, AND gate B is *open*, AND gate C is *open*, then go to Line 80. If any one gate is closed, report that fact by defaulting to Line 60.

Imagine how this simple logic could be used to create a super-simple "computer" consisting of only an electric switch on each gate. Add a battery and put a light bulb in the farmer's house. The bulb could indicate if any of the gates are open. Such a "gate-checking" computer would have only three memory cells -- the switches.

Hmm. It would do the job a lot cheaper than an IBM ... but would be awfully hard to play *Invaders* with.

**EXERCISE 47-1:** Using the above program as a model, and the "OR logic" seen in Figure 47-2, write a program which will report Bess' status as determined by the position of Gates X, Y and Z.

## Teacher's Pet

Here is a simple program which uses > instead of the equals sign in a logical test. The student passes if he has a final grade over 60 OR a midterm grade over 70 AND a homework grade over 75. Enter this NEW program, RUN it a few times, and see how efficiently the logical OR and logical AND tests work in the same program Line (40).

```
10 INPUT "FINAL GRADE";F

20 INPUT "MIDTERM GRADE";M

30 INPUT "HOMEWORK GRADE";H

40 IF (F>60 OR M>70) AND H>75 THEN 70

50 PRINT "FAILED"

60 END

70 PRINT "PASSED"
```

Does this give some idea of the power and convenience of logical math? The actual "cut off" numbers could, of course, be set at any level.

## Logical Variations

This next program example mixes equals, greater-than and less-than signs in the same program. It determines and reports whether the two numbers we INPUT are both positive, both negative, or have different signs.

Analyze the program. Note the parentheses. Although they are not necessary, they tell us to shift our thinking to "logical". Type it in and RUN.

```
10 INPUT "FIRST NUMBER IS";F
20 INPUT "SECOND NUMBER IS";S
30 IF (F>=0) AND (S>=0) THEN 70
40 IF (F<0) AND (S<0) THEN 90
50 PRINT "OPPOSITE SIGNS"
60 END
70 PRINT "BOTH POSITIVE OR ZERO"
80 END
90 PRINT "BOTH NEGATIVE"
```

## NOT

In addition to the logical AND and OR functions, we have what is called logical NOT. Here is how it can be used:

```
10 INPUT "ENTER A NUMBER";N
20 L = NOT(N>5)
30 IF L = 0 GOTO 60
40 PRINT "N WAS NOT GREATER THAN 5"
50 END
60 PRINT "N WAS GREATER THAN 5"
```

...and RUN.

Line 2Ø is obviously the key one, containing NOT. If the statement in Line 2Ø is *true* (namely, that N is NOT larger than 5), the Computer makes the value of L=-1. The test in Line 3Ø then fails.

If, on the other hand, N IS larger than 5, the statement is *false* and the Computer makes the value of L = Ø.

True = -1 and False = Ø. (Time for the primal scream, again. All together, now...)

## More Logical Operators

As if these 3 *logical* operators weren't enough, the IBM Computer allows use of 3 more "Logical" words. They are (in order of appearance):

EQV, XOR, and IMP.

To help see how these things work, let's write a "testbed" program into which we can install them.

```
10 INPUT "ENTER A VALUE FOR X";X
20 INPUT "ENTER A VALUE FOR Y";Y
30 IF (X<10) AND (Y>10) THEN 60
40 PRINT : PRINT"CONDITION WAS FALSE"
50 END
60 PRINT : PRINT"CONDITION WAS TRUE"
```

...and RUN.

INPUT the number 5 for X and 15 for Y. No big deal. Both comparisons were true, which made the AND condition true.

## OR

Replace the AND in Line 3Ø with OR and RUN. Try different numbers to get a feel for the program.

# EQV

There are several more "advanced" logical operators. EQV stands for EQuiVa-lence. Replace the OR in Line 30 with the word EQV.

```
30 IF (X<10) EQV (Y>10) THEN 60
```

The condition in Line 30 will be true only if both arithmetical comparisons are the same. Only if X is less than 10 AND Y is greater than 10, OR if X is *not* less than 10 AND Y is *not* greater than 10.

Try the number 5 for X and 15 for Y. Both tests pass so the overall condition is true.

Try 15 for X and 5 for Y. Both conditions are false, but since they are *both* the same (false in this case) the overall condition is true and execution jumps to Line 60.

# XOR

XOR stands for eXclusive OR. This means that if one *and only one* test passed, the overall condition will be true.

Replace the EQV in Line 30 with the word XOR. RUN with different numbers. Try 5 for X and 15 for Y. Execution falls through to Line 40 because *both* tests pass. Remember if we were using the regular OR, the overall condition would be true.

# IMP

Our final operator is IMP which stands for IMPlication. This is probably the hardest to understand. The IMP condition will be *true* for all conditions except when the first test is *true* and the second test is *false*. The *overall condition* is then *false*. Replace the XOR with an IMP:

```
30 IF (X<10) IMP (Y>10) THEN 60
```

...and RUN.

Try 5 for both X and Y. These numbers give us a *false* condition. All other conditions are *true*.

## Order of Operations

When trying to figure out which gets calculated first in the thick of a "humongous" equation, here's the pecking order:

Those operations buried deepest inside the parentheses get resolved first. The idea is to clear the parentheses as quickly as possible. When it all becomes a big tie, here's the order:

1. Exponentation -- a number raised to a power.

2. Negation, that is, a number having its sign changed. Typically, a number multiplied times -1.

3. Multiplication and division -- from left to right.

4. Addition and subtraction -- from left to right.

5. Less than, greater than, equals, less or equal to, greater or equal to, not equal to -- from left to right.

6. The logical NOT.

7. The logical AND.

8. The logical OR.

9. The logical XOR.

10. The logical EQV.

11. The logical IMP

## And In Conclusion

Logical math is worth the hassle. As one last fun program, enter and RUN this "Midnight Inspection." Line 1ØØ checks each response for a NO answer (instead of a YES). Using logical OR, it branches to the "no-go" statement (Line 12Ø) if any one of the tests is negative ("N").

```
10 CLS
20 PRINT "ANSWER WITH 'Y' OR 'N'."
30 PRINT
40 INPUT "HAS THE CAT BEEN PUT OUT";A$
50 INPUT "PORCH LIGHT TURNED OFF";B$
60 INPUT "ALL DOORS/WINDOWS LOCKED";C$
70 INPUT "IS THE T.V. TURNED OFF";D$
80 INPUT "THERMOSTAT TURNED DOWN";E$
90 PRINT:PRINT
100 IF A$="N" OR B$="N" OR C$="N" OR D$=
    "N" OR E$="N" THEN 120
110 PRINT "           GOODNIGHT":END
120 PRINT "SOMETHING HAS NOT BEEN DONE."
130 PRINT "DO NOT GO TO BED"
140 PRINT "UNTIL YOU FIND THE PROBLEM!"
150 GOTO 30
```

In most cases, AND and OR statements are interchangeable if other parts of a program are rewritten to accommodate the switch.

## Learned in Chapter 47

### Miscellaneous

Logical AND
Logical OR
Logical NOT
Logical EQV
Logical XOR
Logical IMP
Order of Operations

# Chapter 48

# A Study Of Obscurities

IBM BASIC has some features that are not used by most beginning programmers. Their use presumes special applications and requires knowledge which is really beyond the scope of this book. In the interest of completeness, however, abbreviated descriptions of what they are and how they are used are included in this Chapter.

## USR

The USR Function has a variety of uses, most of them having little to do with BASIC. It allows us to "call" or "gosub" a program written in ASSEMBLY language, and "return" back to the main BASIC program when it's finished. To make much sense of USR you'll need ASSEMBLY language skills -- a whole book in itself.

## USR In Use

Without getting out too deep in the water, we must first DEFine the address that our machine language routine starts at with the DEF USR statement. Up to 10 machine language routines can be DEFined at once.

For example, if a program starts at 32000 (offset into the current SEGment), then try:

```
DEF USR3 = 32000
```

To CALL the non-existent machine language program at 32000 from BASIC we would say:

```
X = USR3(1)
```

Hmmm. We've seemed to have lost control.

Press [Alt] [Ctrl] [Del] to Reset the Computer, then return to BASICA.

There is no way to predict what may result from calling a non-existent USR program.

To get a little taste for Machine language let's try the classic example of a screen "White out", or in our case a "Green out". In order to get our Machine language routine ready we will POKE the numbers (or the *object* code) into high memory. Type in:

```
10 DEF SEG
20 DEF USR = 10000
30 FOR X = 0 TO 13
40  READ P
50  POKE 10000+X,P
60 NEXT X
70 INPUT "HIT ENTER TO DO IT"; A$
80 X = USR(0)
90 FOR X = 1 TO 5000 : NEXT X : CLS
100 DATA 183,112,184,0,6,185,0,0
110 DATA 186,79,24,205,16,203
```

SAVE as "GREENOUT" *before* you RUN it. Double check the DATA to be sure it's correct. POKEing around with numbers in memory is the easiest way to lose a program or lock up the Computer.

...and RUN.

In Line 80 we tell the Computer to execute the program beginning at the address we specified with the DEF USR statement (10000 in this example).

Lines 100 and 110 contain the instructions to "green out" the screen.

## CALL

The CALL Function is a lot like USR. CALL allows us to set certain parameters for use in the machine language program. A typical CALL statement might look like this:

```
CALL 58000
```

It tells the Computer to execute the program beginning at memory address 58000.

Without getting out too deep in the water, there are storage areas called registers that hold information needed by a machine language subroutine. This information is passed through the registers to our program via CALL.

```
CALL 58000(A,B,C$,D...etc.)
```

tells the Computer to execute the program at address 58000 and passes the data stored in A,B,C$,D...etc. to the machine language program.

That's as far as we're going to press our luck on this one right now. We don't want to leave so terror-struck that we won't continue.

Machine and Assembly language programming books are readily available for that small percentage of readers who want to pursue the subject. You at least have a sufficient introduction to nod your head and smile knowingly when others try to impress you with their knowledge of these things. Consult your Owner's manual for more details.

## OUT

Let's see what OUT does. Connect a Cassette Recorder to the PC. Remove the Cassette from the recorder, and leave the hatch open so we can see the drive hub. Press the PLAY key, and type in this NEW program:

```
10 INPUT"64 = ON & 72 = OFF";N
20 IF N = 0 GOTO 10
```

```
30 OUT 97,N
40 GOTO 10
```

...and RUN, answering the INPUT? and watching the drive hub.

We are sending directions OUT to Port 97, the recorder Port, and telling the motor to be either ON or OFF.

We have to be careful what numbers are INPUTted in this program.

Some numbers cause the keyboard to lock up tight. If you fell into this trap, turning off the Computer is the only way out.

That's a sample of what OUT does. Nuff said.

## OUT Ports

Here are some of the key Port descriptions.

| PORT | ARGUMENT | DESCRIPTION |
|---|---|---|
| 97 | 64 | Cassette motor ON |
| 97 | 67 | Activate speaker |
| 97 | 72 | Speaker OFF and Cassette motor OFF |
| 952 | 0 | Turn OFF power to screen |
| 952 | 1 | Disable screen, can still use Cursor |
| 952 | 9 | Enable screen display |
| 1010 | 16 | Turn ON drive A |
| 1010 | 33 | Turn ON drive B |

## INP

The PC has 65536 "ports" or channels of communication with the "outside world". They are numbered from 0 to 65535. Because this subject is worthy of an entire book itself, we will only learn enough here to get an elementary "feel" for it.

CompuSoft Publishing will release a book titled *Controlling The World With Your IBM PC* (by your favorite author) which takes the beginner all the way through advanced applications of the IBM using digital information INPut and OUTput via these 65536 ports.

Only two of these ports in the IBM will be considered here. Port numbers 97 and 98 control the Cassette Recorder. Most of the other ports are available to take in information or send it out via adapter boards within the Computer.

You're not going to "Control The World" with what you learn about ports in this Chapter, but enter this program and you may be surprised at what INP (IN Port) can do.

```
10 OUT 97,64        'TURNS ON CASSETTE MOTOR
20 S = INP(98) : PRINT S,
30 IF S<48 GOTO 60
40 PRINT "DATA IS FLOWING FROM CASSETTE"
50 GOTO 20
60 PRINT "NO DATA COMING FROM CASSETTE"
70 A = A+1 : IF A = 100 GOTO 90
80 GOTO 20
90 OUT 97,72        'TURNS OFF CASSETTE MOTOR
```

Place a program tape in the recorder. (The Rolling Stones or any other raucous noise will do nicely. If it sounds like real music this demonstration may not work). Set the volume where you usally do, and press PLAY. Type RUN.

Haha! Didn't expect that, did you?

Here's how it works:

Line 10 Turns on the Cassette motor.

Line 20 Looks at Port #98 and reads a coded message, then PRINTs that code.

---

The Computer cannot take in data from the Cassette Port until the motor is turned on.

---

Line 30 Tests that code number. If it is less than 48, *execution branches to Line 50*. If not, it defaults to:

Line 40 Returns execution to Line 20 where we begin the "polling" of the Port again.

Line 60 Is a counter that will branch to Line 80 after 100 no-data counts are reached.

Line 80 Turns off the Cassette motor.

Astute observers have probably noted that there is a definite pattern to the numbers displayed. Why these particular numbers appear is beyond the scope of this book. The point is, DATA either *is* or *isn't* flowing into the Computer, and this is what INP reads, and acts upon.

If you want to have a little fun, play the tape again but adjust the volume control very carefully (down around 2) so that variations in data flow are sensed and appear as changes in the message on the screen. Doesn't take much imagination to go from this point to different kinds of visual displays.

One more view of INP. Enter this NEW program, and RUN.

```
10 FOR N = 900 TO 959
20 PRINT N; INP(N),
30 NEXT N
```

This program scans a small fraction of the Ports and tells us their status.

## WAIT

The WAIT statement ties right in with INP and OUT. It is used as a Port monitor. When a program encounters the WAIT statement, it WAITs for a certain value to be INPUT from a Port. For example:

```
WAIT 98,16,4
```

tells the Computer to WAIT until a non-zero value is produced when the byte value at Port 98 is eXclusively ORed with the byte value of 4, and the result logically ANDed with the byte value of 16. (Oh well ... back to bird watching!) When this condition is met, program execution continues at the next statement. If the last byte value (4 in the example above) is omitted from the WAIT statement, the Computer assumes its value to be 0.

If you get stuck in an endless loop, just hit [Ctrl] [Break] to get out of it.

Each value listed in the WAIT statement must be between 0 and 255 (the range of values that can be held in an 8 bit memory cell).

## VARPTR

While VARPTR (short for VARiable PoinTeR) is found in this IBM BASIC, it's about as far from main-Line BASIC as anything we have.

## Take A Deep Breath

If a variable is *numeric*, VARPTR tells us the *location* of the *first byte* of the number stored in that variable.

If it's a *string* variable, VARPTR tells us where in memory the *INDEX* to the variable is located. Read that last Line carefully. We don't want anyone getting lost.

VARPTR doesn't have the common decency to point to the location of the *contents* of a *string* variable. Instead, it points to a three byte "index" to the variable. The three bytes contain:

1. The *length* of the string.
2. The least significant byte (LSB) of the *starting location* of the string.
3. The most significant byte (MSB) of the *starting location* of the string.

To actually find the *contents* of the string variable, we have to calculate the location using bytes 2 and 3 of the "index" to that variable. Sound complicated? Well, it is a bit tricky, but this example should clarify matters a bit.

Enter this NEW program:

```
10 REM  * STRING VARIABLE LOCATER *
```

THAT'S PRETTY OBSCURE.
USR
VARPTR
PORTS
LSB MSB

```
20 CLS
30 A$ = "12345"
40 X = VARPTR(A$)
50 PRINT "THE INDEX TO A$ IS AT";X
990 PRINT : LIST
```

...and RUN.

Line 40 uses VARPTR to store the address of the index to A$ in X. Line 50 PRINTs it.

We haven't found the *contents* of A$ yet, just the *index*. Hang in there. Add:

```
60 L = PEEK(X+1) + 256*PEEK(X+2)
70 PRINT "A$ IS HIDING AT LOCATION";L
```

...and RUN.

So that's where the little rascal is. Line 60 uses some fancy footwork to convert bytes two (X+1) and three (X+2) of the index (X) into the actual location L of A$. Line 70 PRINTs the *address* value.

How could we prove that we have found the correct location? Sure. PEEK at the contents of A$ and compare it with "12345". Add:

```
80 FOR I=L TO L+4
90   PRINT CHR$(PEEK(I)),
100 NEXT I : PRINT
```

...and RUN.

Satisfied? The 5 digits in A$ are stored in 5 consecutive memory locations.

Now, knowing where a variable is located in memory may not seem too useful at first blush, but it has some surprising consequences. Once we have found the location of a string variable, we can modify its contents. Try this change:

```
100 READ N : POKE I,N
```

```
110 NEXT I : PRINT A$ : PRINT
120 DATA 204,205,203,206,202,185
```

...and RUN. Then RUN again!

Surprise! We poked graphic codes into an unsuspecting "normal" string variable and transformed it into a pictorial masterpiece. Line 90 PRINTed the 5 "pieces", and Line 110 assembled the puzzle.

Type:

```
PRINT A$
```

to be sure we aren't just dreaming. Yes, we actually modified the contents of A$ by using VARPTR to *find* the string, then POKEing in new numbers. These computers can be downright fun once we get to know them.

Look at Line 30. Did we do that? I'm afraid so. A LISTing containing the actual graphics doesn't affect the program.

Leave with this thought. We packed a "dummy" string with only 5 graphic codes. A string variable *can* hold up to 255 characters (about one eighth of the video display). Just imagine what we could do with strings packed with up to 255 cursor control codes, graphic codes, and special character codes! If that doesn't push your imagination to overload, you might as well trade this computer in for a $4.95 calculator.

## SWAP

The SWAP Function lets us exchange the position of two variables with ease. Type:

```
10 CLS
20 PRINT "INPUT A + B SEPARATED BY COMMA";
30 INPUT A,B
40 PRINT : PRINT "A =";A,"B =";B,
50 SWAP A,B
60 PRINT "SWAPPED",
70 PRINT "A =";A,"B =";B
```

```
80 PRINT : LIST
```

...and RUN.

It works with string variables, too. Try changing every A and B to A$ and B$. INPUT a pair of names and watch what happens.

## Learned In Chapter 48

| Statements | Functions |
| --- | --- |
| OUT | USR |
| INP | VARPTR |
| WAIT | SWAP |
| SOUND | |

# Chapter 49

# Advanced SAVEing, MERGEing, and CHAINing

Everyone type in this NEW program:

```
10 REM LINE 10
20 REM LINE 20
40 REM LINE 40
```

We know this program is not destined for fame, but SAVE it on disk anyway. Each program SAVEd to disk becomes a FILE. Like any file, it is labeled with a file name. We will call this program FIRST. Type:

```
SAVE "FIRST"
```

BASIC programs can be SAVEd on disk in either of 2 "formats". Unless we specify otherwise, the so-called "compressed format" is used.

1. In the *compressed* format, everything that can be abbreviated is stored in a shortened form. All numbers except those enclosed in quotes are stored in a minimum number of bytes, with BASIC keywords like PRINT and GOTO stored as special shorthand "codes". This format is the one usually used, and is fine for most purposes since it conserves disk space. This is all "invisible" to the user.

2. But there are times when we will sacrifice a little disk space for the luxury of saving a program or data on disk in the "character for character" format. It is called the "ASCII format".

ASCII formatted files have several special purposes.

1) They can be loaded directly into word processing programs for easy editing. A word processor's "search and replace" capacity is a great way to make massive "global" changes in BASIC programs or other files.

2) Files in ASCII format can be sent over phone Lines to other computers. Electronic mail is here!

3) And, the ASCII format can be used to MERGE two files -- either hook them end-to-end, overlay one on top of the other, or intermesh their Line numbers. Using ASCII format, we can MERGE a useful routine into several programs without retyping it. (Remember our SGN subroutine?)

## Merging Files

Let's try a MERGEr right now. Type this NEW program:

```
30 REM THIS LINE GOES BEFORE LINE 40
40 REM THIS LINE REPLACES LINE 40
50 REM THIS LINE APPEARS AFTER LINE 40
```

and SAVE it:

```
SAVE "SECOND",A
```
(Look carefully!)

The ",A" causes it to be SAVEd in ASCII format.

Now we can MERGE the two programs. LOAD the original program back into memory:

```
LOAD "FIRST"
```

then:

```
LIST
```

to be sure only the FIRST program is in memory. Now bring in the next program by typing:

```
MERGE "SECOND"
```

LIST to verify that programs were MERGEd.

```
10 REM LINE 10
20 REM LINE 20
30 REM THIS LINE GOES BEFORE LINE 40
40 REM THIS LINE REPLACES LINE 40
50 REM THIS LINE APPEARS AFTER LINE 40
```

Of course it worked! Look very carefully. We have *new* Lines 30 and 50, and the original Line 40 was *replaced* by Line 40 from the incoming file.

Observe that the FIRST program did not have to be in ASCII format, only the second one drawn in for MERGEr. If we wish to MERGE 2 programs and their Line numbers conflict, RENUMber them first.

The combined program can be SAVEd as usual under any name. Let's use:

```
SAVE"MERGER"
```

## Removing Files from the Diskette

The 2 program files, FIRST and SECOND, are now combined into a MERGEd file, "MERGER", and SAVEd on disk. They are no longer necessary. Right?

What's that about a safety copy of the program?

Yes, we *should* keep an extra copy of any important program and right now, FIRST and SECOND are the only protection we have if MERGER should somehow get zapped. What if we erased them and a nasty electrical spike sizzled the MERGER file?

A safety backup copy is normally made on a different diskette. Since we are

W-W-WHAT HAPPENED?
GASP
I MERGED WITH A MACK TRUCK!
WHEEZE

only risking 5 Lines of code at this point, we'll gamble with Murphy's law and make our safety copy of the MERGER program on the *same diskette*.

Since we can't SAVE the same program on the same diskette under the same name, we have to give it another name. Rather than have to remember an excessive number of names, just type:

```
SAVE "MERGER.BAK"
```

By appending the "." and the three letter "extension" "BAK", we create a second file with the same "first name" (MERGER) as our original. The extension "BAK" reminds us that the program is a safety BAcKup, and thus a duplicate, not a different program. .SAF for SAFety, .COP for COPy, .NO1 for Number 1 and other extensions can work as well.

## KILL - KILL!

Now we can erase the 2 original files with a clear conscience. From BASIC, type:

```
KILL "FIRST.BAS"      [ENTER]
KILL "SECOND.BAS"     [ENTER]
```

Check the disk DIRectory by typing:

```
FILES     [ENTER]
```

to make sure FIRST and SECOND have disappeared.

The KILL instruction doesn't actually "erase" FIRST and SECOND from the diskette. It simply removes their *names* from the DIRectory. The result is the same, however; if they can't be found they can't be used. (Sort of like having an unlisted telephone number).

(To answer the question in some readers minds, *YES*, with a special UTILITY program we could conceivably patch up the DIRectory and retrieve our "dead" files. Of course, if another new file is SAVEd first and it happens to use the same place on the disk, the file(s) is lost for good. For all intents and purposes, consider the files KILLed.)

We can also reNAME programs from BASIC. Suppose we want to change the name of the backup copy to NEWMERGE. No problem. Just type:

```
NAME "MERGER.BAK" AS "NEWMERGE"
```

Check the DIRectory with FILES to be sure that MERGER.BAK is gone and NEWMERGE took its place. Note that NEWMERGE has no .BAS or .BAK since none was specified.

## CHAINing

The ability to CHAIN programs is very powerful. Not only can we RUN one program by calling it from another, but the values of the variables can be transferred from one program to the next without being reset to Ø. Try this:

```
NEW

10 REM  * THIS IS THE FIRST PROGRAM

30 CLS : PRINT "PROGRAM ONE"

40 M$ = "IBM PERSONAL COMPUTER"

50 A = 20

60 PRINT "M$ = ";M$

70 PRINT "A =";A

80 RUN "TWO"
```

SAVE as "ONE" but **do not RUN it!** Type NEW and ENTER these Lines:

```
10 REM  * THIS IS THE SECOND PROGRAM

20 PRINT : PRINT "PROGRAM TWO"

30 PRINT "M$ = ";M$

40 PRINT "A =";A : PRINT
```

SAVE it as "TWO", but *do not RUN*. Now, from the command level type:

```
RUN "ONE"
```

Note very carefully that the String and Numeric variables were *not* carried over from the first to the second program. We used a RUN statement to execute "TWO". Remember RUN initializes all variables back to 0 or null. Now:

```
LOAD "ONE"
```

and change Line 80 to:

```
80 CHAIN "TWO",,ALL
```

SAVE as "ONE"

...and RUN.

Wow! The variables passed from ONE to TWO.

By adding the ALL option, program ONE passed ALL variable data to program TWO. Now let's see what gets placed between the two commas.

Add this Line to program TWO:

```
50 CHAIN "ONE",100,ALL
```

and SAVE as "TWO". Line 50 will LOAD program ONE and begin execution at Line 100. If we don't specify a Line number, it would start ONE running at its first Line again and we would be in an endless loop, or endless CHAIN. If the starting Line number is omitted, as we did in Line 80 of the ONE program, we still have to use the commas as place holders.

Now LOAD "ONE" back in and change Line 80 to:

```
80 CHAIN "TWO"
```

and add the following:

```
20 COMMON M$
99 STOP
```

```
100 PRINT "WE ARE NOW BACK IN 'ONE'"

110 PRINT "M$ = ";M$

120 PRINT "A =";A
```

SAVE as "ONE"

...and RUN.

Here's what happened. Program ONE ran up thru Line 80, where it CHAINed to program TWO. Only M$ was forwarded from ONE.

Since the ALL option was removed from Line 80, all variables were not carried over to the CHAINed program. But, by adding Line 20 we made M$ COMMON to both programs. Variable M$ was forwarded, but A was not. Program TWO ran thru Line 50 where it CHAINed back to Line 100 of ONE. ALL variables were forwarded, but A=0 in TWO, so that's what was printed this 2nd time by ONE.

The Line 99 STOP will never be executed and is not necessary. It was placed there as a reminder that program ONE in this case is really executed as 2 different programs under the same name.

The way to forward only selected variables without CHAINing them all is:

```
20 COMMON M$,A        (etc...)
```

Do it, SAVE as "ONE" and RUN again.

LOAD and LIST both ONE and TWO on the screen at the same time and study them very carefully.

CHAINing and MERGEing have real programming value. What you have learned here will satisfy most programming needs. If you need to use more "advanced" CHAIN and MERGE features, refer to the factory manual.

## Learned In Chapter 49

**Statements**

MERGE
CHAIN
COMMON
NAME

**Commands**

KILL

# PART 9
# PROGRAM CONTROL

# Chapter 50

# Flowcharting

Most of the programs written for this book were simple; but, they met simple, specific needs. Suppose we want to write a program to play chess or bridge, evaluate complicated investment alternatives, keep records for a bowling league or a small business, or do stress calculations for a new building? How would we approach writing such a complex program?

We break down a complex program into a series of smaller programs. This is called *modular programming* and the individual programs are called *modules*. But how are the modules related -- and how do we write them, anyway?

---

Module is just a 75-cent word for "section" or "building block".

---

One way to plan a program is to make a picture displaying its logic. Remember, a picture is worth a thousand words (or is it the other way around)? The picture that programmers use is called a *flowchart*.

Flowcharts are most helpful when kept simple. A cluttered flowchart is hard to read and usually isn't much more helpful than an ordinary program LISTing. A good flowchart is also helpful for "documentation" to give us (or others) a picture of how the program works -- for later on, when we've forgotten.

Flowcharts are so widely used that programmers have devised standard symbols. There are many specialized symbols in use, but we will examine only the most common ones.

BEGIN or END

PROCESSING BLOCK
(something the
Computer does without
making any decisions)

DECISION DIAMOND
(branches off in different
directions, depending on the
decision it makes.)

Each decision point asks a question such as *"Is A larger than B?"* or *"Have all the cards been dealt?"* The different branches are marked by YES or NO.

Another useful symbol is:

CONTINUATION

The circle usually has a number inside it which corresponds to a number on another page if the flowchart is too large for a single sheet.

CONNECTOR ARROWS

Arrows indicate the direction in which program execution proceeds.

There are no hard-and-fast rules about what goes into a flowchart and what doesn't. A flowchart is supposed to help, not be more work than it's worth. It helps us plan the *logic* of a program. When it stops helping and makes us feel like we're back in arts and crafts designing mosaics, we've gone as far as the flowchart will take us (or more typically, it's passed its point of usefulness).

Suppose we want to grade a 5-question test by comparing each of the *students'* answers with the *correct* answer. We can put the correct answers in a DATA statement in the program, enter a student's answers through the keyboard, compare (grade) them, then PRINT the % of correct answers. This procedure can be repeated until all the students' papers are graded.

The flowchart might look like this:

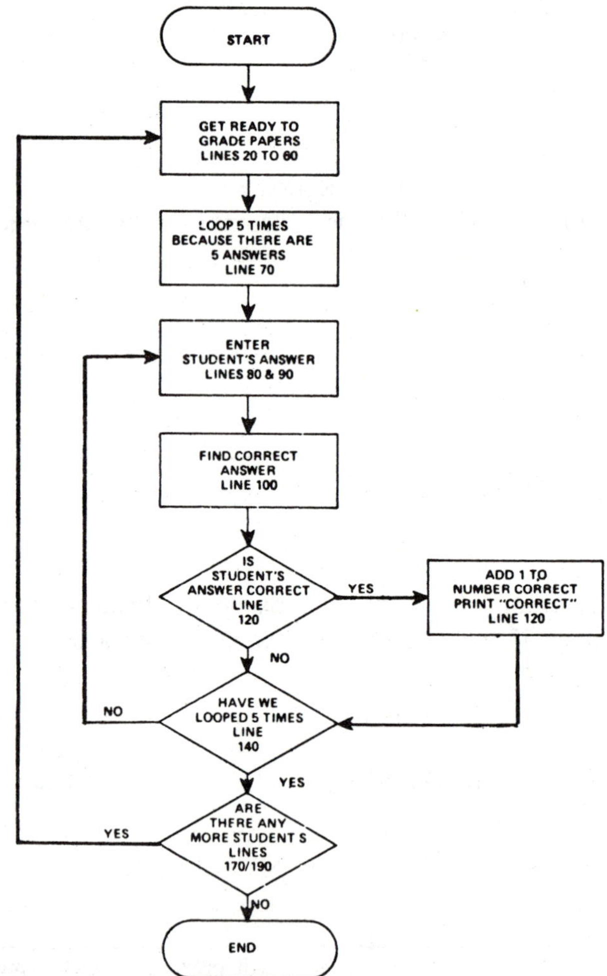

This flowchart has three decision diamonds. In the first, the Computer determines if an answer is correct. In the second, the Computer determines if all the questions in a single student's paper have been graded. The third terminates execution when all tests have been graded.

> **EXERCISE 50-1:** Using the flowchart as a guide, write a program that grades a test having five questions.

For more complicated problems, we may subdivide the flowchart into larger modules. A *master flowchart* will show the relationship between the flowcharts of individual programs.

For example, let's say we want to write a program that calculates the return on various investments. The options might be:

1 - CERTIFICATE OF DEPOSIT

2 - BANK SAVINGS ACCOUNT

3 - CREDIT UNION

4 - MONEY MARKET FUND

The main (or Control) program will select one of these 4 options using an INPUT question, execute the correct sub-program, and PRINT the answer. Its flowchart might be as shown on the next page.

We can now flowchart each of the individual programs in the blocks separately. The Certificate of Deposit program would, for example, have to contain the rate of return, size of deposit, and maturity. The order in which that program INPUTs data and performs the calculations would be specified in its own flowchart.

> **EXERCISE 50-2:** Write the master program as flowcharted, with a branch to a program to calculate the return on a Bank Savings Account paying simple interest.

> **EXERCISE 50-3:** Choose a program from an early Chapter and design your own flowchart.

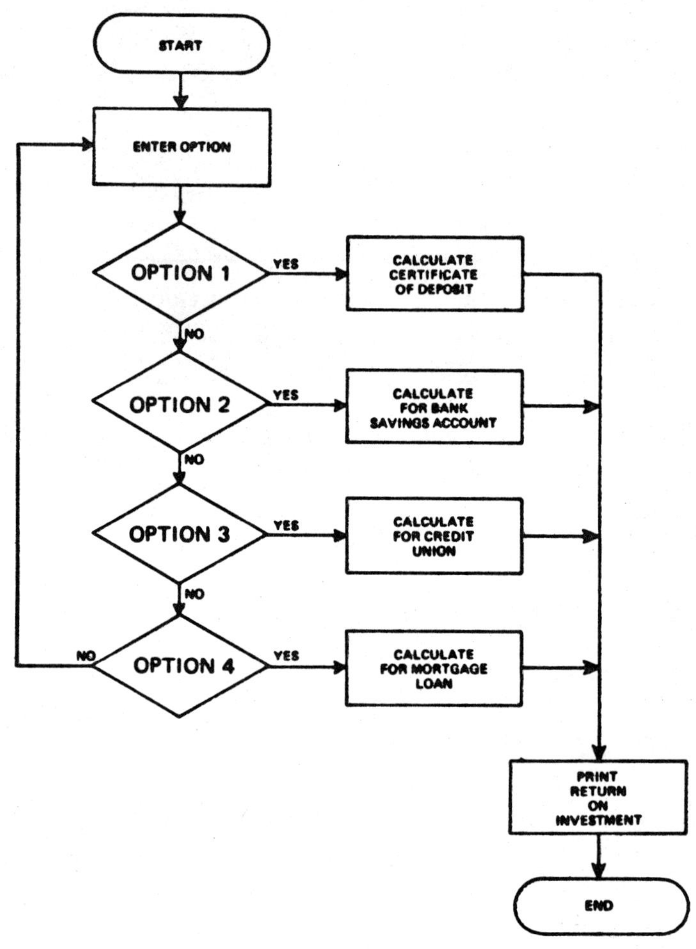
START
ENTER OPTION
OPTION 1
YES
CALCULATE
CERTIFICATE
OF DEPOSIT
NO
OPTION 2
YES
CALCULATE
FOR BANK
SAVINGS ACCOUNT
NO
OPTION 3
YES
CALCULATE
FOR CREDIT
UNION
NO
NO
OPTION 4
YES
CALCULATE
FOR MORTGAGE
LOAN
PRINT
RETURN
ON
INVESTMENT
END

ME
ME
YOU
YOU
I GOT THE MESSAGE! HOO BOY! HE'S EVEN THINKIN' LIKE A PROGRAMMER NOW!

## Learned In Chapter 50

### Miscellaneous

Flowcharting

# Chapter 51

# Debugging Programs

## uick -- The Raid!

The Computer has given us plenty of nasty messages. We know something's wrong, but it isn't always obvious exactly where, or why.

How do we find it? The answer is simple -- *be very systematic. Even experienced programmers make lots of silly mistakes ... but experience teaches how to locate mistakes quickly.*

## Hardware, Cockpit Or Software?

The first step in the "debugging" process is to isolate the problem as being either:

1. A hardware problem,

2. An operator problem, or

3. A software problem.

## Is It Further To Boca Raton Or By Bus?

Starting with the least likely possibility -- is the Computer itself malfunctioning? Chances are very high that the Computer is working perfectly. There are several very fast ways to find out.

*A. Type:*

```
PRINT FRE(0)
```

If there is no program loaded into memory, the answer should be:

```
33402
```

Or the correct value previously noted for your system. If there is a program loaded, the answer should be some lesser value.

If the answer is too large (assuming, of course, you have not added more memory), there may be trouble. Or, it's possible that the answer is a *negative* number. Trouble.

## Possible Solution

In either of the above cases, shut the Computer off. (Or, as they say in the big time, "Take it all the way down.") Let it sit for a full minute before turning it on.

---

Yes, any program in memory will be lost, but at this point it's probably shot anyway. You could *try* to SAVE it before turning OFF the machine if it makes you feel any better.

---

Turn the machine back ON, and try the PRINT FRE(0) test again. If the results are the same, there is probably a chip failure that will require professional troubleshooting and replacement.

*B. One Last Try*

Before full panic sets in, type NEW and enter this program. It assigns almost every free memory location in RAM a specific value, then reads that value back out, comparing it to adjacent values.

Type:

```
5 DIM A(8300)
10 FOR X 1 TO 8300 : A(X) = X : NEXT X
20 FOR Y = 1 TO 8300 : PRINT A(Y);
```

```
30 IF A(Y) - A(Y-1) <> 1 THEN PRINT "BAD" : BEEP
40 NEXT Y
```

After a *short* wait for the array to "spin-up", the monitor should display:

`1 2 3 4 5 6 7 8` (etc. through the value of M)

If the "horn honks" and "BAD" appears, we *may* have found the problem. A bad memory chip.

Type this test program into the Computer, SAVE as "MEMTEST". Try it out *before you need it and hope it will never be used.*

## Video Display Problems?

The Video Display is very similar to its counterpart in a television set. It has adjustments for brightness and contrast on the front of the monitor.

## Idiot Here -- What's Your Excuse?

Of course *you* don't make silly mistakes!

Now that's settled,

1. Is everything plugged in? Correctly? Firmly?

2. Are the drive doors closed?

3. Is the printer turned ON and ON-Line?

4. Are you using "legal" commands?

if so...

Go walk the dog, then check it all over again.

"PHYSICIAN – HEAL THYSELF!"
TSK TSK

## If...Then

If the trouble was not found in the cockpit or with the hardware, there is probably something wrong with the program. Dump out the troublesome program. LOAD in one that is known to work and RUN it as a final hardware and operator check.

## Common Errors

Here are some of the common sources of "computer-detected errors".

1. Assume the error is in a PRINT, or INPUT statement.

Did you:

a. Forget one of the needed pair of quotation marks?
EXAMPLE:

```
10 PRINT "ANSWER IS, X : GOTO 5
```

ERROR: No ending quotation mark after IS

---

Yes, I know it's Ok if the missing quote is the last character in the Line.

---

b. Use an illegal variable name?
EXAMPLE:

```
10 INPUT 6G
```

ERROR: Must be a variable recognizable by the Computer.

c. Forget the Line number, accidentally mix a letter in with the number, or use a Line number larger than 65529?
EXAMPLE:

```
72B3 PRINT "BAD LINE NUMBER."
```

ERROR (pointing to 72B3)

d. Accidentally have a double quotation mark in the text?
EXAMPLE:

```
10 PRINT "HE SAID "HELLO THERE."
```

e. Type a Line more than 255 characters long?

f. Misspell PRINT or INPUT *(It happens!)*

g. Accidentally type a stray character in the Line, especially an extra comma or semicolon?

2. If the error is in a READ statement, almost all the previous possibilities apply, plus:

   a. Is there really a DATA statement for the Computer to read? Remember, it will only read a piece of DATA once unless it is RESTOREd.
   EXAMPLE:

```
10 READ X,Y,Z

20 DATA 2,5
```

   ERROR: There are only two numbers for the Computer to read. If we mean for Z to be zero, we must say so.

```
20 DATA 2,5,0
```

3. If the bad area is a FOR-NEXT loop, most of the previous possibilities apply, plus:

   a. Is there a NEXT statement to match the FOR?
   EXAMPLE:

```
10 FOR A=1 TO N
```

   ERROR: Where's the NEXT A?

Some of these FOR-NEXT loop errors won't trigger actual error messages; the program may just wind up in an endless loop.

   b. Do you have all the requirements for a loop -- a starting point, an ending point, a variable name, and a STEP size if it's not 1?
   EXAMPLE:

```
10 A=1 TO N
```

   ERROR: Must have a FOR and a NEXT.

c. Did you accidentally nest 2 loops using the same variable in both loops?

EXAMPLE:

```
10 FOR X=1 TO 5
20  FOR X=1 TO 3
30   PRINT X
40  NEXT X
50 NEXT X
```

ERROR: The nested loops must have different variables.

d. Does a variable in a loop have the same letter as the loop counter?

EXAMPLE:

```
10 A=22
20 FOR R=1 TO 5
30  R=18
40   Y=R*A
50    PRINT Y
60 NEXT R
```

ERROR: The value of R was changed by another R inside the loop, and NEXT R was overRUN, since 18 is larger than 5.

e. Are the loops nested incorrectly with one not completely inside the other?

EXAMPLE:

```
10 FOR X=1 TO 6
20  FOR Y=1 TO 8
30   PRINT X,Y
40  NEXT X
50 NEXT Y
```

4. If the goofed-up statement is an IF-THEN or GOTO

   a. Does the Line number specified by the THEN or GOTO really exist? Be especially careful of this error when eliminating a Line in the process of "improving" or "cleaning up" a program.

5. The error comes back as "Out of memory" but PRINT FRE(Ø) indicates there is room left. If you are using an array and get an error, remember, **extra room (up to hundreds of bytes) has to be left for processing**. You have probably overRUN the amount of *available* memory.

6. The ERROR comes back as "Subscript out of range".

   a. Did you exceed the limits of one of the built-in functions?

7. Did one of the *values* on the Line exceed the maximum or minimum size for numbers?

To find out whether you did any of these things, PRINT the values for all the variables used in the offending Line. If you still don't see the error, try carrying out the operations indicated on the Line. For example, the error may occur during a multiplication of two very large numbers.

PRINT the operation in calculator mode (no Line number).

These certainly aren't all the possible errors one can make, but at least they give some idea where to look first. Since we can't completely avoid silly errors, it's necessary to be able to recover from them as quickly as possible.

By the way ... a one-semester course in beginning typing can do wonders for your programming speed and typing accuracy.

## From The Ridiculous To The Sublime:

All the Computer can tell us is that we have (or have not) followed all of its rules. Assuming we have, the Computer will not protest even if we're asking it to do something that's quite silly and not at all what we intended. It will dutifully put out garbage all day long if we feed it garbage -- even though we follow its rules. Remember GIGO?

GIGO stands for Garbage In, Garbage Out.

If the program has no obvious errors, what might be the matter?

Typical "unreported" errors are:

1. Accidentally reinitializing a variable -- particularly easy when using loops.
   EXAMPLE:

```
10 FOR N=1 TO 3
20  READ A
30  PRINT A
40  RESTORE
50 NEXT N
60 DATA 1,2,3
```

2. Reversing conditions, i.e. using "=" when we mean "<>", or "greater than" when we mean "less than."

3. Accidentally including "equals", as in "less than or equals", when we really mean only "less than."

4. Confusing similarly named variables, particularly the variable A, the string A$, and the array A(X). *They are not at all related.*

5. Forgetting the order of program execution -- from left to right on each Line, but multiplications and divisions always having priority before additions and subtractions. Intrinsic functions (INT, RND, ABS, etc.) having priority over everything else.

6. Counting incorrectly in loops. `FOR I=0 TO 7` causes the loop to be executed *eight*, not seven, times.

7. Using the same variable accidentally in two different places. This is okay if we don't need the old variable any more, but disastrous if we do. Be especially careful when combining programs or using the special subroutines.

But how do we spot these errors if the Computer doesn't point them out? Use common sense and let the Computer help. The rules are:

1. Isolate the error. Insert temporary "flags". Add STOP, END, and extra PRINT statements until you narrow the error down to one or two Lines.
   EXAMPLES OF USEFUL FLAGS:

```
299 PRINT ,"LINE #299"

399 IF X<Ø THEN PRINT "X OUT OF RANGE AT
     #399" : STOP
```

Line 299 checks whether the Line immediately following Line 299 is executed. Line 399 might be used to locate the point where X goes out of range.

Although the details are different in every program, these techniques can be easily applied.

2. Make "tests" as simple as possible. Don't add "enhancements" until you've found the problem.

3. Check simple cases by hand to test the logic, but let the Computer do the hard work. Don't try to wade through complex calculations with pencil and paper. You'll introduce more new mistakes than you'll find. Use the calculator mode, or a separate hand calculator for that work.

4. Remember that we can force the Computer to start a program at any Line number. Just type:

```
GOTO ###
```

This is a useful tool for working back through a program. Give the variables acceptable values using calculator-mode statements, then GOTO some point midway through the program. If the answers are what are expected, then the error is *before* the "test point". Otherwise, the error is after the test point.

5. Remember that it's not necessary to LIST the entire program just to look at the one section. Type:

```
LIST ###-###
```

6. Practice "defensive programming." Just because a program "runs okay", don't assume it's dependable. Programs that accept INPUT data and process it can be especially deceptive. Make a point of checking a new program at all the critical places.

Examples: A square root program should be checked for INPUTs less than or equal to zero. Math functions should be checked at points where the function is undefined, such as TAN(90°).

## Beware Of Creeping Elegance

Programs grow more elegant with the ego reinforcement of the programmer. This "creeping elegance" increases the chance of silly errors. It's fun to let the mind wander and add some more program here, and some more there, but it's also easy to lose sight of the program's purpose. It is at times like this when the flowchart is ignored and the trouble begins. Nuff said.

### Learned In Chapter 51

**Miscellaneous**

Defensive programming
Computer-detected errors
Flags
Hardware checkout procedures

# Chapter 52

# Chasing Bugs

We have seen that the EDITor is a powerful aid in changing programs once we find out what is wrong. In this and the next Chapter we will learn how to use built-in diagnostic tools to help hunt down the errors.

## TRON/TROFF

The simplicity but power of TRON/TROFF is awesome. Enter this NEW program:

```
10 FOR N = 1 TO 5
20  PRINT "SEE TRON RUN"
30 NEXT N
99 END
```

...and RUN, to be sure it's OK.

Now, type:

```
TRON
```

(which stands for TRacer ON), then RUN. The screen says:

```
[10][20]SEE TRON RUN
[30][20]SEE TRON RUN
```

OH, COME, NOW!

```
[30][20]SEE TRON RUN

[30][20]SEE TRON RUN

[30][20]SEE TRON RUN

[30][99]
```

## What Does It Mean?

The numbers between [ ] are the program Line numbers. TRON traces the sequence of program execution and PRINTs each *Line number* as it is "hit". How's that for powerful?

Now type:

```
TROFF        ⏎
```

(for TRacer OFF) and RUN.

The Tracing has stopped and it's business as usual. TRON is the very essence of simplicity.

Since TRON and TROFF can be imbedded as program *statements* as well as BASIC *commands*, the possibilities for troubleshooting program *logic* are endless. Our little demonstration program is short and error-free, but by adding the following Lines and RUNning.

```
5 TRON

35 TROFF
```

Imagine its value in a program with dozens or hundreds of program Lines all tangled up with IF-THEN's, ON-GOTO's, etc. The errors that drive us wild are those we can't see.

## Learned In Chapter 52

### Commands/Statements

TRON
TROFF

# Chapter 53

# Chasing The Errors

IBM BASIC provides 54 different ERROR messages numbered 1-30 for the Elementary and Intermediate BASIC we have learned, and 50-73 for Advanced or Disk BASIC. There are so many we need a separate Chapter plus an Appendix just to understand what they mean.

Let's quietly tiptoe into the hall of ERRORs by typing this NEW little test program:

```
10  REM * TESTING ERROR CODES *
20 INPUT"CHECK WHICH ERROR CODE";N
30 ERROR N
```

RUN the program a number of times, (entering numbers between 1 and 73), forcing the Computer to PRINT out the message for various types of ERRORs. Don't waste time trying to understand them now. You can study them in detail in Appendix E.

The only new BASIC word is in Line 30. ERROR has little use in life except as above, PRINTing the Error Code from its code number.

## ERROR Trapping

The ON ERROR GOTO statement is of more value. It is used when we think we're on the trail of a specific type of ERROR, but are not sure.

# IBM ERROR CODES

## BASIC ERRORS

| Code | Error |
|---|---|
| 1 | NEXT without FOR |
| 2 | Syntax ERROR |
| 3 | RETURN without GOSUB |
| 4 | Out of DATA |
| 5 | Illegal function call |
| 6 | Overflow |
| 7 | Out of memory |
| 8 | Undefined line number |
| 9 | Subscript out of range |
| 10 | Duplicate definition |
| 11 | Division by zero |
| 12 | Illegal direct |
| 13 | Type mismatch |
| 14 | Out of string space |
| 15 | String too long |
| 16 | String formula too complex |
| 17 | Can't continue |
| 18 | Undefined user function |
| 19 | No RESUME |
| 20 | RESUME without ERROR |
| 21 | Unprintable error |
| 22 | Missing operand |
| 23 | Line buffer overflow |
| 24 | Device timeout |
| 25 | Device fault |
| 26 | FOR without NEXT |
| 27 | Out of paper |
| 29 | WHILE without WEND |
| 30 | WEND without WHILE |
| | **DISK ERRORS** |
| 50 | FIELD overflow |
| 51 | Internal error |
| 52 | Bad file number |
| 53 | File not found |
| 54 | Bad file mode |

| Code | Error |
|---|---|
| 55 | File already open |
| 57 | Device I/O Error |
| 58 | File already exists |
| 61 | Disk full |
| 62 | Input past end |
| 63 | Bad record number |
| 64 | Bad file name |
| 66 | Direct statement in file |
| 67 | Too many files |
| 68 | Device unavailable |
| 69 | Communication buffer overflow |
| 70 | Disk write protect |
| 71 | Disk not ready |
| 72 | Disk media error |
| 73 | Advanced feature |

Suppose we suspect that someplace in the program there is an accidental square rooting of a negative number, and it's goofing up the results. Type in this NEW test program:

```
10 CLS : ON ERROR GOTO 70
20 PRINT
30 INPUT "FIND THE SQUARE ROOT OF";N
40 A = SQR(N)
50 PRINT "SQUARE ROOT OF";N;"=";A
60 GOTO 30
70 BEEP
80 PRINT "SQR ROOT OF NEGATIVE IS ILLEGAL!"
99 END
```

...and RUN.

Try positive values, and 0, then try a negative value.

ON ERROR GOTO is acting much as our old friend ON X GOTO did, so there are no big surprises here.

Change Line 10 to a REM Line and try assorted values, ending with a negative number. Again, no big surprise. An ERROR message was delivered, pinpointing both the nature and location of the ERROR, and execution was terminated. Lines 70 and 80 were *not* executed, however.

Change Line 10 back to:

```
10 CLS : ON ERROR GOTO 70
```

and add:

```
90 RESUME 20
```

...and RUN with various values, including negative.

Although the Computer was forced to operate with an ERROR (negative square root), execution did not terminate. The ERROR message was delivered but the Computer kept on going, thanks to RESUME. This is the essence of good ERROR trapping -- identifying the ERROR without "crashing" the program. There may be several interrelated ERRORs that can be found easily only by continuing the RUN.

Change Line 90 to:

```
90 RESUME NEXT
```

...and RUN.

Although the results are similar to those obtained with:

```
RESUME 20
```

there is a subtle difference.

RESUME NEXT causes execution to RESUME at the NEXT Line immediately following the Line which made the ERROR. Thus Line 50 is PRINTed, even though (in this case) it gives a wrong answer. RESUME 20 directed execution to a very specific Line. With a little head-scratching we can quickly see how both of these features are useful in difficult debugging situations.

Next, change Line 90 to:

```
90 RESUME
```

...and RUN.

As we see and hear, RESUME by itself (or RESUME 0) sends execution back to the Line in which the ERROR is being made. The Computer keeps trying to take the square root of the same negative number. (If you are having difficulty visualizing what is taking place in any of these examples, turn on TRON and read the road map.)

## ERL

Change Line 90 back to:

```
90 RESUME 20
```

and add:

```
85 PRINT "ERROR IS IN LINE #";ERL
```

...and RUN.

The program now informs us that the

```
ERROR IS IN LINE # 40
```

ERL is a "reserved" word that PRINTs the *Line number* in which the ERROR occurs. For my money, this little jewel in combination with ON ERROR GOTO to snag 'em, and RESUME NEXT (or RESUME Line number) to keep the program from crashing, makes this whole hassle worthwhile.

## ERR

A final esoteric touch may be obtained by adding the ERR (not ERL) statement. ERR produces the ERROR code number.

We've gone almost full cycle. Add Line 87:

```
87 PRINT "AND ERROR CODE IS";ERR
```

...and RUN.

Finally, to complete this loop begun several pages ago, add:

```
88 PRINT "WHICH STANDS FOR" : ERROR ERR
```

...and RUN.

...which brings us back to Do, a deer, a female deer...(it must be time to STOP this book -- getting too silly!) Notice that program execution STOPs after the ERROR statement.

## More Variations on the Theme

A very useful application of ERROR traps allows the program to automatically LIST the program if there is an ERROR. It requires the addition of 2 temporary program Lines using all 3 ERROR statements.

From Appendix E (which covers the Error messages) comes an example of what happens when there is an ERROR in a FOR-NEXT loop. Type in:

```
NEW
10 FOR A = 1 TO 5
20  PRINT "THERE IS NO 'NEXT A'"
30 NEXT Z
```

...and RUN.

The Computer responds with:

```
NEXT without FOR in 30
```

There is a FOR-NEXT Error in Line 30. Add the following Lines to approximate the same result, plus cause an automatic program LISTing:

```
5 ON ERROR GOTO 100          to 'set' the ERROR trap

99 END                       to END execution if all is well

100 PRINT ERL,ERR : LIST
```

Line 100 PRINTs the Line # with the ERROR, and the ERROR code (found in Appendix E) and LISTs the program (or LIST ##-##).

Try this "trapping" and "reporting" routine. If all is well in the program, nothing will be different. If there is an ERROR, it will be trapped and reported on the screen. Can you think of ways to make the "reporting" more elegant?

**EXERCISE 53-1:** Enter the following NEW program:

```
20 CLS
30 FOR I=1 TO 10
40   X = RND(21) : F = X-10/X
50   PRINT I,"X=" X,"F(X)= "F;
60   IF F<0 THEN PUNT ELSE PRINT
70   IF X = 20 THEN READ A
80 NEXT I
90 INPUT "PRESS ENTER TO CONTINUE";Z : GOTO 20
```

Write an ERROR trapping routine that recovers from both ERRORs and PRINTs:

```
OUT OF DATA ERROR IN LINE ##
SYNTAX ERROR IN LINE ##
```

or as appropriate.

HINT -- Syntax ERROR is code 2, and Out of DATA is code 4.

## Learned In Chapter 53

| Statements | Functions | Miscellaneous |
|---|---|---|
| ERROR | ERL | ERROR codes |
| ON ERROR GOTO | ERR | |
| RESUME | | |

CONGRATULATIONS, PAL, WE DID IT!! MIND IF I RIP OFF A FEW NOTES OF POMP and CIRCUMSTANCE?
(I ARE A REAL PROGRAMMER)

# SECTION B

# ANSWERS TO EXERCISES

**SAMPLE ANSWER FOR EXERCISE 7-1:**

```
50 PRINT D
```

**SAMPLE RUN FOR EXERCISE 7-1:**

```
6000
```

Note: You may have used a different Line number in your answer but the way to get the answer PRINTed on the screen is by using the PRINT statement. If you didn't get it right the first time don't be discouraged. Type in Line 50 above and RUN the program. Then return to Chapter 7 and continue.

**SAMPLE ANSWER FOR EXERCISE 7-2:**

```
10 REM * TIME SOLUTION KNOWING DISTANCE AND RATE *
20 D = 6000
30 R = 500
40 T = D / R
50 PRINT "THE TIME REQUIRED IS";T;"HOURS."
```

Note: Remember to [↵] each Line.

**SAMPLE RUN FOR EXERCISE 7-2:**

```
THE TIME REQUIRED IS 12 HOURS.
```

Note: In order to arrive at the formula in Line 40 it is necessary to transpose D = R * T and express in terms of T.

**SAMPLE ANSWER FOR EXERCISE 7-3:**

```
10 REM * CIRCUMFERENCE SOLUTION *
20 P = 3.14
30 D = 35
40 C = P * D
50 PRINT "THE CIRCLE'S CIRCUMFERENCE IS";C;"FEET."
```

**SAMPLE RUN FOR EXERCISE 7-3:**

```
THE CIRCLE'S CIRCUMFERENCE IS 109.9 FEET.
```

Note: Since pi is not included in IBM BASIC, we have to set a variable (in this case P was used) equal to the value pi (3.14).

**SAMPLE ANSWER FOR EXERCISE 7-4:**

```
10 REM * CIRCULAR AREA SOLUTION *
20 P = 3.14
30 R = 5
40 A = P * R * R
50 PRINT "THE CIRCLE'S AREA IS";A;"SQUARE INCHES."
```

**SAMPLE RUN FOR EXERCISE 7-4:**

```
THE CIRCLE'S AREA IS 78.5 SQUARE INCHES.
```

Note: Some BASICs do not have a function which means "raise to the power" to handle $R^2$ (IBM BASIC does.) In easy cases like this one, we can simply use R times R EXPONENTIATION function as we proceed.

**SAMPLE ANSWER FOR EXERCISE 7-5:**

```
10 B = 225
20 C = 17 + 35 + 225
30 D = 40 + 200
40 N = B - C + D
50 PRINT "YOUR NEW BALANCE IS $";N
```

**SAMPLE RUN FOR EXERCISE 7-5:**

```
YOUR NEW BALANCE IS $ 188
```

**SAMPLE ANSWER FOR EXERCISE 8-1:**

```
10 REM * CAR MILES SOLUTION PROGRAM *
20 N = 1000000
30 D = 10000
40 T = N * D
50 PRINT "THE TOTAL NUMBER OF MILES DRIVEN IS";T
```

**SAMPLE RUN FOR EXERCISE 8-1:**

```
THE TOTAL NUMBER OF MILES DRIVEN IS 1E+10
```

Note: As discussed earlier, the answer is the number 1 followed by ten zeros. 10,000,000,000. Ten Billion. The Computer will not print any numbers over 999,999 without converting them to exponential notation.

**SAMPLE ANSWER FOR EXERCISE 9-1:**

```
10 REM * FAHRENHEIT TO CELSIUS CONVERSION *
20 F = 65
30 C = (F-32) * (5/9)
40 PRINT F;"DEGREES FAHRENHEIT =";C;"DEGREES CELSIUS."
```

**SAMPLE RUN FOR EXERCISE 9-1:**

```
65 DEGREES FAHRENHEIT = 18.3333 DEGREES CELSIUS.
```

Observe carefully how the parentheses were placed. As a general rule, when in doubt -- use parentheses. The worst they can do is slow down calculating the answer by a few millionths of a second.

**SAMPLE ANSWER FOR EXERCISE 9-2:**

```
30 C = F - 32 * (5 / 9)
```

**SAMPLE RUN FOR EXERCISE 9-2:**

```
65 DEGREES FAHRENHEIT = 47.2222 DEGREES CELSIUS.
```

Note how silently and dutifully the Computer came up with the wrong answer. It has done as we directed, and we directed it wrong. A common phrase in computer circles is GIGO (pronounced "gee-goe"). It stands for "Garbage In - Garbage Out". We have given the Computer garbage and it gave it back to us by way of a wrong answer. Phrased another way, "Never in the history of mankind has there been a machine capable of making so many mistakes so rapidly and confidently." A computer is worthless unless it is programmed correctly.

**SAMPLE ANSWER FOR EXERCISE 9-3:**

```
30 C = (F - 32) * 5 / 9
```

**SAMPLE RUN FOR EXERCISE 9-3:**

```
65 DEGREES FAHRENHEIT = 18.3333 DEGREES CELSIUS.
```

## SAMPLE ANSWER FOR EXERCISE 9-4:

Two possible answers:

```
30 - (9 - 8) - (7 - 6) = 28
30 - (9 - (8 - (7 - 6))) = 28
```

Sample programs:

```
10 A = 30 - (9 - (8 - (7 - 6)))
20 PRINT A
```

Or Line 10 might be

```
10 A = 30 - (9 - 8) - (7 - 6)
```

Try a few on your own.

## SAMPLE ANSWER FOR EXERCISE 10-1:

```
10 A = 5
20 IF A <> 5 THEN 50
30 PRINT "A EQUALS 5."
40 END
50 PRINT "A DOES NOT EQUAL 5."
```

## SAMPLE RUN FOR EXERCISE 10-1:

```
A EQUALS 5.
```

## SAMPLE ANSWER FOR EXERCISE 10-2:

```
10 A = 6
20 IF A <> 5 THEN 50
30 PRINT "A EQUALS 5."
40 END
50 PRINT "A DOES NOT EQUAL 5."
60 IF A < 5 THEN 90
70 PRINT "A IS LARGER THAN 5."
80 END
90 PRINT "A IS SMALLER THAN 5."
```

## SAMPLE RUN FOR EXERCISE 10-2:

```
A DOES NOT EQUAL 5.
A IS LARGER THAN 5.
```

Note: We had to put in another END statement (Line 80) to keep the program from running on to Line 90 after PRINTing Line 70.

## SAMPLE ANSWER FOR EXERCISE 15-1:

```
1 CLS
2 INPUT "HOW MANY SECONDS DELAY DO YOU WISH";S
3 P = 800
4 D = S * P
5 FOR X = 1 TO D
6 NEXT X
7 PRINT "DELAY IS OVER.  TOOK";S;"SECONDS."
```

Explanation:

Line 2 used the INPUT statement to obtain desired delay, S in seconds.

Line 3 defined P, the number of passes required to for a one second delay.

Line 4 multiplied the delay for one second times the number of seconds desired, and called that product D.

Line 5 began the FOR-NEXT loop from 1 to whatever is required.

Line 6 is the other half of the loop.

Line 7 reports the delay is over, and prints S, the number of seconds. Obviously, S is only as accurate as the program itself since it merely copies the value of S you entered in Line 2.

## SAMPLE ANSWER FOR EXERCISE 15-2:

```
60 PRINT "RATE", "TIME"
65 PRINT "(MPH)","(HOURS)"
```

If you honestly had trouble with this one, better go back and start all over because you've missed the real basics.

**SAMPLE ANSWER FOR EXERCISE 15-3:**

```
5 CLS
10 PRINT "   ***   S A L A R Y   R A T E   C H A R T   ***"
20 PRINT
30 PRINT "YEAR","MONTH","WEEK","DAY"
40 PRINT
50 FOR Y = 5000 TO 25000 STEP 1000
55  REM * CONVERT YEARLY INCOME INTO MONTHLY *
60  M = Y / 12
65  REM * CONVERT YEARLY INCOME INTO WEEKLY *
70  W = Y / 52
75  REM * CONVERT WEEKLY INCOME INTO DAILY *
80  D = W / 5
100  PRINT Y,M,W,D
110 NEXT Y
```

**SAMPLE RUN FOR EXERCISE 15-3:**

```
   ***   S A L A R Y   R A T E   C H A R T   ***

YEAR          MONTH         WEEK          DAY

 5000          416.6667      96.15384      19.23077
 6000          500           115.3846      23.07692
 7000          583.3333      134.6154      26.92308
 8000          666.6667      153.8462      30.76923
```

**SAMPLE ANSWER FOR EXERCISE 15-4:**

```
10 R = .01
20 D = 1
30 T = .01
35 CLS
40 PRINT "DAY","DAILY","TOTAL"
50 PRINT "  #","RATE","EARNED"
60 PRINT
70 PRINT D,R,T
80 IF R > 1E+06 THEN END
90 R = R * 2
100 D = D + 1
110 T = T + R
120 GOTO 70
```

## SAMPLE RUN FOR EXERCISE 15-4:

```
DAY          DAILY          TOTAL
 #           RATE           EARNED

 1           .01            .01
 2           .02            .03
 3           .04            .07
 4           .08            .15
 5           .16            .31
 6           .32            .63
```

## SAMPLE ANSWER FOR EXERCISE 15-5:

```
5 CLS
10 PRINT "WIRE FENCE","LENGTH","WIDTH","AREA"
20 PRINT " (FEET)","(FEET)","(FEET)","(SQ. FEET)"
30 F = 1000
40 FOR L = 0 TO 500 STEP 50
50  W = (F - 2 * L ) / 2
60  A = L * W
70  PRINT F,L,W,A
80 NEXT L
90 END
```

## SAMPLE RUN FOR EXERCISE 15-5:

```
WIRE FENCE     LENGTH         WIDTH          AREA
 (FEET)        (FEET)         (FEET)         (SQ. FEET)
 1000           0              500            0
 1000           50             450            22500
 1000           100            400            40000
 1000           150            350            52500
 1000           200            300            60000
```

## ADDENDUM TO EXERCISE 15-5:

Here's a program that lets the Computer do the comparing:

```
5 CLS
9 REM * SET MAXIMUM AREA AT ZERO *
10 M = 0
14 REM * SET DESIRED LENGTH AT ZERO *
```

```
15 N = Ø
19 REM * F IS TOTAL FEET OF FENCE AVAILABLE *
2Ø F = 1ØØØ
24 REM * L IS LENGTH OF ONE SIDE OF RECTANGLE *
25 FOR L = Ø TO 5ØØ STEP 5Ø
29  REM * W IS WIDTH OF ONE SIDE OF RECTANGLE *
3Ø  W = (F - 2 * L) / 2
35  A = W * L
39  REM * COMPARE WITH A CURRENT MAXIMUM, REPLACE IF NECESSARY *
4Ø  IF A <= M THEN GOTO 55
45  M = A
49  REM * ALSO UPDATE CURRENT DESIRED LENGTH *
5Ø  N = L
55 NEXT L
6Ø PRINT "FOR LARGEST AREA USE THESE DIMENSIONS:"
65 PRINT N;"FT. BY";5ØØ-N;"FT. FOR TOTAL AREA OF";M;"SQ. FT."
```

**SAMPLE ANSWER FOR OPTIONAL EXERCISE 15-6:**

```
1Ø REM * FINDS OPTIMUM LOAD TO SOURCE MATCH *
2Ø CLS
3Ø PRINT "LOAD","CIRCUIT","SOURCE","LOAD"
4Ø PRINT "RESISTANCE","POWER","POWER","POWER"
5Ø PRINT "(OHMS)","(WATTS)","(WATTS)","(WATTS)"
6Ø PRINT
7Ø FOR R = 1 TO 2Ø
8Ø  I = 12Ø / (1Ø + R)
9Ø  C = I * I * (1Ø + R)
1ØØ  S = I * I * 1Ø
11Ø  L = I * I * R
12Ø  PRINT R,C,S,L
13Ø NEXT R
```

## SAMPLE RUN FOR OPTIONAL EXERCISE 15-6:

| LOAD RESISTANCE (OHMS) | CIRCUIT POWER (WATTS) | SOURCE POWER (WATTS) | LOAD POWER (WATTS) |
|---|---|---|---|
| 1 | 1309.091 | 1190.083 | 119.0083 |
| 2 | 1200 | 1000 | 200 |
| 3 | 1107.692 | 852.071 | 255.6213 |
| 4 | 1028.571 | 734.6939 | 293.8775 |
| 5 | 960 | 640 | 320 |
| 6 | 900 | 562.5 | 337.5 |
| 7 | 847.0588 | 498.2699 | 348.7889 |
| 8 | 800 | 444.4444 | 355.5556 |
| 9 | 757.8947 | 398.8919 | 359.0028 |
| 10 | 720 | 360 | 360 |
| 11 | 685.7143 | 326.5306 | 359.1837 |

## SAMPLE ANSWER FOR EXERCISE 16-1:

```
10 PRINT "THE                   TOTAL                SPENT"
20 PRINT "BUDGET","YEAR'S","THIS"
30 PRINT "CATEGORY";TAB(17);"BUDGET";TAB(33);"MONTH"
```

## SAMPLE ANSWER FOR EXERCISE 16-2:

```
30 PRINT " YEAR";TAB(18);"MONTH";TAB(34);"WEEK";
40 PRINT TAB(50);"DAY";TAB(66);"HOUR"
85 REM * CONVERT WEEKLY INCOME INTO HOURLY *
90 H = W / 40
100 PRINT Y,M,W,D,H
```

## SAMPLE RUN FOR EXERCISE 16-2:

*** S A L A R Y   R A T E   C H A R T ***

| YEAR | MONTH | WEEK | DAY | HOUR |
|---|---|---|---|---|
| 5000 | 416.6667 | 96.15384 | 19.23077 | 2.403846 |
| 6000 | 500 | 115.3846 | 23.07692 | 2.884616 |
| 7000 | 583.3333 | 134.6154 | 26.92308 | 3.365385 |
| 8000 | 666.6667 | 153.8462 | 30.76923 | 3.846154 |
| 9000 | 750 | 173.0769 | 34.61538 | 4.326923 |

```
10000      833.3333     192.3077     38.46154      4.807693
11000      916.6667     211.5385     42.30769      5.288461
12000      1000         230.7692     46.15385      5.769231
13000      1083.333     250          50            6.25
```

**SAMPLE ANSWER FOR EXERCISE 16-3:**

```
30 PRINT "INTER";TAB(10);"LOAD";TAB(21);"CIRCUIT";
35 PRINT TAB(36);"SOURCE";TAB(51);"LOAD"
40 PRINT "RESIST";TAB(10);"RESIST";TAB(21);"POWER";
45 PRINT TAB(36);"POWER";TAB(51);"POWER"
50 PRINT "(OHMS)";TAB(10);"(OHMS)";TAB(21);"(WATTS)";
55 PRINT TAB(36);"(WATTS)";TAB(51);"(WATTS)"
120 PRINT "  10";TAB(11);R;TAB(20);C;TAB(35);S;TAB(50);L
```

**SAMPLE RUN FOR EXERCISE 16-3:**

```
INTER     LOAD      CIRCUIT          SOURCE         LOAD
RESIST    RESIST    POWER            POWER          POWER
(OHMS)    (OHMS)    (WATTS)          (WATTS)        (WATTS)

  10         1      1309.091         1190.083       119.0083
  10         2      1200             1000           200
  10         3      1107.692         852.071        255.6213
  10         4      1028.571         734.6939       293.8775
  10         5      960              640            320
  10         6      900              562.5          337.5
  10         7      847.0588         498.2699        348.7889
  10         8      800              444.4444       355.5556
```

**SAMPLE ANSWER FOR EXERCISE 17-1:**

```
10 FOR A = 1 TO 3
20  PRINT "A LOOP"
30   FOR B = 1 TO 2
40    PRINT ,"B LOOP"
42     FOR C = 1 TO 4
44      PRINT ,,"C LOOP"
48     NEXT C
50   NEXT B
60 NEXT A
```

## SAMPLE ANSWER FOR EXERCISE 17-2:

The program will be the same as the answer to Exercise 17-1 with the following additions:

```
45          FOR D = 1 TO 5
46           PRINT ,,,"D LOOP"
47          NEXT
```

Note: To get the full impact of this "4-deep" nesting, stop the RUN frequently to examine the nesting relationships between each of the loops.

## SAMPLE ANSWER FOR EXERCISE 18-1:

Addition of the following single Line gives a nice clean PRINTout with all the values "rounded" to their integer value:

```
55 A = INT(A)
```

Worth all the effort to learn it, wasn't it?

## SAMPLE ANSWER FOR EXERCISE 18-2:

```
55 A = INT(10 * A ) / 10
```

When 3.14159 was multiplied times 10 it became 31.4159. The INTeger value of 31.4159 is 31. 31 divided by 10 is 3.1, etc.

## SAMPLE ANSWER FOR EXERCISE 18-3:

This was almost too easy.

```
55 A = INT(100 * A) / 100
```

## SAMPLE ANSWER FOR EXERCISE 19-1:

```
10 INPUT "TYPE ANY NUMBER";X
20 T = SGN(X)
30 ON T+2 GOTO 50,70,90
40 END
50 PRINT "THE NUMBER IS NEGATIVE."
60 END
```

```
70 PRINT "THE NUMBER IS ZERO."
80 END
90 PRINT "THE NUMBER IS POSITIVE."
```

**SAMPLE ANSWER FOR EXERCISE 23-1:**

```
10 PRINT CHR$(73);CHR$(66);CHR$(77);
20 PRINT CHR$(32);CHR$(80);CHR$(67);
```

**SAMPLE ANSWER FOR EXERCISE 23-2:**

```
10 INPUT "ENTER A NUMBER";A$
20 A = ASC(A$)
30 IF A<48 THEN 10
40 IF A>57 THEN 10
50 PRINT "ASCII VALUE OF ";A$;" IS";A
```

**SAMPLE ANSWER FOR EXERCISE 24-1:**

```
10 CLS
20 INPUT "FIRST STRING";A$
30 INPUT "SECOND STRING";B$
40 PRINT : PRINT "ALPHABETICAL ORDER:"
50 IF A$<B$ THEN PRINT A$,B$ : END
60 PRINT B$,A$
```

**SAMPLE ANSWER FOR EXERCISE 25-1:**

```
10 CLS
20 INPUT "INPUT STRING";A$
30 IF LEN(A$)>10 THEN PRINT "THE 10 CHARACTER
LIMIT WAS EXCEEDED."
```

**SAMPLE ANSWER FOR EXERCISE 25-2:**

```
10 CLS
20 INPUT "ENTER PASSWORD";A$
30 FOR X=1 TO 11
40  READ N
50  P$ = P$ + CHR$(N)
60 NEXT X
70 IF A$ = P$ THEN 100
```

```
80 PRINT "WRONG PASSWORD, GET LOST!"
90 END
100 PRINT "CORRECT PASSWORD, YOU MAY ENTER"
110 DATA 79,80,69,78,32,83,69,83,65,77,69
```

## SAMPLE ANSWER FOR EXERCISE 26-1:

```
10 CLS
20 INPUT "INPUT YOUR STREET ADDRESS";A$
30 A = VAL(A$)
40 PRINT: PRINT "YOUR NEIGHBOR'S STREET NUMBER IS ";A+4
50 PRINT : LIST
```

## SAMPLE ANSWER FOR EXERCISE 26-2:

```
10 CLS
20 FOR X = 101 TO 120
30  A$ = STR$(X)
40  PRINT A$+"WT",
50 NEXT X
60 PRINT : LIST
```

## SAMPLE RUN FOR EXERCISE 26-2:

```
101WT      102WT      103WT      104WT      105WT      106WT
107WT      108WT      109WT      110WT      111WT      112WT
113WT      114WT      115WT      116WT      117WT      118WT
119WT      120WT
```

## SAMPLE ANSWER FOR EXERCISE 27-1:

```
10 CLS
20 INPUT "ISN'T THIS A SMART COMPUTER";A$
30 B$ = LEFT$(A$,1)
40 IF B$ = "Y" THEN PRINT "AFFIRMATIVE":END
50 IF B$ = "N" THEN PRINT "NEGATIVE":END
60 PRINT "THIS IS A YES OR NO QUESTION"
70 GOTO 20
```

## SAMPLE ANSWER FOR EXERCISE 27-2:

```
10 CLS : MAX$ = ""
20 FOR I = 1 TO 3
30  READ A$
40  N$ = MID$(A$,2,3)
50  IF N$>MAX$ THEN MAX$ = N$: P$ = A$
60 NEXT I
70 PRINT "THE PART NUMBER WITH THE LARGEST NUMERIC
PORTION IS ";P$
80 PRINT : LIST
90 DATA N106WT,A208FM,Z154DX
```

## SAMPLE ANSWER FOR EXERCISE 27-3:

Choice C. P-

## SAMPLE ANSWER FOR EXERCISE 27-4:

```
1 CLS
10 A$ = STRING$(30,42)
20 PRINT TAB(40-LEN(A$)/2);A$
30 PRINT : LIST
```

## SAMPLE ANSWER FOR EXERCISE 28-1:

```
10 CLS
20 LOCATE 12,20 : PRINT "DATE: ";DATE$,;
30 PRINT "TIME: ";TIME$
40 GOTO 20
```

## SAMPLE ANSWER FOR EXERCISE 30-1:

```
10 CLS
20 A = 5 : B = 12
30 C = SQR(A^2 + B^2)
40 PRINT "THE SQUARE ROOT OF";A;
50 PRINT "SQUARED PLUS";B;"SQUARED IS";C
60 PRINT : LIST
```

## SAMPLE ANSWER FOR EXERCISE 30-2:

```
10 INPUT "ENTER A NUMBER";N
20 PRINT "LOG (EXP (";N;") ) =";LOG(EXP(N))
30 PRINT "EXP (LOG (";N;") ) =";EXP(LOG(N))
40 PRINT
50 GOTO 10
```

## SAMPLE ANSWER FOR EXERCISE 35-1:

```
50 U$ = "####.##       "
50 U$ = "$####.##       "
50 U$ = "$$###.##       "
50 U$ = "$$,###.##       "
50 U$ = "**$,###.##       "
```

## SAMPLE ANSWER FOR EXERCISE 35-2:

```
10 CLS : PRINT TAB(24)"CREDITS    TAX      TOTAL"
20 FOR I = 1 TO 3
30  READ A$,X,Y,Z
39  REM    12345678901234567890123456789012345678901234
40  U$ = "\                  \       ##.#      .#
##.#"
50  PRINT USING U$; A$,X,Y,Z
60 NEXT I
70 READ A$,N
79 REM    1234567
80 V$ = "\  \    ###.##"
90 PRINT TAB(35);:PRINT USING V$;A$,N
100 DATA ASTRAL COMPUTER, 18.30, .70, 19.00
110 DATA BIOFEEDBACK ADAPTER, 1.80, 00, 1.80
120 DATA PERSONALITY MODULE, 7.20, .30, 7.50
130 DATA "DUE", 28.30
```

## SAMPLE ANSWER FOR EXERCISE 36-1:

```
10 CLS
20 A$ = "REVENUES" : B$ = "EXPENSES" : C$ = "ASSETS"
30 U$ = "     \        \        \        \              \
      \"
40 PRINT USING U$; A$,B$,C$
50 A# = 1203104.22# : B# = 560143.8# : C = 0
60 V$ = "######,###.##     ####,###.##
#####,###.##-"
70 PRINT USING V$; A#,C,A#
80 PRINT USING V$; C,B#,-B#
90 PRINT : LIST
```

## SAMPLE ANSWER FOR EXERCISE 39-1:

Add or change the following Lines:

```
10 DIM A(210) : CLS
20 INPUT "WHICH CAR TO EXAMINE ";W
30 FOR L = 1 TO 10
40  READ A(L)
50 NEXT L
60 FOR S = 101 TO 110
70   READ A(S)
80 NEXT S
90 FOR B = 201 TO 210
100   READ A(B)
110 NEXT B
130 PRINT
140 PRINT "CAR#","ENG. SIZE","COLOR","BODY STYLE"
150 PRINT W,A(W),A(W+100),A(W+200)
200 DATA 300,200,500,300,200
210 DATA 300,400,400,300,500
220 DATA 3,1,4,3,2,4,3,2,1,3
230 DATA 20,20,10,20,30,20,30,10,20,20
```

## SAMPLE ANSWER FOR EXERCISE 39-2:

Delete Lines 500 - 540, and change Line 30 to:

```
30 FOR C=1 TO 52 : A(C)=C : NEXT C
```

## SAMPLE ANSWER FOR EXERCISE 40-1:

Change Line 50 to:

```
50 IF A$(F) >= A$(S) THEN 90 'TEST FOR LARGER ASCII #
```

An approach is to reserve the order of printing:

```
110 FOR D=N TO 1 STEP-1 : PRINT A$(D), : NEXT D
```

but that's not what we had in mind.

## SAMPLE ANSWER FOR EXERCISE 41-1:

```
10 CLS
20 FOR E=1 TO 4
30  FOR D=1 TO 3
40    REM ENTRY DATA: NAME, NUMBER, $$$$
50    READ R$(E,D)
60    PRINT R$(E,D),
70  NEXT D : PRINT
80 NEXT E : PRINT
1000 REM * DATA FILE *
1010 DATA "JONES, C.", 10439, 100.00
1020 DATA "ROTH, J.", 10023, 87.24
1030 DATA "BAKER, H.", 12936, 398.34
1040 DATA "HARMON, D.", 10422, 23.17
```

## SAMPLE ANSWER FOR EXERCISE 41-2:

Add:

```
100 REM *** SORT ***
110 FOR F=1 TO 3
120  FOR S=F+1 TO 4
130   IF R$(F,1) <= R$(S,1) THEN 190
140    FOR J =1 TO 3
```

```
150       T$ = R$(F,J)
160       R$(F,J) = R$(S,J)
170       R$(S,J) = T$
180      NEXT J
190   NEXT S
200 NEXT F
210 PRINT : PRINT "ALPHA SORT" : PRINT
220 FOR E=1 TO 4
230   FOR D=1 TO 3
240     PRINT R$(E,D),
250   NEXT D : PRINT
260 NEXT E : PRINT
```

**SAMPLE ANSWER FOR EXERCISE 41-3:**

Change these lines:

```
130 IF VAL(R$(F,3)) <= VAL(R$(S,3)) THEN 190
210 PRINT : PRINT "NUMERIC SORT": PRINT
```

**SAMPLE ANSWER FOR EXERCISE 47-1:**

```
10 INPUT "IS GATE 'X' OPEN";A$
20 INPUT "IS GATE 'Y' OPEN";B$
30 INPUT "IS GATE 'Z' OPEN";C$
40 PRINT
50 IF A$="Y" OR B$="Y" OR C$="Y" THEN 80
60 PRINT "OLD BESSIE IS SECURE IN PASTURE #1"
70 END
80 PRINT "A GATE IS OPEN, OLD BESSIE IS FREE TO ROAM."
```

**SAMPLE ANSWER FOR EXERCISE 50-1:**

```
10 REM * TEST GRADER *
20 CLS
30 PRINT "THIS IS A TEST GRADING PROGRAM"
40 PRINT "ENTER THE STUDENT'S FIVE ANSWERS AS REQUESTED"
50 RESTORE
60 N = 0
70 FOR I=1 TO 5
80  PRINT "ANSWER NUMBER";I;
90  INPUT A
100  READ B
110  PRINT A,B,
```

```
120  IF A=B THEN PRINT "CORRECT": N=N+1 ELSE PRINT ,"WRONG"
130  PRINT
140 NEXT I
150 PRINT N;"RIGHT OUT OF 5 WHICH IS";
160 PRINT N/5 * 100;"%"
170 PRINT "ANY MORE TESTS TO GRADE";
180 INPUT "--1=YES, 2=NO";Z
190 IF Z=1 THEN CLS: GOTO 50
200 DATA 65,23,17,56,39
```

## SAMPLE ANSWER FOR EXERCISE 50-2:

```
100 CLS
110 PRINT : PRINT
120 PRINT "ENTER THE NUMBER OF ONE OF THE FOLLOWING
INVESTMENTS"
130 PRINT
140 PRINT "   1 - CERTIFICATE OF DEPOSIT"
150 PRINT "   2 - BANK SAVINGS ACCOUNT"
160 PRINT "   3 - CREDIT UNION"
170 PRINT "   4 - MORTGAGE LOAN"
180 PRINT : INPUT "INVESTMENT";F
190 ON F GOTO 1000, 2000, 3000, 4000
200 GOTO 100 : REM IF NUMBER NOT BETWEEN 1 AND 4
1000 REM * CERTIFICATE OF DEPOSIT PROGRAM GOES HERE *
1010 PRINT "THE C.D. PROGRAM HAS YET TO BE WRITTEN."
1020 GOSUB 10000 : GOTO 100
2000 REM * BANK SAVINGS ACCOUNT PROGRAM *
2010 CLS : PRINT : PRINT "THE ROUTINE CALCULATES SIMPLE
INTEREST ON"
2020 PRINT "DOLLARS HELD IN DEPOSIT FOR SPECIFIED PERIOD"
2030 PRINT "USING A SPECIFIED PERCENTAGE OF INTEREST." : PRINT
2040 PRINT : INPUT "HOW LARGE IS THE DEPOSIT (IN DOLLARS)";P
2050 INPUT "HOW LONG WILL YOU LEAVE IT IN (IN DAYS)";D
2060 INPUT "WHAT INTEREST RATE DO YOU EXPECT (IN %)";R
2070 CLS : PRINT : PRINT : PRINT "FOR A STARTING
PRINCIPAL OF $";P;"AT A"
2080 PRINT "RATE OF";R;"% FOR";D;"DAYS, THE INTEREST"
2090 PRINT "AMOUNTS TO ";
```

```
2100 REM INTEREST = (%/YR)/(DAYS/YR) * DAYS * PRINCIPAL
2200 I = R / 100 / 365 * D * P
2300 PRINT : PRINT "    "," $ ";I
2400 END
3000 REM * CREDIT UNION PROGRAM GOES HERE *
3010 PRINT "THE C.U. PROGRAM HAS YET TO BE WRITTEN."
3020 GOSUB 10000 : GOTO 100
4000 REM * MORTGAGE LOAN PROGRAM GOES HERE *
4010 PRINT "THE M.L. PROGRAM HAS YET TO BE WRITTEN."
4020 GOSUB 10000 : GOTO 100
10000 FOR I = 1 TO 1000 : NEXT I : RETURN
```

## SAMPLE ANSWER FOR EXERCISE 53-1:

```
10 ON ERROR GOTO 100
20 CLS
30 FOR I = 1 TO 10
40  X = INT(RND*21) : F = X - 10/X
50  PRINT I, "X=";X,"F(X)=";F;
60  IF F<0 THEN PUNT ELSE PRINT
70  IF X=20 THEN READ A
80 NEXT I
90 INPUT "PRESS ENTER TO CONTINUE";Z : GOTO 20
100 IF ERR=2 THEN 140
110 IF ERR=4 THEN 130
120 PRINT "ERROR" : END
130 PRINT "OUT OF DATA ERROR IN LINE ";ERL: RESUME NEXT
140 PRINT : PRINT "SYNTAX ERROR IN LINE ";ERL: RESUME NEXT
```

# SECTION C

# PREPARED USER PROGRAMS

# 12-Hour Clock

```
1 REM * COPYRIGHT (C) 1984 BY COMPUSOFT. ALL RIGHTS RESERVED.*
3 REM *                  <<<<< 12-HOUR CLOCK >>>>>          *
10 INPUT "THE HOUR IS"; E
20 F = INT(E/10) : E = E - (F*10)
30 INPUT "THE MINUTES ARE"; C
40 D = INT(C/10) : C = C - (D*10)
50 INPUT "THE SECONDS ARE"; A
60 CLS
70 B = INT(A/10) : A = A - (B*10)
80 FOR N=1 TO 690 : NEXT N
90 A = A + 1
100 IF A>9 THEN 120
110 GOTO 310
120 A = 0
130 B = B + 1
140 IF B>5 THEN 160
150 GOTO 310
160 B = 0
170 C = C + 1
180 IF C>9 THEN 200
190 GOTO 310
200 C = 0
210 D = D + 1
220 IF D>5 THEN 240
230 GOTO 310
240 D = 0
250 E = E + 1
260 IF E>9 THEN 280
270 GOTO 300
280 E = 0
290 F = F + 1
300 IF (F=1) AND (E=3) THEN A=0 : B=0 : C=0 : D=0 :
    E=1 : F=0
310 LOCATE 11,29 : PRINT F;E;":";D;C;":"B;A;
320 GOTO 80
```

## Checksum For Business

For those responsible for inventory numbers or check clearing and balancing in business, a checksum is a most useful testing "code". This simple program calculates error-free checksums almost instantly. It is designed for 6-digit numbers and so can be used for stock number verification or other applications.

```
1 REM * COPYRIGHT (C) 1984 BY COMPUSOFT. ALL RIGHTS RESERVED. *
3 REM        <<<<< CHECKSUM FOR BUSINESS >>>>>
10 PRINT
20 INPUT "THE FIRST DIGIT IS ";A
30 INPUT "THE SECOND DIGIT IS ";B
40 INPUT "THE THIRD DIGIT IS ";C
50 INPUT "THE FOURTH DIGIT IS ";D
60 INPUT "THE FIFTH DIGIT IS ";E
70 INPUT "THE SIXTH DIGIT IS ";F
80 PRINT
90 PRINT "THE NUMBER IS ";A;B;C;D;E;F
100 S = A+2*B+C+2*D+E+2*F
110 T = INT(S/10)
120 U = S - T * 10
130 S = T + U
140 IF S>9 THEN 110
150 PRINT "   THE CHECKDIGIT IS "; S
```

## Speed Reading

Your Computer is your own personal Tachistoscope, a device used to practice speed reading. Study this sample program carefully to see how easy it is for you to substitute your own reading material at whatever reading level you want. The variable time loop lets you input the desired reading speed in words-per-minute.

```
1 REM * COPYRIGHT (C) 1984 BY COMPUSOFT.  ALL RIGHTS RESERVED. *
3 REM                <<<<< SPEED READING PROGRAM >>>>>
10 GOTO 30
20 FOR I=1 TO B : NEXT I : LOCATE 10,1 : BEEP : RETURN
30 INPUT "HOW MANY WORDS PER MINUTE DO YOU READ";W
40 B=(12*60/W)*800
50 REM 800= # OF LOOPS IN 1 SECOND
60 REM ADJUST THE 800 IN LINE 50 TO MATCH YOUR SYSTEM
70 CLS : GOSUB 20
100 PRINT "FIRST PARAGRAPH FROM 'GONE WITH THE WIND'.": GOSUB 20
110 PRINT "   SCARLETT O'HARA WAS NOT BEAUTIFUL, BUT MEN
    SELDOM   ":GOSUB 20
120 PRINT "REALIZED IT WHEN CAUGHT BY HER OWN CHARM AS THE
    TARLETON ":GOSUB 20
130 PRINT "TWINS WERE.  IN HER FACE WERE TOO SHARPLY BLENDED
    THE    ":GOSUB 20
140 PRINT "DELICATE FEATURES OF HER MOTHER, A COAST ARISTOCRAT
    OF ":GOSUB 20
150 PRINT "FRENCH DESCENT, AND THE HEAVY ONES OF HER FLORID
    IRISH   ":GOSUB 20
160 PRINT "FATHER.  BUT IT WAS AN ARRESTING FACE, POINTED OF
    CHIN  ":GOSUB 20
170 PRINT "SQUARE OF JAW.  HER EYES WERE PALE GREEN WITHOUT A
    TOUCH ":GOSUB 20
180 PRINT "OF HAZEL, STARRED WITH BRISKLY BLACK LASHES AND
    SLIGHTLY ":GOSUB 20
190 PRINT "TITLED AT THE ENDS. ABOVE THEM, HER THICK BLACK
    BROWS    " : GOSUB 20
200 PRINT "SLANTED UPWARDS, CUTTING A STARTLING OBLIQUE LINE
    IN HER ":GOSUB 20
210 PRINT "MAGNOLIA-WHITE SKIN--THAT SKIN SO PRIZED BY
    SOUTHERN     ":GOSUB 20
220 PRINT "WOMEN AND SO CAREFULLY GUARDED WITH BONNETS, VEILS,
    AND  ":GOSUB 20
230 PRINT "MITTENS AGAINST HOT GEORGIA SUNS.
        ":GOSUB 20
240 CLS
```

## Craps

The game is as old as history. A testimonial to the intelligence and ingenuity of our ancient ancestors. An excellent way to demonstrate the running of twin Random Number Generators.

You don't need to know how to play the game -- the Computer will quickly teach you.(...There's one born every minute...)

```
1 REM * COPYRIGHT (C) 1984 BY COMPUSOFT. ALL RIGHTS RESERVED. *
3 REM *              <<<<<  CRAPS  >>>>>                 *
10 CLS
20 INPUT "PRESS <ENTER> TO CONTINUE"; A$
30 CLS : GOSUB 150 : P=N
40 PRINT : PRINT "YOU ROLLED "; P ;"  ",
50 ON P GOTO 60,90,90,70,70,70,80,70,70,70,80,90
60 REM USED FOR THE ON STATEMENT IF P=1 (WHICH IT CAN'T)
70 PRINT "YOUR POINT IS "; N : GOTO 100
80 PRINT "YOU WIN!!" : PRINT : GOTO 20
90 PRINT "YOU LOSE." : PRINT : GOTO 20
100 GOSUB 150 : M=N
110 PRINT : PRINT "YOU ROLLED "; M,
120 IF P=M THEN 80
130 IF M=7 THEN 90
140 GOTO 100
150 A = INT(RND*6+1) : B= INT(RND*6+1) : N = A+B : RETURN
```

# Dow-Jones Industrial Average Forecaster

There is no guarantee that this program will make you instantly wealthy, but it is an example of converting a financial magazine article into a usable computer program. The article describing the market premises on which this program is built appeared in Forbes Magazine.

```
1 REM * COPYRIGHT (C) 1984 BY COMPUSOFT.  ALL RIGHTS RESERVED. *
3 REM     <<<<< DOW-JONES AVERAGE FORECASTER >>>>>
10 CLS
20 PRINT "*** PROJECTS TARGET DOW-JONES INDUSTRIAL AVERAGE
   AS A FUNCTION OF YEARS DJI "
30 PRINT "EARNINGS AND INFLATION RATE ***"
40 PRINT
50 REM * K = COST OF MONEY. ASSUME 3% *
60 K = .03
70 REM * P = RISK PREMIUM OF STOCK OVER BONDS. ASSUME 1% *
80 P = .01
90 PRINT "DO YOU KNOW YEARS PROJECTED EARNINGS OF 30 DJI (Y/N)";
100 INPUT A$
110 IF A$="Y" THEN 290
120 PRINT
130 PRINT "THIS METHOD WILL GIVE EARNINGS APPROXIMATIONS USING
    THE NEWSPAPER PRICES AND"
140 PRINT "P/E RATIOS.  BETTER FORECASTS OF EACH COMPANY'S
    EARNINGS MAY GIVE AN IMPROVED"
150 PRINT "OVERALL FORECAST"
160 PRINT
170 D=0
180 FOR N= 1 TO 30
190   READ A$
200   PRINT "WHAT IS THE CURRENT PRICE OF >--> ";A$;" <--<;
210   INPUT P
220   PRINT "THE CURRENT P/E RATIO: ";
230   INPUT R
240   E=P/R
250   D=E+D
260 NEXT N
270 PRINT
280 GOTO 330
290 PRINT "WHAT IS THE TOTAL PROJECTED EARNINGS FOR 1 SHARE OF
    EACH";
```

```
300 INPUT D
310 REM * I = ESTIMATED INFLATION RATE *
320 PRINT "WHAT IS THE INFLATION RATE";
330 INPUT I
340 T=D/(K+P+I*.01)
350 R=T/D
360 PRINT
370 PRINT "INFL. RATE","DJI EARN.","PROJ DJ AVE.","AVE./EARN.
    RATIO"
380 PRINT
390 PRINT I,D,T,R
400 DATA ALLIED CHEM., ALCOA, AMER. BRANDS, AMER. CAN, AMER. BELL
410 DATA BETH. STEEL, CHRYSLER, DUPONT, E. KODAK, ESMARK, EXXON
420 DATA GEN. ELECT., GEN. FOODS, GEN. MOTORS, GOODYEAR, INCO
430 DATA INT. HARV., INT. PAPER, JOHNS-MAN, MINN. MM., OWENS-ILLS.
440 DATA PROCTOR & GAM., SEARS, STD. OIL CAL., TEXACO, UNION
    CARBIDE
450 DATA U.S. STEEL, UNITED TECHNOL., WESTINGHOUSE, WOOLWORTH
```

## Termites

A malicious sense of humor helps on this one. Its avowed purpose is to demonstrate turning off the "lights" in a random fashion, but it's not without other redeeming value. If you don't like to sit by the fire and watch it snow while reading good poetry, you can always watch the termites eat your house down.

```
1 REM * COPYRIGHT (C) 1984 BY COMPUSOFT.  ALL RIGHTS RESERVED *
3 REM *                <<<<< TERMITES >>>>>                  *
10 DEF SEG = 45056!  '  VIDEO DISPLAY MEMORY
20 CLS : KEY OFF
30 FOR P=160 TO 3998 STEP 2  : POKE P,219 : NEXT P   ' FILL SCREEN
40 N = 1920   '  NUMBER OF BITES
50 LOCATE 1,1
60 PRINT TAB(10); "SEE THE TERMITES EAT",,"ONLY      BITES LEFT!";
70 X = INT(RND*1920)
80 A = X * 2 + 160    '  ADDRESS
90 IF PEEK(A) = 32 THEN 70    '  IF ALREADY BLANK, FIND NEXT ONE
100 POKE A,32
110 N = N - 1
120 LOCATE 1,61 : PRINT N;
130 IF N>0 THEN 70
```

```
140 LOCATE 13,37 : COLOR 0,7
150 PRINT "BURP!!" : COLOR 7,0
160 GOTO 160
```

## Automatic Ticket Number Drawer

Like to make a big splash at the next Rotary Club, County Fair, or other ticket drawing giveaway? This program uses the random number generator to pick the lucky number(s) and eliminate charges of stuffing the ticket box, besides giving the whole affair some pizzaz. If your own number comes up and you are charged with rigging the Computer, you're on your own.

```
1 REM * COPYRIGHT (C) 1984 BY COMPUSOFT.  ALL RIGHTS RESERVED *
3 REM *  <<<<< AUTOMATIC TICKET NUMBER DRAWER >>>>>  *
10 CLS : RANDOMIZE
20 REM * PICKS WINNER(S) BY DRAWING TICKET NUMBER *
30 REM * NO MORE THAN 32767 TICKETS CAN BE SOLD *
40 REM * BUT TICKET NUMBERS CAN RANGE TO 99999 & BEYOND *
50 INPUT "THE LOWEST NUMBER IS "; B
60 PRINT
70 INPUT "THE HIGHEST NUMBER IS "; H
80 PRINT
90 E = H-B+1
100 IF E<32768 THEN GOTO 120
110 PRINT "TOO MANY TICKETS SOLD!" : END
120 INPUT "HOW MANY WINNERS DO YOU WANT ";W
130 CLS
140 IF W>E THEN GOTO 280
150 PRINT : PRINT : PRINT : PRINT
160 PRINT "*   A N D   T H E   W I N N I N G   ";
170 IF W>1 THEN GOTO 200
180 PRINT "T I C K E T   I S   *"
190 GOTO 210
200 PRINT "   T I C K E T S   A R E   *"
210 PRINT
220 FOR N= 1 TO W
230 Z = INT(RND*E)
240 PRINT
250 PRINT TAB(12) ; ">----->>>  "; Z+B
260 NEXT N
270 END
280 CLS : PRINT TAB(8);"YOU HAVE MORE WINNERS THAN ";
290 PRINT "TICKETS - DUMMY !"
```

# Wheel of Fortune
## (Or ... Never Give a Sucker an Even Break.)

Modeled after the large wheels of fortune found at carnivals and other such gatherings, this graphics program accurately replicates its odds. The numbers are read from a DATA bank and "rotated" through "windows" as the wheel is "spun".

As commonly played, a $1 bet on any number, 1, 2, 5, 10, 20 or 40 (the joker and IBM) returns those amounts -- if that number comes up. If not -- it's a cheap education.

Step right up, stranger. Try your luck at the wheel of fortune.

```
1 REM * COPYRIGHT (C) 1984 BY COMPUSOFT. ALL RIGHTS RESERVED. *
3 REM *                <<<<< THE WHEEL OF FORTUNE >>>>>          *
5 RANDOMIZE
10 DIM A(60)
20 CLS : KEY OFF
30 PRINT "STEP RIGHT UP, STRANGER.  TRY YOUR HAND AT THE   ":
   PRINT : PRINT
40 PRINT "        W H E E L  O F  F O R T U N E" : PRINT : PRINT
50 PRINT "PAYOFFS IN DOLLARS FOR A $1 BET ARE 1,2,5,10,20."
60 PRINT : PRINT "SPECIALS ARE THE JOKER (13) AND THE IBM (99),
   EACH PAYING $40!"
70 PRINT : INPUT "ENTER YOUR CHOICE AS A 1, 2, 5, 10, 13,
   20, OR 99"; G
80 IF G=1 OR G=2 OR G=5 OR G=10 OR G=13 OR G=20 OR G=99 THEN 90
   ELSE 70
90 CLS
100 T=65 : P = INT(RND*54+1)
110 COLOR 31 : PRINT TAB(32)"WHEEL OF FORTUNE" : COLOR 7
120 LOCATE 3,36 : PRINT ">>----<<"
130 RESTORE : FOR I = 1 TO 54 : READ A(I) : NEXT I
140 RESTORE : FOR I = 55 TO 60 : READ A(I) : NEXT I
150 FOR J=1 TO 48 : READ K : NEXT J
160 FOR C=1 TO 7
170 READ Y,X
180 LOCATE Y,X
190 GOSUB 600
200 NEXT C
210 LOCATE 17,29 : PRINT "ROUND AND ROUND IT GOES...";
220 LOCATE 20,34 : PRINT "JOKER (13) &"
230 LOCATE 21,36 : PRINT "IBM (99)"
```

```
240 LOCATE 22,32 : PRINT "BOTH PAY 40 TO 1";
250 FOR I=0 TO 6
260 READ Y(I),X(I)
270 NEXT I
280 FOR S=1 TO 100 + INT (RND * 2 + 1)
290 FOR I=0 TO 6
300 LOCATE Y(I),X(I)
310 PRINT A(P+I); : NEXT I
320 IF S < T THEN 370
330 R = (S-T)^2
340 IF S > 98 THEN LOCATE 17,32:PRINT"PAYOFFS GO TO THE" :
    GOTO 360
350 LOCATE 17,28 : PRINT "       ALMOST THERE . . . .    ";
360 IF S<102 THEN FOR Z=1 TO R : NEXT Z
370 P = P - 1 : IF P=0 THEN P=54
380 NEXT S : PRINT TAB(39);: Q=A(P+4) : GOSUB 500 : X=0
390 LOCATE 20,30 : PRINT "YOUR CHOICE WAS "; : Q=G : GOSUB 500
400 LOCATE 21,35 : PRINT STRING$(20,32)
410 LOCATE 20,30 : IF G=A(P+4) THEN PRINT "YOU WIN AT"; ODDS;
    "TO 1   " : LOCATE 22,32 : PRINT STRING$(20,32); : GOTO 430
420 LOCATE 22,32 : PRINT "    YOU LOSE.      "
430 LOCATE 23,27 : PRINT "PRESS <";
440 COLOR 31
450 PRINT "ENTER";: COLOR 7: INPUT"> TO CONTINUE"; A$
460 GOTO 20
470 DATA 1,2,99,1,5,1,2,1,10,1,2,1,5,1,2,1,5,1,2,1,20,1,2,10
480 DATA 1,2,1,5,1,2,1,5,1,2,13,1,2,1,10,1,2,1,2
490 DATA 1,20,1,2,5,1,2,10,1,2,5
500 ODDS = Q : IF (Q<>13) AND (Q<>99) THEN PRINT " ";Q : RETURN
510 ODDS = 40 : A$="JOKER" : IF Q=99 THEN A$ = "IBM"
520 PRINT TAB(38) A$ : RETURN
530 DATA 10,1,7,12,5,24,4,36,5,48,7,60,10,72
540 DATA 12,3,9,14,7,26,6,38,7,50,9,62,12,74
600 REM DRAW THE SQUARES
610 PRINT STRING$(8,220);
620 FOR TOP=1 TO 3
630  LOCATE Y+TOP,X : PRINT CHR$(221)STRING$(6,32)CHR$(222);
640 NEXT TOP
650 LOCATE Y+TOP,X : PRINT STRING$(8,223);
660 RETURN
```

## Alexander's Ragtime Band

This utilizes the SOUND statement to reproduce the old Dixieland favorite.

```
1 REM * COPYRIGHT (C) 1984 BY COMPUSOFT.  ALL RIGHTS RESERVED. *
3 REM          <<<<< ALEXANDER'S RAGTIME BAND >>>>>
10 ON ERROR GOTO 80
20 CLS : DEFINT A
30 REM CLOCK TICKS 18.2 TIMES PER SECOND
40 READ A,L
50 TL=L*18.2
60 SOUND A,TL
70 GOTO 40
80 IF ERR=4 THEN END
90 RESUME 100
100 GOSUB 120
110 GOTO 40
120 RESTORE
130 IF ERR=4 THEN END
140 FOR X=1 TO 22
150 READ A,L
160 IF A=32767 THEN A=32767/1.3348
170 SOUND A*1.3348,L*18.2
180 NEXT X
190 READ B$,C
200 RETURN
210 END
220 REM DATA IS NOTE (IN HZ CONCERT PITCH), LENGTH (IS SECONDS)
230 DATA 262,1,440,1,349,1
240 DATA 466,.125,494,.375,466,.125,494,1,32767,.375
250 DATA 466,.125,494,.375,587,.125,494,1.32767,.375
260 DATA 466,.125,494,.375,587,.125,466,.375,440,.125,392..375,
    330,.125
270 DATA 466,.25,440,.25,32767,.25,392,1,.25,32767,.375
280 DATA ERROR,2
290 DATA 494,.125,523,.375,554,.125,587,.25,32767,.25
300 DATA 659,.375,494,.125,587,.25,659,.5,494,.25
310 DATA 587,.325,32767,.05,587,.125,659,.375,494,.125,.587,
    .5,32767,.5
320 DATA 392,.5,493,.375,294,.125,392,.375,466,.125,392,.375,294,
    .125
330 DATA 392,.375,466,.125,494,.25,587,.5,37567,1.25
```

```
340 DATA 440,.125,32767,.05,440,.45,32767,.05,440,.45,494,.5
350 DATA 554,.25,440,.375,32767,.125,440,.25,494,.325,32767,
    .05,494,.125
360 DATA 554,.375,32767,.125,587,1.5,32767,1.875
370 DATA 466,.125,494,.375,466,.125,494,1,32767,.375
380 DATA 466,.125,494,.375,587,.125,494,1,32767,.375
390 DATA 466,.125,494,.375,587,.125,466,.375,440,.125,392,.375,
    330,.125
400 DATA 466,.25,440,.25,32767,.25,392,.75,32767,.05,587,.5,32767,
    .05,784,1
```

## Sorry

SORRY is a popular board game by Parker Brothers. This program demonstrates how to load a deck of cards into a numerical array, draw them out in a random fashion, "reshuffle" the deck after the last card is drawn, and continue drawing. The program will pause between each drawing of the cards, allowing as much time as desired to actually move the pieces on your own SORRY board. Have fun!

```
1 REM * COPYRIGHT (C) 1984 BY COMPUSOFT.  ALL RIGHTS RESERVED *
3 REM                  <<<<< SORRY >>>>>
10 RANDOMIZE : CLS : DIM A(45)
20 PRINT "STAND BY FOR THE SHUFFLING OF THE DECK OF CARDS"
30 PRINT : PRINT : PRINT
40 FOR N = 1 TO 45 : READ A(N) : NEXT N
50 PRINT : PRINT : PRINT
60 Y=1
70 PRINT "SHUFFLING COMPLETED . . . . GAME BEGINS!" : PRINT
80 R = INT(RND*45+1)
90 M = A(R)
100 IF M=0 THEN 80
110 A(R)=0 : T=0
120 FOR Z = 1 TO 45
130   T=A(Z) + T
140 NEXT Z
150 PRINT TAB(34);"PRESS ENTER ";:INPUT A$
160 IF T=0 THEN 180
170 GOTO 210
180 PRINT "END OF THE DECK.  THE CARDS ARE BEING RESHUFFLED"
190 RESTORE
200 GOTO 30
210 IF Y<0 THEN 240
```

```
220 PRINT TAB(10); "RED"
230 GOTO 250
240 PRINT TAB(60);"GREEN"
250 IF M=13 THEN 270
260 PRINT TAB(B+10); M
270 ON M GOTO 290,310,540,360,540,540,380,540,410,430,540,450
280 GOTO 520
290 PRINT TAB(B);"MAY MOVE A PIECE OUT"
300 GOTO 540
310 PRINT TAB(B);"MAY MOVE A NEW PIECE OUT"
320 PRINT : PRINT
330 PRINT TAB(B+5);"DRAW AGAIN . . ."
340 PRINT
350 GOTO 580
360 PRINT TAB(B);"MUST BACK UP 4 SPACES"
370 GOTO 540
380 PRINT TAB(B);"MAY SPLIT THE 7 BETWEEN"
390 PRINT TAB(B+3);" 2 PIECES"
400 GOTO 540
410 PRINT TAB(B);"MAY MOVE BACKWARDS 1 SPACE"
420 GOTO 540
430 PRINT TAB(B);"CAN SWAP A PIECE WITH OPPONENT"
440 GOTO 540
450 PRINT : PRINT
460 IF B=0 THEN 510
470 PRINT "     GOTCHA            <<<====<<<    <<<====<<<";
480 PRINT TAB(60);"S O R R Y !"
490 PRINT : PRINT
500 GOTO 540
510 PRINT "S O R R Y !        >>>====>>>    >>>====>>>";
520 PRINT TAB(70);"GOTCHA !"
530 PRINT TAB(40);"*"
540 FOR T = 1 TO 1000 : NEXT T : FOR X= 1 TO 4
550 PRINT TAB(40);"*"
560 NEXT X
570 Y = Y * (-1)
580 IF Y>0 THEN B=0 ELSE B=51
590 GOTO 80
600 DATA 1,1,1,1,1,2,2,2,2,3,3,3,3,4,4,4,4,5,5,5,5,7,7,7,7,8,8
610 DATA 8,8,10,10,10,10,11,11,11,11,12,12,12,12,13,13,13,13
```

SECTION D

# APPENDICES

# Using Cassette BASIC

## Part I -- Startup Procedure

Hook up the Computer as shown in the reference manual and turn it ON. After giving itself a perfunctory check-up, the Computer will beep at us, display a copyright message, tell us we're using Cassette BASIC (Version C1.00), and tell us how much memory we have. A 64K machine will have 61404 Bytes free.

Before moving on to Chapter 2, take a quick look at the keyboard.

The ENTER key is the one with the left arrow and a stem, right above the key that says [PrtSc], on the right part of the keyboard. The SHIFT keys have an outline of an up arrow on them, and are found on either side of the lower middle portion of the keyboard.

[←┘] equals ENTER.

Now return to Chapter 2 to join Disk BASIC readers coming in from *their* startup section.

## Part II -- Using Cassette Tape

We will soon write and run long and powerful programs. It becomes tedious to type them in accurately just once, let alone each time we want to use them. Impressing your friends with this super-whazzoo Computer is somewhat more difficult if they sit watching TV reruns of Star-Trek while you take an hour to type in a program. There has to be a better way.

The IBM has a built-in "Cassette Tape Interface" which allows us to record and store any program on high quality cassette tape. A full "4K" of memory can be DUMPed onto tape, or LOADed from tape, in under 3 minutes. Most programs are shorter and take even less time. That isn't enough time to get through the deodorant ads. Besides building up your own tape library of computer programs, you can exchange favorite programs with other IBM owners by exchanging tapes.

---

DUMPed and LOADed are everyday terms used by computer people for storing and "playing back" computer programs.

---

## Recording

Only a little practice is required. Follow the yellow brick road:

1. Obtain a recorder, cassette tape, and interconnecting cable such as Radio-Shack part number 26-1207.

2. Connect the cable between the TAPE jack on the back of the IBM and the cassette tape recorder. For the RS cable:

   A. The small gray plug goes into the MIC jack on the recorder.

   B. The large gray plug goes into the AUX jack.

   C. The black plug goes into the EAR jack.

3. Type any program into the Computer, preferably one that is at least several lines long. RUN it to be sure it is entered correctly.

4. Press the PLAY and RECORD buttons *at the same time* until they lock.

5. "Dump" the program onto tape by typing the command:

```
SAVE "CAS1:TEST"
```

The motor on the recorder will start and you'll be recording the Computer's program onto tape.

NOTE: The CAS1 prefix on the save command is unnecessary if you are using Cassette BASIC, since CAS1 is the only place you can save programs. Disk BASIC users *must* insert the prefix, or the program will be SAVEd on Disk.

Watch the Video screen when:

```
Ok

_
```

returns and the motor stops, the program is recorded on tape. It is also still in the Computer's memory. It has only been "copied" out.

6. Rewind the tape. Disconnect the plug from the EAR jack and play the tape so you hear what digital data sounds like. Sounds terrible, doesn't it?

*You were expecting maybe Lawrence Welk?*

## Loading

Reversing the process and loading (copying) the program from tape into the Computer is just as easy.

1. Be sure the tape is fully rewound and the plugs are all in place.

2. Push down the PLAY button until it locks. Set the volume control to about midrange or louder.

IMPORTANT: Too little volume will cause a bad "data LOAD": too much volume may result in distortion in the Tape Recorder and also goof-up the "LOAD".

3. Type NEW (to clear out any existing program).

4. Type the command:

```
LOAD"CAS1:TEST"
```

The tape recorder's motor will start and data will flow from the tape into the Computer's memory.

As soon as the Computer senses the DATA, the screen will display:

```
TEST    .B Found.
```

This means the Computer is beginning to LOAD the program in memory. The .B is there to tell us that it's a Basic program. If it were a data file (See Appendix D) it would have a .D on the end.

Watch the Video Display. The program is entered when:

```
OK

_
```

returns and the recorder motor stops.

5. RUN the program to see that the data transfer was successful. In the event that it was not, repeat the above steps, being sure that all cables are properly connected, *the volume level* is Ok and the tape recorder heads are clean. (Listen to the tape to be sure there is a program on it.)

---

NOTE: If the recorder does not stop, press [Break]. This will take the Computer out of the LOAD or SAVE mode with a Device Timeout error and return control to the keyboard.

---

To get a "DIRectory" of what's on the tape, rewind it, hit PLAY and type:

```
LOAD"CAS1:?????"
```

This will look for a program called "?????" (which you know isn't on the tape) and will tell you what *is* on the tape. The screen will show:

```
TEST    .B Skipped.
```

and will continue running until you hit [Break] ( [Ctrl] [Scroll Lock] ).

About 20 seconds after the recorder stops, you will get a Device Timeout error.

With the new DOS 1.10, if the recorder doesn't pick up any data, even if the cassette is still running, you will also get a Device Timeout error after 20 seconds.

As a final test, try rewinding the tape again and type:

```
LOAD"CAS1:TEST",R
```

The screen will display:

```
TEST     .B Found
```

and then immediately RUN the program when it's all loaded in. This can also be accomplished by:

```
RUN"CAS1:TEST"
```

which will also LOAD and RUN the program TEST.

## Miscellaneous Tape Palaver

To minimize the chance of hitting a "soft spot" on a tape, where the oxide may be thin or have flaked off, experienced operators routinely do a "double dump" when copying from Computer to tape. This simply means copying the program twice on the same tape -- one recording right after the other.

With fairly long programs, this might take some time. So try:

```
SAVE "CAS1:TEST" : SAVE "CAS1:TEST"
```

Then go feed the cat while it SAVEs.

Also on long dumps, one is made in one direction, the cassette flipped over, and recorded in the other direction. For extra safety, very important programs are recorded on more than one tape. Your own experience should be your guide.

You may have noticed that specially wound Computer Tape has no plastic leader on the ends. This is because when you begin "dumping" data from memory onto tape there must be real live tape there to record it.

---

Normal audio tape has lead-ins on both ends (typically non-magnetic mylar material). *You cannot record on the leader portion of tapes.* Advance the tape past the leader before recording a program.

---

**If one little bit of data is lost the entire program can be lost.** Computer Tape is wound in shorter than usual lengths, with the C-10 being standard. It will record 5 minutes in each direction -- far more than enough for most programs.

Experienced "computerists" have found that it is better to use a separate cassette (or at least a separate side) for each program rather than try to search through long tapes for a desired program. Since computer data on tape is not readable by the human ear, separate cassettes solve the problem.

---

If you record programs on long audio cassettes, use the Tape Recorder's Counter to aid in locating programs.

---

When you are not using the recorder for loading or recording, do not leave the RECORD or PLAY keys down (press STOP).

**Do not expose recorded tapes to magnetic fields.**

Do not attempt to re-record on a pre-recorded Computer data tape. Even though the new recording process erases the old recording, just enough information may be left to confuse the new recording. If you want to use the same tape a second or third time, use a bulk tape eraser to be sure all old data is erased.

If you want to save a taped program permanently, break off the Erase Protect tab on the Cassette (see the Tape Recorder's Manual). When the tab(s) has been broken off, you cannot press down the RECORD key (to keep from accidentally erasing that tape).

## Part III -- "CHAIN"ing Programs

An extraordinarily valuable feature of our cassette is to be able to "CHAIN" programs together. When we say "CHAIN" we mean that we can RUN one program, and then the last statement could be RUN another program, which in turn would RUN a third program...

The most common example of this feature is the use of a menu. We are then offered a choice of programs to RUN and the Computer automatically RUNs them for us. For example:

```
10 CLS : LOCATE 2,32
20 PRINT ">>> MAIN MENU <<<" : PRINT
30 FOR X=1 TO 5
40 READ A$ : PRINT "-" A$
50 NEXT X
60 PRINT : INPUT "WHICH PROGRAM WOULD YOU LIKE TO RUN"; P$
70 RUN "CAS1:" + P$
100 DATA CHECK BOOK, RECIPES, ACCOUNTS PAYABLE
110 DATA STAR TREK, PAC MAN
```

We are given the 5 choices, we type in which one we want, and then it's RUN.

# The ASCII Chart

| ASCII value | Character | ASCII value | Character |
|---|---|---|---|
| 000 | (null) | 032 | (space) |
| 001 | ☺ | 033 | ! |
| 002 | ☻ | 034 | " |
| 003 | ♥ | 035 | # |
| 004 | ♦ | 036 | $ |
| 005 | ♣ | 037 | % |
| 006 | ♠ | 038 | & |
| 007 | (beep) | 039 | ' |
| 008 | (backspace) | 040 | ( |
| 009 | (tab) | 041 | ) |
| 010 | (line feed) | 042 | * |
| 011 | (home) | 043 | + |
| 012 | (form feed) | 044 | , |
| 013 | (carriage return) | 045 | - |
| 014 | ♫ | 046 | . |
| 015 | ☼ | 047 | / |
| 016 | ► | 048 | 0 |
| 017 | ◄ | 049 | 1 |
| 018 | ↕ | 050 | 2 |
| 019 | ‼ | 051 | 3 |
| 020 | ¶ | 052 | 4 |
| 021 | § | 053 | 5 |
| 022 | ▬ | 054 | 6 |
| 023 | ↨ | 055 | 7 |
| 024 | ↑ | 056 | 8 |
| 025 | ↓ | 057 | 9 |
| 026 | → | 058 | : |
| 027 | ← | 059 | ; |
| 028 | (cursor right) | 060 | < |
| 029 | (cursor left) | 061 | = |
| 030 | (cursor up) | 062 | > |
| 031 | (cursor down) | 063 | ? |

| ASCII value | Character | ASCII value | Character |
|---|---|---|---|
| 064 | @ | 095 | _ |
| 065 | A | 096 | ' |
| 066 | B | 097 | a |
| 067 | C | 098 | b |
| 068 | D | 099 | c |
| 069 | E | 100 | d |
| 070 | F | 101 | e |
| 071 | G | 102 | f |
| 072 | H | 103 | g |
| 073 | I | 104 | h |
| 074 | J | 105 | i |
| 075 | K | 106 | j |
| 076 | L | 107 | k |
| 077 | M | 108 | l |
| 078 | N | 109 | m |
| 079 | O | 110 | n |
| 080 | P | 111 | o |
| 081 | Q | 112 | p |
| 082 | R | 113 | q |
| 083 | S | 114 | r |
| 084 | T | 115 | s |
| 085 | U | 116 | t |
| 086 | V | 117 | u |
| 087 | W | 118 | v |
| 088 | X | 119 | w |
| 089 | Y | 120 | x |
| 090 | Z | 121 | y |
| 091 | [ | 122 | z |
| 092 | \ | 123 | { |
| 093 | ] | 124 | ¦ |
| 094 | ∧ | 125 | } |

| ASCII value | Character | ASCII value | Character |
|---|---|---|---|
| 126 | ~ | 159 | ƒ |
| 127 | ⌂ | 160 | á |
| 128 | Ç | 161 | í |
| 129 | ü | 162 | ó |
| 130 | é | 163 | ú |
| 131 | â | 164 | ñ |
| 132 | ä | 165 | Ñ |
| 133 | à | 166 | ª |
| 134 | å | 167 | º |
| 135 | ç | 168 | ¿ |
| 136 | ê | 169 | ⌐ |
| 137 | ë | 170 | ¬ |
| 138 | è | 171 | ½ |
| 139 | ï | 172 | ¼ |
| 140 | î | 173 | ¡ |
| 141 | ì | 174 | « |
| 142 | Ä | 175 | » |
| 143 | Å | 176 | ░ |
| 144 | É | 177 | ▒ |
| 145 | æ | 178 | ▓ |
| 146 | Æ | 179 | │ |
| 147 | ô | 180 | ┤ |
| 148 | ö | 181 | ╡ |
| 149 | ò | 182 | ╢ |
| 150 | û | 183 | ╖ |
| 151 | ù | 184 | ╕ |
| 152 | ÿ | 185 | ╣ |
| 153 | Ö | 186 | ║ |
| 154 | Ü | 187 | ╗ |
| 155 | ¢ | 188 | ╝ |
| 156 | £ | 189 | ╜ |
| 157 | ¥ | 190 | ╛ |
| 158 | Pts | 191 | ┐ |

| ASCII value | Character | ASCII value | Character |
|---|---|---|---|
| 192 | └ | 225 | β |
| 193 | ┴ | 226 | Γ |
| 194 | ┬ | 227 | π |
| 195 | ├ | 228 | Σ |
| 196 | ─ | 229 | σ |
| 197 | ┼ | 230 | μ |
| 198 | ╞ | 231 | τ |
| 199 | ╟ | 232 | Φ |
| 200 | ╚ | 233 | θ |
| 201 | ╔ | 234 | Ω |
| 202 | ╩ | 235 | δ |
| 203 | ╦ | 236 | ∞ |
| 204 | ╠ | 237 | Ø |
| 205 | ═ | 238 | ∈ |
| 206 | ╬ | 239 | ∩ |
| 207 | ╧ | 240 | ≡ |
| 208 | ╨ | 241 | ± |
| 209 | ╤ | 242 | ≥ |
| 210 | ╥ | 243 | ≤ |
| 211 | ╙ | 244 | ⌠ |
| 212 | ╘ | 245 | ⌡ |
| 213 | ╒ | 246 | ÷ |
| 214 | ╓ | 247 | ≈ |
| 215 | ╫ | 248 | ° |
| 216 | ╪ | 249 | • |
| 217 | ┘ | 250 | · |
| 218 | ┌ | 251 | √ |
| 219 | █ | 252 | $^{n}$ |
| 220 | ▄ | 253 | $^{2}$ |
| 221 | ▌ | 254 | ■ |
| 222 | ▐ | 255 | (blank 'FF') |
| 223 | ▀ | | |
| 224 | α | | |

SPECIAL FUNCTION KEYS

Rows: 1 2 3 4 5 6 7 8 9 10 11 12 13 14 15 16 17 18 19 20 21 22 23 24 25

Columns: 1 2 3 4 5 6 7 8 9 10 11 12 13 14 15 16 17 18 19 20 21 22 23 24 25 26 27 28 29 30 31 32 33 34 35 36 37 38 39 40 41 42 43 44 45 46 47 48 49 50 51 52 53 54 55 56 57 58 59 60 61 62 63 64 65 66 67 68 69 70 71 72 73 74 75 76 77 78 79 80

# Appendix C

# IBM Reserved Words

| | | |
|---|---|---|
| ABS | AND | ASC |
| ATN | AUTO | BEEP |
| BLOAD | BSAVE | CALL |
| CDBL | CHAIN | CHR$ |
| CINT | CIRCLE | CLEAR |
| CLOSE | CLS | COLOR |
| COM | COMMON | CONT |
| COS | CSNG | CSRLIN |
| CVD | CVI | CVS |
| DATA | DATE$ | DEF |
| DEFDBL | DEFINT | DEFSNG |
| DEFSTR | DELETE | DIM |
| DRAW | EDIT | ELSE |
| END | EOF | EQV |
| ERASE | ERL | ERR |
| ERROR | EXP | FIELD |
| FILES | FIX | FNxxxxxxx |
| FOR | FRE | GET |
| GOSUB | GOTO | HEX$ |
| IF | IMP | INKEY$ |
| INP | INPUT | INPUT# |
| INPUT$ | INSTR | INT |
| KEY | KILL | LEFT$ |
| LEN | LET | LINE |
| LIST | LLIST | LOAD |
| LOC | LOCATE | LOF |
| LOG | LPOS | LPRINT |
| LSET | MERGE | MID$ |
| MKD$ | MKI$ | MKS$ |

| | | |
|---|---|---|
| MOD | MOTOR | NAME |
| NEW | NEXT | NOT |
| OCT$ | OFF | ON |
| OPEN | OPTION | OR |
| OUT | PAINT | PEEK |
| PEN | PLAY | POINT |
| POKE | POS | PRESET |
| PRINT | PRINT# | PSET |
| PUT | RANDOMIZE | READ |
| REM | RENUM | RESET |
| RESTORE | RESUME | RETURN |
| RIGHT$ | RND | RSET |
| RUN | SAVE | SCREEN |
| SGN | SIN | SOUND |
| SPACE$ | SPC( | SQR |
| STEP | STICK | STOP |
| STR$ | STRIG | STRING$ |
| SWAP | SYSTEM | TAB( |
| TAN | THEN | TIME$ |
| TO | TROFF | TRON |
| USING | USR | VAL |
| VARPTR | WAIT | WEND |
| WHILE | WIDTH | WRITE |
| WRITE# | XOR | |

# Appendix D

# Storing Data Files On Cassette

The material in this Appendix is optional and yet very important. The more practical programming you do, the more you'll appreciate your IBM's data file capabilities. They allow you to go from the world of programming to the larger world of *data processing*.

---

What we mean is, you'll be able to do lots more with larger quantities of information.

---

Up to now we've relied on BASIC's numeric variables, string variables and DATA lines to store the data our programs need. This leaves us with two limitations:

1. The Computer's memory may not be large enough to hold all the data we need (for example, an inventory list).

2. When we turn off the Computer, the values of all variables are lost.

Cassette data files solve both of these problems. We can save huge quantities of information on tape and retrieve them later, just as we save and reload programs. Only instead of the commands SAVE and LOAD, we'll need to learn some special statements.

---

To perform the exercises in this Appendix, you'll need to keep your Tape Recorder connected and set in the proper mode -- RECORD, PLAY or STOP -- as indicated in the text. Insert a blank cassette tape and set the tape counter to zero so you'll know where you started the data file.

---

## Open The Door, Richard

The first one is the OPEN statement. The OPEN statement is a powerful medicine. It handles all the details of creating a new file. It communicates 3 things to the system:

1 - What we plan to *do* with the file (i.e. INPUT data from it or PRINT information into it).

2 - What *number* (1 - 15) we assign to the file. (More on that in a second ...)

3 - The file's *name*.

Type:

```
100 OPEN "O",1,"CAS1:TESTDATA"
```

but don't RUN yet. The letter "O" indicates that we intend to OUTPUT information from memory, OUT to a data file. If we wanted to INPUT information from disk to memory we would use the letter "I". We'll learn how to INPUT a little later.

## File Buffers

Line 100 assigns the Number 1 to our file, along with the filename CAS1:TESTDATA. Any number from 1 to 15 may be assigned, but the file number cannot be greater than the number of files we reserved when entering BASIC. The default is 3.

The OPEN statement is our written agreement with the Computer to refer to CAS1:TESTDATA as file #1 in all our other program statements, until notified otherwise. In addition, the OPEN statement assigns a 256 byte area of memory (called a file "buffer") to file #1. The file buffer acts as a Policeman and Traffic Director for information traveling to and from the CAS1:TESTDATA file on disk. Though there are a maximum of 15 buffers available, we can control an unlimited number of files by reassigning the file buffers in memory to different disk files as needed. Very clever.

## Close The Barn Door

The opposite of OPENing a file is "CLOSE"ing it. It's a good habit to

CLOSE all files while they aren't in use. And we can all use an extra good habit or two. Better add:

```
200 CLOSE 1
```

OPEN simply assigns CAS1:TESTDATA a buffer and file number (#1 in this case), and prepares CAS1:TESTDATA for either Output (as in this case) or Input from tape to Computer memory. CAS1:TESTDATA will stay on the tape indefinitely under that name, but its assignment of an exclusive buffer and file number ceases each time it is CLOSEd.

## CLOSE

The CLOSE statement severs the association of a file with its assigned number and buffer.

There are a few options we can exercise when dealing with more than one data file in a single BASIC program. For example:

`CLOSE 1,3` closes only files numbered 1 and 3.

`CLOSE N` closes file number N.

`CLOSE` closes all files currently open.

It's not a bad idea to use:

```
CLOSE
```

in your programs since it CLOSEs everything in sight. To fully understand the value of the CLOSE statement, we need to take a closer look at the way data is transferred to the tape.

To store the data to a tape file, we need 3 additional BASIC statements.

## PRINT#

Writing to the file is done with the BASIC PRINT# statement. We know that our old friend PRINT directs output to the screen and LPRINT directs it to the printer. The third member of the PRINT family, PRINT#, sends output to tape.

Remember the file number that we assigned in the OPEN statement? It is used by the PRINT# statement to direct output to that same file. We assigned buffer #1 to the file CAS1:TESTDATA, so we'll use:

```
PRINT #1,
```

to send information to the CAS1:TESTDATA file.

But what do we want to print and how do we do it?

Writing DATA into a sequential file is almost exactly like writing to the screen. We can think of a sequential file as one

```
V....E....R....Y.......................................
```

long line on the screen.

Numbers, strings, and variables can be separated by commas or semicolons, and these "formatters" have precisely the same effect on the disk file as they do on the screen.

On the other hand, if we have the tape space to spare *and* special formatting requirements, we can use PRINT #1, USING. That's right, just like the PRINT USING we learned for the screen and printer. For example,

```
PRINT #1, USING "###.##";A
```

and

```
PRINT #3, USING "! ! \    \"; X$, Y$, Z$
```

work just fine for tape files. (See Chapters 35 and 36 for a review if your PRINT USING skills have grown dull.)

Press RECORD and PLAY keys on your Recorder at the same time, then add the following lines and RUN:

```
50 A=1:B=2:C=3
```

```
110 PRINT #1, A, B, C
```

This program causes three things to happen:

1. The Tape Recorder is automatically started (assuming you have it set in the RECORD mode).

2. The values of A, B and C are written onto the cassette.

3. The Recorder is automatically stopped. (You should then press STOP on the Recorder to disengage the recording head.)

You now have a permanent record which can easily be read back into the Computer. Note that the variables A, B and C are *not* written onto the tape -- just the *values* of those variables (in this case, 1, 2 and 3) are stored.

## INPUT#

The next step in this process is to INPUT our DATA back from tape, into memory. After all, the only reason to store something on disk is so we can retrieve it later.

Once file number 1 is CLOSEd in Line 200, the number 1 and its corresponding buffer are no longer associated with the disk file CAS1:TESTDATA. They are free to be used with any file specified in a new OPEN statement. Change:

```
100 OPEN "I",1,"CAS1:TESTDATA"
```

We are reOPENing the same file, CAS1:TESTDATA, as file number 1, but this time for INPUTting. Note that with sequential files, we must CLOSE the file, then reopen it when switching from reading to writing, and vice versa.

To read the contents of a sequential DATA file, we use the INPUT# statement.

Make the program read:

```
100 OPEN "I",1,"CAS1:TESTDATA"

110 INPUT #1, A, B, C
```

```
120 PRINT "THE DATA HAS BEEN READ FROM THE TAPE"
130 PRINT "A =";A, "B =";B, "C =";C
200 CLOSE 1
```

...and LIST. The significant Lines are:

1. Line 100 - ReOPEN the file for Computer INPUT
2. Line 110 - INPUT its contents to Computer memory
3. Line 130 - PRINT those contents on the screen
4. Line 200 - CLOSE the file again ... (always!)

To read back the data from tape, you must first press REWIND on the Recorder to rewind the tape to the point where the data file started.

Now press PLAY on the Recorder and type:

```
RUN
```

If the data from the earlier program was stored and read properly, the Computer should display:

```
THE DATA HAS BEEN READ FROM THE TAPE

A = 1          B = 2          C = 3
OK
_
```

Line 110 causes the Recorder to start, loading three numbers into the variables A, B and C. When the three numbers have been read, the Recorder motion is stopped.

Line 120 prints a reassuring message. This is important when the Computer is using an external device such as a Tape Recorder. Print messages are also valuable as prompting instructions to the user regarding the control of the Recorder. For example, before the

Computer executes a PRINT # statement, we can have it print a message telling the user to put the Recorder in the Record mode.

Line 130 prints the data that was read from the tape.

NOTE: If the Recorder is not in the PLAY mode (with proper connections made) when it executes in INPUT # statement, the Computer will keep trying to read the tape until it gets something. To regain control of the Computer, press [Break].

## LINE INPUT#

BASIC provides an alternate way of INPUTting data into *string* variables that avoids the confusion of delimiters. The BASIC statement is:

```
LINE INPUT#
```

and the rules are simple, but first a little background.

LINE INPUT (without the #) which we met in an earlier chapter accepts data from the keyboard. Unlike INPUT, LINE INPUT accepts *everything* typed until it receives a CR [←]. LINE INPUT accepts an entire Line of text, terminated by a carriage return.

In the same way, LINE INPUT# loads all characters into a single string variable until a CR in the file is hit. *All other data separators are ignored.* Powerful stuff, and couldn't be easier to use.

Of course, LINE INPUT# will not read past the End Of the File, nor cram more than 255 characters into the string variable.

That's it. All commas and quotes are included in the string. It eats up file data like a garbage truck.

NOTE: Only one variable is allowed for each LINE INPUT# statement.

One last word of advice: If you PRINT# a list of, say, 10 values onto tape, you should INPUT# a list of 10 values also. If you don't match up the number of PRINT# items with the number of INPUT# items, you'll end up either losing data or having to press [Break] to regain control of your system.

The following program demonstrates how a data file can be used to create a list of data items, process and update it. Study it carefully and think how similar programs might handle inventories, or any sequential lists.

```
10 REM  * TEMPERATURE AND HUMIDITY RECORDING PROGRAM *
20 REM  * DATA STORAGE MUST START ON THE 1ST DAY OF MONTH *
40 CLS : INPUT "WHAT DAY OF THE MONTH IS IT"; D
50 INPUT "WHAT IS TODAY'S TEMPERATURE"; T
60 INPUT "WHAT IS TODAY'S HUMIDITY"; H
70 PRINT : PRINT
80 IF D = 1 GOTO 430              'ON FIRST DAY IS NO
   PRIOR DATA
100 REM * INPUTTING DATA STORED ON CASSETTE TAPE *
110 PRINT "WE MUST LOAD PRIOR DAYS TEMP & HUMIDITY FROM"
120 PRINT "THE DATA TAPE.  BE SURE IT'S REWOUND AND THE
    RECORDER"
130 PRINT "IS SET TO 'PLAY'." : PRINT : PRINT
140 INPUT "PRESS 'ENTER' WHEN EVERYTHING IS READY TO GO.";
    A$
160 CLS : PRINT "DATA IS NOW FLOWING INTO THE COMPUTER
    FROM TAPE."
170 PRINT : PRINT : PRINT "DATE", "TEMP", "HUMIDITY" :
    PRINT
180 FOR X = 1 TO D - 1
190  OPEN "I", 1, "TEMPDATA"
200  INPUT #1, Y, Z             'BRINGS IT IN FROM TAPE
210  PRINT X, Y, Z               'PRINTS IT ON THE SCREEN
220  B = B + Y : C = C + Z       'KEEPS RUNNING TOTALS
230  CLOSE 1
240 NEXT X
300 REM * MONTHS AVERAGES TO-DATE *
```

```
310 B = (B+T)/D : C = (C+H)/D   'COMPUTES THE AVERAGES
320 PRINT D, T, H
330 PRINT : PRINT "    **    THIS MONTH AVERAGES    **"
340 PRINT TAB(7); "TEMP"; TAB(17); "HUMIDITY"
350 PRINT TAB(7); B; TAB(19); C
400 REM * STORING TODAY'S TEMP & HUMIDITY ON TAPE *
410 PRINT:PRINT:INPUT "PRESS 'ENTER' WHEN READY TO
    CONTINUE";A$
420 CLS : PRINT : PRINT
430 PRINT "TODAY'S TEMPERATURE AND HUMIDITY WILL NOW BE
    PRINTED"
440 PRINT "ON THE DATA TAPE.  BE SURE 'RECORD' & 'PLAY'
    ARE"
450 PRINT "PRESSED.  DO NOT REWIND THE TAPE, YET." : PRIN
460 INPUT "WHEN ALL IS READY, PRESS 'ENTER'"; A$ : CLS
470 PRINT "TODAY'S DATA IS NOW FLOWING FROM THE COMPUTER
    TO THE"
480 PRINT "TAPE.  WE WILL INPUT THIS PLUS THE EARLIER
    DATA"
490 PRINT "TOMORROW." : PRINT
500 OPEN "O", 1, "TEMPDATA"
510 PRINT #1, T, H                'PRINTS TODAY'S DATA
    ON TAPE
520 CLOSE 1
530 PRINT "TODAY'S NUMBERS HAVE BEEN ADDED TO THE TAPE."
540 PRINT "REWIND THE TAPE IN PREPARATION FOR TOMORROW."
```

Line 200 reads back all the previous days' numbers, two at a time. When all the information is read in, the average temperature and humidity are calculated (using the current day's info as well). Line 510 then writes the current day's information at the end of the list.

For a sample run of the program, assume it is the first day of the month. Enter plausible temperature and humidity figures. Continue running the program until you've got a cumulative listing for several days. Getting the feel for data files?

Be sure to SAVE this program as "TEMPHUMD" since it's a valuable lesson.

## Suggestions For Further Use Of Data Files

1. TEACHING/TESTING. Write a program that gives a multiple-choice test, for example, a vocabulary test. Include ten questions. The program should write the student's name and all ten responses onto a cassette data file. Design the program so that any number of students may take the test in sequence. Include instructions about when to use the RECORD, PLAY and STOP keys.

   Write a grader program that uses the data file created above to read each student's name and responses, grade the test, and then read the next student's test. Be sure to leave time for the teacher to mark down the names and grades in his or her little black book.

2. INVENTORY. Write a program that sets up an array in which you store the following information about a group of cars:

   License No. Engine Size Color Code Body Style

   The program should then store the array in a data file.

   Write another program which:

   1. Asks you which car you're interested in (you enter the license number).

   2. Reads the data file until it comes to the correct license number.

   3. Prints out all the information about that particular car.

# Appendix E

## Error Messages

| Code | Error |
|---|---|
| 1 | NEXT without FOR |
| 2 | Syntax error |
| 3 | RETURN without GOSUB |
| 4 | Out of DATA |
| 5 | Illegal function call |
| 6 | Overflow |
| 7 | Out of memory |
| 8 | Undefined Line number |
| 9 | Subscript out of range |
| 10 | Duplicate definition |
| 11 | Division by zero |
| 12 | Illegal direct |
| 13 | Type mismatch |
| 14 | Out of string space |
| 15 | String too long |
| 16 | String formula too complex |
| 17 | Can't continue |
| 18 | Undefined user function |
| 19 | No RESUME |
| 20 | RESUME without error |
| 21 | Unprintable error |
| 22 | Missing operand |
| 23 | Line buffer overflow |
| 24 | Device timeout |
| 25 | Device fault |
| 26 | FOR without NEXT |
| 27 | Out of paper |
| 29 | WHILE without WEND |
| 30 | WEND without WHILE |

| Code | Error |
|---|---|
| 50 | FIELD overflow |
| 51 | Internal error |
| 52 | Bad file number |
| 53 | File not found |
| 54 | Bad file mode |
| 55 | File already open |
| 57 | Device I/O Error |
| 58 | File already exists |
| 61 | Disk full |
| 62 | Input past end |
| 63 | Bad record number |
| 64 | Bad file name |
| 66 | Direct statement in file |
| 67 | Too many files |
| 68 | Device Unavailable |
| 69 | Communication buffer overflow |
| 70 | Disk Write Protect |
| 71 | Disk not Ready |
| 72 | Disk Media Error |
| 73 | Advanced Feature |

## Code

1. **NEXT without FOR:** an attempt was made to RUN a program containing a FOR-NEXT loop, but the word "FOR" was missing.

2. **Syntax error:** a command, statement or function is misspelled or an operator is omitted.

3. **RETURN without GOSUB:** the Computer reads a RETURN statement and there is no corresponding GOSUB.

4. **Out of DATA:** the Computer is told to READ more items from the DATA statement than are available.

5. **Illegal function call:** illegal values are used with the built-in math functions or the Computer cannot figure out what to compute because of the values it received.

6. **Overflow:** the Computer is unable to use a number because it is either too large or too small. An overflow condition can also be created by routine mathematical calculations at either the statement or command levels.

7. **Out of memory:** an attempt is made to store a program larger than the Computer's memory storage space. It is also displayed when a matrix variable is assigned more elements than there is space in memory to store it.

8. **Undefined Line number:** a branching statement such as GOTO or GOSUB calls for a Line number that does not exist.

9. **Subscript out of range:** the elements in a numeric or string matrix are beyond the range of values reserved in the DIM statement.

10. **Duplicate definition:** the Computer is told to DIMension a numeric or string Matrix after it has already been DIMensioned earlier in the same program.

11. **Division by zero:** the Computer is asked to divide a number by Ø. You may think of your Computer as the smartest thing going, but it is not capable of handling numbers of infinite value.

12. **Illegal direct:** the Computer is asked to INPUT a value or string in the Immediate or Direct mode.

13. **Type mismatch:** a numeric value is assigned to a string variable or a string is assigned to a numeric variable.

14. **Out of string space:** more letters or characters are assigned to a string variable than it is capable of storing.

15. **String too long:** an attempt is made to store more than 255 letters or characters in a string variable.

16. **String formula too complex:** string manipulation has become too complicated or too long for the Computer.

17. **Can't continue:** the command CONT is typed and there no program to continue, the program had just been EDITed, or a line has just been added or deleted.

18. **Undefined user function:** a function is called before it was defined with a DEF FN statement.

19. **No RESUME:** an ON ERROR GOTO statement is used to branch to a specified program line, and the Computer does not encounter a RESUME statement before the program stops.

20. **RESUME without error:** the Computer encounters a RESUME statement without first finding an ON ERROR GOTO statement.

21. **Unprintable error:** the ERROR statement is used to self-inflict an error and the resulting error code is not one used by the Computer.

22. **Missing operand:** the Computer is not given all the information required to carry out its directive.

23. **Line buffer overflow:** a line has been entered that has too many characters.

24. **Device timeout:** BASIC was not given information from an input/output device within a predetermined amount of time. In Cassette BASIC, this wouid only occur while trying to read the cassette or write to the printer.

25. **Device fault:** a hardware error indication returned by an interface adapter. In Cassette BASIC, this will only occur when a fault status is returned from the printer interface adapter.

26. **FOR without NEXT:** an attempt is made to RUN a program containing a FOR-NEXT loop, but the word "NEXT" is missing.

27. **Out of paper:** the printer is either out of paper or it is not turned on. Insert paper if you need to, check to see the printer is properly connected and the power is on. Continue with the program.

29. **WHILE without WEND:** a WHILE statement does not have a matching WEND. A WHILE was executing when an END, STOP, or RETURN statement was found.

30. **WEND without WHILE:** a WEND was found before a matching WHILE was executed.

50. **FIELD overflow:** a FIELD statement is attempting to allocate more bytes than were specified for the record length of a random file in the OPEN statement. Or, the end of the FIELD buffer was encountered while doing sequential I/O (PRINT#,WRITE#,INPUT#,etc.) to a random file.

51. **Internal error:** there has occured an internal malfunction in BASIC. The conditions under which the message appeared need to be reported to your Computer dealer.

52. **Bad file number:** a statement references a file with a file number that isn't OPEN or is out of range of possible file numbers which was specified at initialization. Or, the device name in the file specification is too long or invalid, or the filename was too long or invalid.

53. **File not found:** a statement such as LOAD, KILL, NAME, FILES, or OPEN has referenced a file that does not exist on the specified drive.

54. **Bad file mode:** statements PUT or GET were used with a sequential file or a closed file, to MERGE a non-ASCII file, or to execute an OPEN with a file mode other than input, output, append, or random.

55. **File already open:** you tried to OPEN a file for sequential output or append, and the file is already OPEN. Or, you tried to KILL a file that is open.

57. **Device I/O error:** an error occurred on a device I/O operation. DOS can't recover from the error.

58. **File already exists:** a NAME statement has specified a filename that is identical to a filename already used on the diskette.

61. **Disk full:** there is no more storage space on diskette. When this error occurs files will be closed.

62. **Input past end:** this is an end of file error. An input statement was executed for a null (empty) file, or after all the data in a sequential file was already input. To avoid this error, use the EOF function to detect the end of file. This error also occurs if you try to read from a file that was opened for output or append.

63. **Bad record number:** the record number in a PUT or GET statement is either greater than the maximum allowed (32767) or equal to zero.

64. **Bad file name:** An invalid form is used for the filename with BLOAD, BSAVE, KILL, OPEN, NAME, or FILES (e.g., a filename starting with a period).

66. **Direct statement in file:** a direct statement was encountered while LOADing or CHAINing to an ASCII format file. The LOAD or CHAIN is terminated. The ASCII file should consist only of statements preceded by line numbers. This may occur because of a line feed character in the input stream.

67. **Too many files:** using SAVE or OPEN an attempt was made to create a new file when all directory entries on the diskette are full, or the file specificaton is invalid.

68. **Device unavailable:** you tried to OPEN a file to a device which doesn't exist. Either you do not have the hardware to support the device (such as printer), or a device is disabled. (For example, you may have used /C:0 on the BASIC command to start Disk BASIC. That would disable communications devices.)

69. **Communication buffer overflow:** a communication input statement was executed but the input buffer was already full. You should use an ON ERROR statement to retry the input when this condition occurs. Subsequent inputs will attempt to clear this faster than the program can process them.

70. **Disk Write Protect:** Tried to write to a diskette with a write protect tab on it.

71. **Disk not ready:**

72. **Disk media error:**

73. **Advanced feature:** The programs contains a function or statement used only in Advanced BASIC, and you're in Disk BASIC. You'll have to reload BASICA.

# SECTION E
# INDEX

# FREE
## Update Information For
## *LEARNING IBM BASIC*

We can sit here and ponder and speculate and wonder all day long, but we'll never really know how we can improve this book in future editions unless you tell us. Please help us help you by giving us your suggestions for improvements. Honest, we really do read and learn from them!

What do you like about the book?____________________

________________________________________

________________________________________

What don't you like?____________________________

________________________________________

________________________________________

Is the book complete? (If not, what should be added?) __________

________________________________________

________________________________________

Did you find any mistakes? (If so, where?) ________________

________________________________________

________________________________________

What other books, manuals or computer aids could be developed to help you?

________________________________________

Anything else? ________________________________

________________________________________

If you would like to receive the latest update memorandum (when available) and information regarding new releases, complete the following:

Name: ____________________________________

Address: __________________________________

City/State/Zip: ______________________________

For your convenience, our address and return postage have been printed on the back of this card. Please drop it in the nearest mail box. Thanks for your help.

Ctrl Alt Del for "restart"

in Basic FILES "B:*.*"

To get out of a Loop Ctrl ScrLock

page# 75

Beginners
All-purpose
Symbolic
Instruction
Code

**BUSINESS REPLY MAIL**
FIRST CLASS PERMIT NO. 100 EL CAJON, CA

POSTAGE WILL BE PAID BY ADDRESSEE

**CompuSoft® Publishing**
535 Broadway
El Cajon, CA 92021-9990

Key off
F-9 OFF

NO POSTAGE
NECESSARY
IF MAILED
IN THE
UNITED STATES